Steven Raichlen's

HIGH-FLAVOR,
LOW-FAT COOKING

by Steven Raichlen

photography by Ken Winokur
styling by Jane Gillooly

CAMDEN
◆HOUSE◆

PUBLISHING

Camden House Publishing, Inc.
A division of Telemedia Communications (USA) Inc.

Camden House Publishing, Inc.
Ferry Road
Charlotte, Vermont 05445

Library of Congress Cataloging-in-Publication Data
Raichlen, Steven.
[High-flavor, low-fat cooking]
Steven Raichlen's high-flavor, low-fat cooking / Steven Raichlen,
p. cm.
Includes index.
ISBN 0-944475-32-9 (h/c) : $24.95 – ISBN 0-944475-31-0 (s/c) : $18.95
1. Cookery, International. 2. Low-fat diet – Recipes. I. Title.
II. Title: High-flavor, low-fat cooking.
TX725.A1R278 1992

641.5'638 – dc20   92-10733
                                                         CIP

Edited by Georgia Orcutt
Designed by Debra Wright

Typeset by
Fletcher Typesetting
Depot Square
Peterborough, New Hampshire 03458

Trade distribution by
Firefly Books Ltd.
250 Sparks Avenue
Willowdale, Ontario
Canada M2H 2S4

Printed and bound in Canada
by D.W. Friesen & Sons, Altona, Manitoba
Fourth Printing, November 1993

To my mother, Frances Raichlen,
who would have loved this book.

CONTENTS

ACKNOWLEDGMENTS

"NO MAN IS AN ISLAND," OBSERVED THE JEFFERSON Airplane (and John Donne before them). Likewise, no cookbook author works alone. This book has been inspired by fabulous meals at hundreds of restaurants, street vendors, markets, and private homes, from my native Baltimore to Bangkok. I'm equally indebted to dozens of talented individuals who helped shape this book from its inception to the final copy.

First and foremost, I want to thank my photographer, Ken Winokur, and stylist, Jane Gillooly, who translated my recipes into gorgeous color images. They came all the way from Boston to Miami to take the pictures and produced miracles in less than 2 weeks.

Didi Emmons ran the photo kitchen, tested recipes, fed the staff, and proved as indispensable here in Miami as she had when she assisted me in Boston. Her palate is as unerring as her sense of humor.

Elida Proenza proved equally indispensable, sharing her practical wisdom, keen taste buds, boundless energy, and culinary skills from her native Cuba.

The children did their part, too. Jake Klein dutifully appeared at mealtimes with Brett in tow, while Betsy Klein showed remarkable forbearance in not eating the food for the photo shoot. My mother-in-law, Miriam Seldin, graciously allowed us to clean her out of serving dishes and cookware.

Three wonderful grandparents helped with the shoot: Grammie Ethel, Dear, and Granddad Winokur. Their combined ages (264 years!) in no way diminished their willingness to help.

Mark and Kiki Ellenby supplied us with splendid exotic fruits; Tim "The Herb Man" Mumford, with fresh herbs.

Maida Heatter and Charlie Cinnamon provided moral support. Jane Wooldridge, Shirley Drevich, Eleanor Rieza, and Allen Herman were willing guinea pigs for my recipes, as was the entire cast of "Those Were the Days."

Every author should be as lucky as I am to have a publisher like Howard White, an editor like Georgia Orcutt, a copy editor like Barbara Jatkola, an art director like Debra Wright, and typesetters like Sheryl Fletcher and Chris Landry.

An all-star team of testers, including Diane Koss, Liz Lowe, Kim Norland, Mimi Powell, Karen Reynolds, Jocelyn Secker-Walker, and Suzy White, made sure the recipes worked. Nancy Sykes coordinated recipe testing and nutritional analyses, Susan Walker served as marketing coordinator, Karen Brasel provided the nutritional analyses for all the recipes, and Sandy Taylor lent her editorial expertise from start to finish.

Above all, I thank my wife, Barbara Seldin, who nurtured this book with patience, fed it with inspiration, and helped harvest it with love. I hereby award her a Purple Heart for enduring a photo shoot in our living room and a steady diet of low-fat food when she really craved butter, eggs, and cream!

PHOTO CREDITS

The author would like to thank the following individuals and businesses for help with styling and props:

Carroll's Jewelers in Coral Gables, Florida

The Cook Shop in South Miami, Florida

Yvette Kalinowski of Iberia Tiles in Coral Gables, Florida

Carole Kotkin

Jeanee Redmond, ceramics

Anthony Perez and Michael Roberge of Blumen Haus in Cambridge, Massachusetts

Dick and Judy Silver of the Mayflower Poultry Co. in Cambridge, Massachusetts

Becky Luigart-Stayner, photographer in Burlington, Vermont

Susan Herr, food stylist in Shelburne, Vermont

PREFACE

MY FATHER-IN-LAW, THE LATE PHIL SELDIN, LIVED his life by this maxim: "There's no such thing as 'can't.'" Five years ago, if someone had asked me to write a 200-recipe cookbook using no cream, 2 egg yolks, and less than a stick of butter, I would have pronounced it impossible. (I probably would have said other things, too, that wouldn't have been fit to print.)

But times change, and so do people. Like many Americans, I've dramatically reduced my fat intake. To give my food the richness to which I was accustomed, I've increasingly come to rely on herbs, spices, condiments, marinades, and other high-flavor ingredients. I've replaced traditional dairy products with nonfat yogurt, extra-virgin olive oil, and even chicken stock.

This book is the result of 3 years of experimenting with what I call "high-flavor, low-fat cooking." Many low-fat or low-calorie cookbooks leave one with a sense of deprivation. They focus on what you can't eat as much as on what you can. I've tried to make this book the exception to the rule by emphasizing flavor over fat. I believe that food not only should be good for you, but it also should taste and look great. In this book, you'll find recipes that are bursting with flavor as well as color photographs that prove this food looks as good as it tastes.

For me, *High-Flavor, Low-Fat Cooking* isn't just another cookbook. It's a healthy and rewarding way of life.

INTRODUCTION

I SUPPOSE IT WAS BOUND TO HAPPEN. YOU DON'T review restaurants and teach cooking classes for 15 years without eventually paying a price. My time of reckoning came just after my 35th birthday. In the space of a year my waist size mushroomed 3 inches. My cholesterol level was dangerously close to 300.

Life threatening? Not for the moment, but I certainly had cause for concern. Hadn't more portly family members warned that my profligate cooking and feasting would catch up with me? Suppose a 280-milligram cholesterol level and buying new belts were just the beginning, not a comfortable plateau?

For better or worse, I had done my culinary training in France in the 1970s, when eggs, butter, and cream were considered a chef's staunchest allies. Meals routinely began with brioche and foie gras and ended with buttercream tortes. Back in the B.C. (Before Cholesterol) era, no one suspected that soufflés and hollandaise sauce might actually be detrimental to your health.

Many Americans have undergone a similar change of heart about fat. Unfortunately, fat is delicious. The world's most gorgeous sauces—béarnaise, hollandaise, and beurre blanc—have butter as the main ingredient. Pastry making would be almost inconceivable without eggs and whipped cream. Even in simple foods such as grilled steak or roast rack of lamb the most flavorful part is the fat.

I've written about food and cooking for my entire adult life. Never once have I used the word "diet." I've always been a firm believer in the virtues of home-cooked meals made with fresh, natural ingredients. I have never used synthetic, dietetic, or highly processed foods, and I wasn't about to start. I knew I had to make a dramatic change in my eating habits, but I didn't want to sacrifice flavor.

As I reviewed my cooking practices, the central question became "How can I retain bold flavors while reducing or eliminating fat?" I looked for ways to replace the inherent richness of animal fat by using herb mixtures, spice pastes, marinades, and other intense flavorings. I abandoned classical cooking techniques such as sautéing and deep-fat frying and concentrated on low-fat methods such as smoking, grilling, and stir-frying. The nonstick frying pan became a close friend—once I realized that I could make the same potato pancake with 2 tablespoons of olive oil instead of half a stick of butter.

I began to replace high-fat ingredients with low-fat substitutes: butter with olive oil, heavy cream with nonfat yogurt. I also discovered that sauces could be thickened with puréed vegetables and that custards and soufflés could be set with egg whites instead of yolks.

My guiding principle in cooking was to use flavor instead of fat. Much to my surprise, my cooking actually improved from what it had been under the influence of Bocuse and Escoffier. I learned that food tasted brighter and fresher without an artery-clogging shroud of fat. And so, what began as a health necessity became a pleasurable way of life.

This book is a celebration of high-flavor, low-fat cooking. It is not a diet book, at least not in the conventional sense, although it will probably help you lose weight. It will definitely help you prepare tasty, full-flavored, deeply satisfying food without using butter, cream, egg yolks, artificial sweeteners, and chemical additives and with only a minimum of fat.

CULINARY MATH

*The following numbers are given to help interpret
the nutritional analysis included with each recipe.*

	Per day for a 120-pound person	Per day for a 170-pound person
Calories	1,800	2,550
Protein	Min. 44 g	Min. 62 g
Fat*	Max. 60 g	Max. 85 g
Carbohydrate	Min. 248 g	Min. 351 g
Sodium**	Max. 6,000 mg	Max. 6,000 mg
Cholesterol	Max. 300 mg	Max. 300 mg

*An easy way to limit fat consumption to the recommended 30 percent of calories is to divide your ideal weight in half. This number is an estimate of the allowed fat in grams per day for a moderately active person. The above values are given as a reference only, since calories needed to maintain ideal body weight vary from person to person.

**Unlike fat, there is no general consensus for healthy people to reduce sodium below this moderate level.

ABOUT THE RECIPES

THE RECIPES IN THIS BOOK WERE INSPIRED BY many sources: my travels in Europe, Asia, the Caribbean, and Latin America; meals at hundreds of restaurants and private homes; intriguing new ingredients I discovered at markets here and abroad.

Three cuisines have had an especially profound impact on the recipes: Asian (especially Southeast Asian), Mediterranean, and Middle Eastern. All are intensely flavorful, all make relatively limited use of saturated fats, and all are well suited for large-scale entertaining or for cooking for one. I'm a firm believer in the virtues of home-cooked food for single people. After all, if you're not special enough to cook for, who is?

The world is a smaller place now than it was when I did my culinary training in the 1970s. Fifteen years ago, few North Americans had ever tasted Thai or Indian food. Today ethnic restaurants serving these and other cuisines have sprung up around the country like mushrooms after a rainstorm. Many of the ingredients we once considered exotic, such as sesame oil and balsamic vinegar, can be found at any major supermarket. Thanks to increased air freight and air travel, North Americans have access to ingredients used all over the world.

These ingredients play a big part in this book. My style of cooking is international and multiethnic. I like big, brash, vibrant flavors, and I use elements from any cuisine in the world to achieve them. I love the bold tastes of fish sauce, lemongrass, cardamom, and rose water. I delight in igniting my food with ginger, horseradish, wasabi, and scotch bonnet chilies.

But these big flavors aren't solely for gustatory gratification. They're also valuable allies in the fight against fat. When you eliminate or reduce fat from a recipe, you also reduce its flavor. What may seem like a profligate, or at least generous, use of spices and seasonings in these recipes is actually a strategy for replacing the flavor lost with the fat.

Many of my recipes call for a lot of ingredients. Don't be intimidated; this doesn't make them more complicated or time-consuming. It simply makes them taste better. I'm tired of timid cookbooks that call for ¼ teaspoon of this flavoring or a few drops of that. If you want food with big flavors, you have to use herbs, spices, and condiments with largesse.

You may not be familiar with some of the ingredients called for, especially if you live in a small town or away from the East or West Coast. Don't be discouraged. Refer to the Cook's Notes (pages 229–245) for definitions and descriptions, and turn to the list of Mail-Order Sources (page 246) to find places that sell what you need.

Finally, a word about the fat content in these recipes. I am not a physician, nutritionist, or dietitian. My first concern has been to create recipes that taste great. With that goal in mind, I have developed recipes that contain a minimum amount of saturated fat and that fall within the current health goal of limiting calories from fat to 30 percent of your total food intake.

A nutritional analysis appears at the end of each recipe. Use it as a guide in balancing meals, but remember that individual recipes need to be considered in the context of a total meal. The Culinary Math box (preceding page) will help you to interpret the nutritional information.

APPETIZERS AND DIPS

EGGPLANT CAKE

*This eggplant "cake" is a lovely low-fat ratatouille baked in a cake pan. The pan is lined
with the eggplant skins, arranged to look like flower petals when the cake is unmolded.
(Allow 2 hours for preparation.) Most ratatouille comes dripping with oil, but this one acquires
its richness from balsamic vinegar and tomato paste, not fat. Serve with Tomato Vinaigrette (page 181).*

5 long (6 to 8"), skinny eggplants (about
   2½ pounds)
2 teaspoons kosher salt
1½ tablespoons extra-virgin olive oil
1 onion, finely chopped
2 cloves garlic, minced (2 teaspoons)
1 red bell pepper, cored, seeded, and diced
1 green bell pepper, cored, seeded, and diced
2 small zucchini, thinly sliced
3 ripe tomatoes, peeled, seeded, and
   chopped (save the skin from one to make
   a tomato rose for garnish; see Note)

2 tablespoons tomato paste
1 tablespoon balsamic vinegar (or to taste)
¼ cup finely chopped fresh herbs (basil,
   oregano, chervil, rosemary, parsley,
   and/or chives)
¼ cup lightly toasted bread crumbs
   (preferably homemade)
1 egg white, lightly beaten with a fork
salt, freshly ground black pepper, and
   cayenne pepper

Cut the eggplants in half lengthwise. Deeply score the flesh with a paring knife, without cutting the skin. Sprinkle the scored sides with kosher salt and let stand 30 minutes. Rinse off any brown juices that form on the surface and blot the eggplants dry. (This is called disgorging, and it helps remove the bitter juices.)

Preheat the oven to 375 degrees F. Place the eggplants, cut side down, on a lightly oiled baking sheet (or one lined with parchment paper). Bake for 30 minutes, or until very soft. Let cool.

Carefully scrape out the flesh and coarsely chop it, leaving the skins intact. Line a 9" cake pan with a circle of parchment paper. Arrange a layer of eggplant skins on top of the paper, skinny end toward the center, overlapping one skin with the next to form a flower-petal design. Let any excess skin hang over the edge of the pan.

Heat the oil in a nonstick frying pan. Cook the onion and garlic over medium heat for 2 to 3 minutes, or until soft but not brown. Stir in the peppers, zucchini, and chopped eggplant, and

Eggplant Cake with Tomato Vinaigrette (page 181)

cook for 3 minutes. Stir in the tomatoes, tomato paste, and balsamic vinegar, and cook for 15 minutes, or until most of the liquid has evaporated and the vegetables are soft. Let the eggplant mixture cool. Stir in the herbs, bread crumbs, and egg white. Add salt, pepper, cayenne, and vinegar to taste. (The mixture should be highly seasoned.)

Preheat the oven to 350 degrees F. Spoon the eggplant mixture into the cake pan and fold any overhanging eggplant skins over the top. Bake for 40 minutes, or until a skewer inserted in the center comes out clean. Let the cake cool to room temperature on a wire rack, then refrigerate for at least 3 hours.

Place a round platter over the pan and invert the cake onto it. (Don't forget to peel off the parchment paper.) Garnish with the tomato rose. Cut into wedges and serve with Tomato Vinaigrette spooned on the side.

Although I normally serve this cake cold, if you prefer, you can warm it at 400 degrees F for 20 minutes, or until a skewer inserted in the center comes out hot.

Serves 8.

Note: To make a tomato rose, use a sharp knife to cut the peel off the tomato in one continuous strip (the strip should be 1" wide), starting at the round end opposite the stem. Loosely roll up this strip from the top to form a rose.

72 CALORIES PER SERVING: 2 G PROTEIN, 2 G FAT, 14 G CARBOHYDRATE; 572 MG SODIUM; 0 MG CHOLESTEROL.

GRILLED QUESADILLAS

Quesadillas are the Mexican version of a grilled cheese sandwich. Grilling imparts a smoky flavor that makes up for the relative blandness of low-fat cheese. (You could also broil the quesadillas or sauté them in a nonstick frying pan brushed with a little olive oil.)

2–3 ounces low-fat Monterey Jack or cheddar cheese, coarsely grated
1 large ripe tomato, peeled, seeded, and finely chopped
1 yellow or red bell pepper, cored, seeded, and finely diced

¼ cup finely chopped cilantro
3 scallions, finely chopped
2 pickled jalapeño chilies (or to taste), thinly sliced
8 flour tortillas
salt and freshly ground black pepper

Place the cheese, tomato, yellow or red pepper, cilantro, scallions, and jalapeños in a bowl and toss to mix.

Preheat the grill. Just before serving, spread four tortillas with the cheese mixture and season with salt and pepper. Place the remaining tortillas on top, sandwich-style. Grill the quesadillas over medium heat for 1 minute per side, or until the cheese is melted and the tortillas are lightly browned. Cut into wedges and serve at once.

Serves 4 as an appetizer, 2 as a light entrée.

244 CALORIES PER SERVING: 10 G PROTEIN, 7 G FAT, 37 G CARBOHYDRATE; 113 MG SODIUM; 10 MG CHOLESTEROL.

KELP CRISPIES

When my assistant and friend Didi Emmons served this appetizer, I wanted to include her recipe. After all, kelp (also known by its Japanese name, kombu) is a good source of calcium, iron, magnesium, potassium, iodine, and vitamins A, C, and D. What's more, it's delicious.

2 ounces dried kelp pieces
¼ cup honey
¼ cup maple syrup
¼ cup sesame seeds

¼ cup coarsely chopped nuts (pecans, pistachios, and/or walnuts)
¼ cup Grape-Nuts or other crunchy cereal

Soak the kelp in cold water to cover for 1 hour, or until soft, changing the water 3 times. Drain in a colander and pat dry with paper towels. Cut each piece into a 2" square.

Preheat the oven to 250 degrees F. Combine the honey and maple syrup in a bowl and whisk until smooth. Dip the kelp pieces in the syrup mixture or brush the syrup on with a paintbrush. Arrange on a baking sheet lined with parchment paper. Sprinkle some of the crispies

with sesame seeds, others with chopped nuts, and the remainder with Grape-Nuts. Bake for 1½ to 2 hours, or until crisp. (To test for doneness, let the piece cool on a wire rack for 5 minutes before tasting.)

Transfer to a wire rack to cool, then store in a cookie tin or another airtight container. (Ours never last long enough to be stored!)

Serves 8 to 10.

99 CALORIES PER SERVING: 2 G PROTEIN, 4 G FAT, 16 G CARBOHYDRATE; 43 MG SODIUM; 0 MG CHOLESTEROL.

WILD MUSHROOM CROSTINI

Crostini are Italian toast points. (Actually, they're more apt to be oval than pointed.) This recipe arose from a "care package" I received from my friends Amy and Thierry Farges, owners of a New York–based exotic mushroom business called Aux Délices des Bois. You can also use common button mushrooms or dried exotic mushrooms (soak them in warm water for 1 hour).

1 loaf French or Italian bread (preferably baguette-shaped)
4 teaspoons extra-virgin olive oil
1 clove raw or roasted garlic
3 cloves garlic, minced (1 tablespoon)
3 scallions, finely chopped, or 3 tablespoons chopped fresh chives

12 ounces exotic mushrooms (about 8 cups)
¼ cup finely chopped flat-leaf parsley, plus a few sprigs for garnish
1 teaspoon finely chopped fresh thyme (or 1 teaspoon dried)
salt, freshly ground black pepper, and cayenne pepper

Preheat the barbecue grill or oven to 400 degrees F. Cut the bread sharply on the diagonal into ½" slices. Very lightly brush each side with oil, using no more than 2 teaspoons in all. Grill for 2 to 3 minutes per side, or until golden brown. Or bake the crostini in the oven for 10 to 12 minutes, or until golden brown, turning once. Let cool on a wire rack. Rub each slice with raw or roasted garlic.

Just before serving, heat the remaining 2 teaspoons oil in a large skillet. Add the minced garlic and scallions, and cook over medium heat for 30 seconds, or until fragrant but not brown. Stir in the mushrooms, herbs, and a little salt and pepper. Increase the heat to high and cook for 3 to 4 minutes, or until the mushrooms are soft and have lost most of their liquid. (There should be about 2½ to 3 cups.) Correct the seasoning, adding salt, pepper, and cayenne to taste.

Mound the mushroom mixture on the crostini and garnish with sprigs of parsley.

Serves 4 to 6.

255 CALORIES PER SERVING: 9 G PROTEIN, 7 G FAT, 41 G CARBOHYDRATE; 392 MG SODIUM; 0 MG CHOLESTEROL.

LOW-FAT CHEESE FONDUE

Traditional Swiss cheese fondue is loaded with fat, but in this recipe low-fat cheese is substituted for the traditional Emmenthaler and Gruyère. Since low-fat cheese is rather bland, I've bolstered the flavor with garlic, nutmeg, and a generous spoonful of mustard.

FOR DIPPING
½ loaf French bread
1 small head broccoli, cut into florets
½ head cauliflower, cut into florets
2 carrots, peeled and cut into ½" pieces
salt
4 ounces fresh mushrooms, large ones halved or quartered, small ones left whole
1 Granny Smith apple, cut into wedges and sprinkled with lemon juice

8 ounces low-fat Swiss or cheddar cheese, or a mixture of both
1 tablespoon flour
1 teaspoon olive oil
1 cup dry white wine
1 clove garlic, minced (1 teaspoon)
1 tablespoon Dijon-style mustard
salt and freshly ground black pepper
pinch of cayenne pepper
pinch of freshly grated nutmeg
1 tablespoon kirsch (cherry brandy) or kümmel (caraway-flavored liqueur)

Cut the bread into 1" cubes and place on a baking sheet for toasting at the last minute. Cook the broccoli, cauliflower, and carrots separately in boiling salted water for 2 minutes, or until tender-crisp. Refresh under cold water and drain. Attractively arrange the cooked vegetables, mushrooms, and apple wedges on a platter.

Grate the cheese into a bowl and toss with the flour. Oil the fondue pot to prevent the cheese from sticking.

Just before serving, lightly toast the bread in a 400 degree F oven. Bring the wine to a boil with the garlic in the fondue pot. Stir in the cheese using a wooden spoon. Boil the fondue for 1 minute. When the cheese is completely melted, stir in the mustard and salt, pepper, cayenne, and nutmeg to taste. Stir in the kirsch and serve at once. Invite each guest to dip toasted bread, vegetables, and apples into the fondue.
Serves 4.

403 CALORIES PER SERVING: 25 G PROTEIN, 9 G FAT, 39 G CARBOHYDRATE; 351 MG SODIUM; 20 MG CHOLESTEROL.

FONDUE RAPPERSWIL WITH SPICY SOY SAUCE

The citizens of Rapperswil on the Zurichsee in northern Switzerland cook paper-thin slices of beef in simmering broth instead of oil, using a fraction of the fat found in traditional fondue bourguignonne. What makes fondue fun are the sauces. Here's a Spicy Soy Sauce to get you started. Other sauce possibilities include Horseradish "Cream" (page 183), Lemon Chili Sauce (page 184), and Romesco Sauce (page 185). The more the merrier!

1 pound beef tenderloin or sirloin,
  partially frozen
sprigs of parsley, for garnish

FOR THE SAUCE
1 or 2 jalapeño chilies (or to taste), seeded
  and minced
2 cloves garlic, minced (2 teaspoons)
2 scallions, minced

1 tablespoon minced fresh ginger
¾ cup chicken or veal stock
2 tablespoons soy sauce
2 tablespoons rice vinegar
1 tablespoon honey

6 cups beef, veal, or chicken broth or stock
  (pages 237–238)
salt and freshly ground black pepper

Slice the meat across the grain as thinly as possible. (If you have a good relationship with your butcher, ask him to slice it on a meat slicer.) Arrange the sliced beef in an attractive pattern on a platter. Garnish with parsley sprigs, cover with plastic wrap, and refrigerate until using.

To make the sauce, combine all the ingredients and stir until the honey is dissolved.

Just before serving, bring the broth to a boil in a fondue pot. (If the fondue flame isn't strong enough, bring the broth to a boil on the stove.) Add salt and pepper to taste. Invite each guest to cook the beef to taste in the simmering broth.

Serves 4.

Note: Most fondue burners aren't hot enough to keep the broth boiling. Use an electric hot plate, tabletop gas burner, or camping stove.

193 CALORIES PER SERVING: 23 G PROTEIN, 8 G FAT, 7 G CARBOHYDRATE; 869 MG SODIUM; 64 MG CHOLESTEROL.

WHITE PIZZA

Here's a switch from the usual red pizza. The topping is made with nonfat ricotta cheese, plus a little goat cheese for flavor. Make the dough in a food processor or by hand.

FOR THE DOUGH
1 tablespoon (1 envelope) dry yeast, or
  ½ ounce compressed yeast
1 tablespoon sugar
2 tablespoons warm water
3 cups unbleached white flour
½ cup whole wheat flour
1½ teaspoons salt
1 cup cold water (approximately)
cornmeal

FOR THE TOPPING
1 pound low-fat or nonfat ricotta cheese
1 tablespoon olive oil

3 cloves garlic, minced (1 tablespoon)
2 scallions, minced
2 ounces goat cheese, crumbled (optional)
3 tablespoons minced fresh herbs, or
  2 teaspoons dried (optional)
salt and freshly ground black pepper
1 red bell pepper, seeded
1 yellow bell pepper, seeded
1 green bell pepper, seeded
1 cup broccoli florets
½ cup pitted black olives, cut in half
  lengthwise (optional)

To make the dough, combine the yeast with the sugar and warm water in a small bowl and let stand for 5 minutes, or until frothy.

Place the flours and salt in the bowl of a food processor. With the machine running, add the dissolved yeast and cold water. Process for 1 minute, or until the dough comes together into a smooth ball. (If the dough is too dry, add a little more water.) Knead the dough for 1 to 2 minutes in the food processor or for 4 to 5 minutes by hand. The dough can also be made in a heavy-duty mixer fitted with a dough hook.

Place the dough in a lightly oiled bowl and cover with plastic wrap. Let rise in a warm, draft-free spot for 1 hour, or until doubled in bulk.

To make the topping, drain the ricotta in a yogurt funnel (see Mail-Order Sources) or a cheesecloth-lined colander for 20 minutes. Heat the oil in a skillet. Cook the garlic and scallions over medium heat for 2 to 3 minutes, or until soft but not brown. Transfer the ricotta to a mix-

ing bowl and stir in the garlic, scallions, goat cheese, and herbs (if using). Add salt and pepper to taste.

Cut the peppers into rings or fanciful shapes. Cook the broccoli florets in boiling salted water for 2 minutes, or until tender-crisp. Refresh under cold water and drain.

Preheat the oven to 525 degrees F, or as high as it will go. (If you have a baking stone, preheat it in the oven.) A half hour before serving, punch down the dough and roll it into two 12" circles or four 7" circles. Transfer the circles to a baker's peel or pizza pan liberally sprinkled with cornmeal. Spread each circle with the ricotta mixture and arrange the peppers, broccoli, and olives (if using) on top. Let rise 10 to 15 minutes.

Slide the pizzas onto the baking stone (or place the pans in the oven). Bake for 15 to 20 minutes, or until the edges and bottom are golden brown. Cut the pizzas into wedges and serve at once.

Serves 8 as an appetizer, 4 as an entrée.

630 CALORIES PER SERVING: 27 G PROTEIN, 14 G FAT, 100 G CARBOHYDRATE; 953 MG SODIUM; 35 MG CHOLESTEROL.

GRILLED EGGPLANT DIP

Baba ganooj (eggplant dip) is well known in North America, but few people prepare it the correct way, which is to char the eggplant on a grill to give it a rich smoky flavor. Once you try this recipe, you'll never go back to oven-baked eggplant. Serve with fresh or toasted pita bread wedges and fresh vegetables for dipping.

2 large eggplants (about 2 pounds)
2 cloves garlic, minced (2 teaspoons)
2 scallions, minced
¼ cup minced flat-leaf parsley, plus a few
    sprigs for garnish
3–4 tablespoons fresh lemon juice
    (or to taste)

2 tablespoons nonfat yogurt
2 tablespoons extra-virgin olive oil
½ teaspoon ground cumin
salt and freshly ground black pepper

Prick the eggplants in a few spots with a fork. (This keeps them from exploding.) Grill them over a medium flame, turning often, until the skin is charred on all sides and the flesh is soft. Let cool.

Cut the eggplants in half lengthwise and scoop out the flesh. (There should be about 2 cups.)

Purée the flesh in a food processor, or finely chop it by hand. Mix the garlic, scallions, and parsley with the eggplant. Add the lemon juice, yogurt, olive oil, and cumin. Season with salt and pepper to taste. Spoon into a shallow bowl and garnish with parsley sprigs.

Serves 6 to 8.

11 CALORIES PER TABLESPOON: 0 G PROTEIN, 1 G FAT, 1 G CARBOHYDRATE; 1 MG SODIUM; 0 MG CHOLESTEROL.

SPINACH SOUFFLÉ

Soufflé might seem like an unlikely dish for a low-fat cookbook. The secret to my version is to replace the egg yolks with puréed roasted onions. The egg whites, which are almost pure protein, provide the puff. Serve with Tomato Vinaigrette (page 181) or Red-Hot Tomato Sauce (page 93).

1 medium-sized onion
2 cloves garlic
1 teaspoon butter, melted, or vegetable
    oil spray
2 tablespoons lightly toasted sesame seeds
    or bread crumbs
12 ounces fresh spinach (or 1 package frozen)
3 tablespoons flour

1 cup skim milk
1 tablespoon Dijon-style mustard
salt and freshly ground black pepper
cayenne pepper
freshly grated nutmeg
6 egg whites
¼ teaspoon cream of tartar

Preheat the oven to 350 degrees F. Roast the onion in its skin for 1 hour, or until soft. After 30 minutes, add the garlic cloves in their skins and roast until soft. Let cool.

Meanwhile, brush a 5-cup soufflé dish with the melted butter or spray with vegetable oil. Sprinkle the inside of the dish with sesame seeds. Steam the spinach until tender, refresh in ice water, and drain. Squeeze the spinach in your hand, wringing out as much liquid as possible. Peel the onion and garlic, and purée them in a food processor with the spinach and flour.

Transfer the purée to a saucepan and bring it to a boil. Stir in the milk and boil for 2 minutes,

or until the mixture thickens. Whisk in the mustard, salt, pepper, cayenne, and nutmeg. (The mixture should be very highly seasoned.) Keep warm. Preheat the oven to 400 degrees F.

Beat the egg whites almost to stiff peaks, adding the cream of tartar after 20 seconds. Stir ¼ of the whites into the hot spinach mixture. Gently fold this mixture into the remaining whites. Spoon the soufflé mixture into the prepared dish and smooth the top with a wet spatula. Bake for 20 to 30 minutes, or until puffed and cooked to taste. Serve at once.

Serves 4.

130 CALORIES PER SERVING: 12 G PROTEIN, 4 G FAT, 13 G CARBOHYDRATE; 223 MG SODIUM; 4 MG CHOLESTEROL.

LEBANESE YOGURT DIP

This recipe comes from my Greek friend Dina Hannah. It is made with yogurt cheese, a great low-fat alternative to cream cheese, and is very easy to prepare, but you need to start the day before you plan to serve it. Serve with fresh or toasted wedges of pita bread.

2 cups nonfat yogurt
¼ cup bulgur (cracked wheat)
2 scallions, minced
2 tablespoons minced flat-leaf parsley
1 clove garlic, minced (1 teaspoon)

2 tablespoons fresh lemon juice (or to taste)
1½ tablespoons extra-virgin olive oil (or to taste)
salt and freshly ground black pepper

Drain the yogurt in a yogurt funnel (see Mail-Order Sources) or a cheesecloth-lined colander for 2 hours. Transfer the resulting yogurt cheese to a bowl and stir in the bulgur. Refrigerate overnight.

The next day, beat the remaining ingredients into the yogurt mixture. Correct the seasoning, adding salt, pepper, lemon juice, and olive oil to taste.

Serves 4 to 6.

33 CALORIES PER TABLESPOON: 2 G PROTEIN, 1 G FAT, 3 G CARBOHYDRATE; 19 MG SODIUM; 2 MG CHOLESTEROL.

BEAN GUACAMOLE

Here's a low-fat twist on a Mexican favorite: guacamole made with puréed beans instead of avocado. Use chick-peas, kidney beans, or white beans. If you're in a hurry, buy them canned (choose a brand low in sodium) and be sure to drain them thoroughly. Using my oven-baked method, even the tortilla chips are low in fat. For a fanciful presentation, cut one of the tortillas into a cactus shape with a sharp knife.

1 cup dried white beans, soaked in water to cover overnight (or 2 cups cooked beans)
1 or 2 cloves garlic, minced (1 or 2 teaspoons)
salt and freshly ground black pepper
1½ tablespoons plus 1–2 teaspoons extra-virgin olive oil
4–5 tablespoons fresh lime juice

2 tablespoons chicken stock or water (approximately)
1 or 2 jalapeño chilies, cored, seeded, and minced
2 scallions, minced
¼ cup finely chopped cilantro, plus several sprigs for garnish
1 package (1 pound) corn tortillas

Boil the soaked beans for 20 minutes, or until tender. (For complete instructions on cooking beans, see page 230).

Purée the beans, garlic, salt, and pepper in a food processor, adding the 1½ tablespoons olive oil, lime juice, and enough stock or water to obtain a smooth, thick purée. Stir in the chilies, scallions, and cilantro. (It's best to do this by hand. If you use a food processor, the dip will turn green.) Transfer the dip to a bowl and garnish with sprigs of cilantro.

Preheat the oven to 350 degrees F. Lightly brush the tortillas on both sides with olive oil. Cut each tortilla into 6 wedges. Arrange the wedges on a baking sheet and bake for 10 to 15 minutes, or until crisp, turning once. Let cool on a wire rack. Serve the chips on the side for dipping.

Serves 6 to 8.

204 CALORIES PER SERVING: 9 G PROTEIN, 5 G FAT, 33 G CARBOHYDRATE; 117 MG SODIUM; 0 MG CHOLESTEROL.

FRENCH HERBED CHEESE DIP

I first tasted this garlic-laden dip at a smoky, low-ceilinged restaurant in the Marais district of Paris. A specialty of Lyons, it bears the curious name cervelles de canuts, *literally "weavers' brains." It can be made in the food processor, but the herbs should be chopped by hand and added separately so they don't turn the cheese green. Traditionally spread on rye bread or served over boiled potatoes, this is an excellent dip for Homemade Breadsticks (page 75).*

2 cups nonfat yogurt
8 ounces low-fat, small-curd cottage cheese
4 cloves garlic, minced (4 teaspoons)
1½ tablespoons extra-virgin olive oil
1 tablespoon white wine vinegar or
  rice wine vinegar

1 tablespoon fresh lemon juice (or to taste)
salt and freshly ground black pepper
½ cup finely chopped fresh herbs (tarragon,
  thyme, oregano, basil, chervil, chives,
  scallions, and/or flat-leaf parsley)

Drain the yogurt in a yogurt funnel (see Mail-Order Sources) or cheesecloth-lined colander for 2 hours. Drain the cottage cheese in a fine-meshed strainer for 2 hours.

Purée the yogurt and cottage cheese in a food processor. Work in the garlic, olive oil, vinegar, lemon juice, salt, and pepper. Correct the seasoning, adding lemon juice and salt to taste. Stir in the herbs. The dip can be served right away, but its flavor will improve if you let it ripen with the herbs for 2 to 3 hours.

Serves 8.

23 CALORIES PER TABLESPOON: 2 G PROTEIN, 1 G FAT, 2 G CARBOHYDRATE; 34 MG SODIUM; 2 MG CHOLESTEROL.

CRAB-STUFFED ARTICHOKES

This dish dates from my student days at the Cordon Bleu in Paris. Shrimp, lobster, or chicken breast can be substituted for the crab. For the best results, use homemade bread crumbs. Serve with Lemon Chili Sauce (page 184) or Horseradish "Cream" (page 183).

4 large artichokes
½ lemon
salt

FOR THE STUFFING
½ pound crabmeat
1 teaspoon freshly grated lemon zest
3 tablespoons lightly toasted fresh
  bread crumbs

3 tablespoons finely chopped flat-leaf parsley
2 tablespoons finely chopped fresh dill,
  or more parsley
2 scallions, finely chopped
1 tablespoon Dijon-style mustard
salt and freshly ground black pepper
pinch of cayenne pepper
2 teaspoons olive oil

Cut the stems and crowns (the top third) off the artichokes. With scissors, cut the barbs off the leaves. Rub the artichokes with the lemon to prevent browning. Cook in at least 3 quarts of boiling salted water for 30 to 40 minutes, or until the leaves pull away easily and you can easily pierce the heart with a skewer. Refresh under cold water, invert, and drain.

To make the stuffing, pick through the crabmeat, removing any bits of shell. Combine the crabmeat with the zest, bread crumbs, herbs, scallions, mustard, salt, pepper, and cayenne in a bowl and mix well. Correct the seasoning, adding salt, pepper, and cayenne to taste.

Remove the inside leaves of the artichokes to make a 1½" cavity. Use a melon baller or grapefruit spoon to scrape out the fibrous "choke" at the bottom, taking care not to pierce the heart. Spoon the filling into the artichokes and sprinkle ½ teaspoon oil over each. The artichokes can be prepared ahead to this stage.

Preheat the oven to 400 degrees F. Bake the stuffed artichokes for 10 to 15 minutes, or until thoroughly heated. Serve warm or at room temperature.

Serves 4.

122 CALORIES PER SERVING: 8 G PROTEIN, 4 G FAT, 18 G CARBOHYDRATE; 303 MG SODIUM; 8 MG CHOLESTEROL.

LIPTAUER CHEESE

Lipto, a region in northern Hungary famed for its sheep cheese, is the home of Liptauer cheese, a tangy spread flavored with paprika and caraway seeds. This version uses low-fat cottage cheese as a base. (Some people add a spoonful of anchovy paste as well.) Serve it surrounded by light and dark party rye bread arranged in alternating and overlapping circles. It tastes best served as soon as possible.

1 pound low-fat, large-curd cottage cheese
1 tablespoon minced onion
1 teaspoon Hungarian paprika
½–1 teaspoon dry mustard
¼ teaspoon caraway seeds

1–2 teaspoons fresh lemon juice (or to taste)
freshly ground black pepper
1 tablespoon chopped chives or scallions, for garnish

Drain the cottage cheese in a strainer for 1 hour. Purée in a food processor. Work in the remaining ingredients except the chives. Correct the seasoning, adding mustard and lemon juice to taste. The cheese should be very spicy. Transfer the cheese to a bowl or crock, sprinkle with the chopped chives, and serve immediately.

Serves 6 to 8.

58 CALORIES PER TABLESPOON: 10 G PROTEIN, 1 G FAT, 3 G CARBOHYDRATE; 307 MG SODIUM; 3 MG CHOLESTEROL.

CREAMY TOFU DIP WITH GINGER AND SCALLIONS

Here's a tofu dish that's designed to turn skeptics into believers. Piped in rosettes on rice wafers, it acquires the elegance of foie gras. This dip is equally tasty served with vegetable sticks or toasted pita chips, or piped onto rice crackers and decorated with cilantro sprigs or sliced nori seaweed.

1 pound tofu (preferably medium or soft), drained
1 jalapeño chili, cored, seeded, and minced
1 or 2 cloves garlic, minced (1 or 2 teaspoons)
2 teaspoons minced fresh ginger
2 scallions, whites minced, greens finely chopped for garnish

2–3 tablespoons tamari or soy sauce
2 tablespoons rice wine vinegar
1 tablespoon sesame oil
2 teaspoons sugar (or to taste)
salt and freshly ground black pepper
1–2 tablespoons water (if needed)

Combine all the ingredients except the scallion greens and water in a food processor or blender. Purée until smooth, adding water as necessary to obtain a creamy consistency. Transfer to a bowl and garnish with scallion greens. Serve as soon as possible; the dip tends to darken as it sits.

Serves 4.

11 CALORIES PER TABLESPOON: 1 G PROTEIN, .7 G FAT, 1 G CARBOHYDRATE; 43 MG SODIUM; 0 MG CHOLESTEROL.

SOUPS

GRAPE GAZPACHO

To most people, gazpacho means an icy purée of tomatoes and other vegetables. Not so in Málaga, in southern Spain, where grapes, garlic, and almonds are turned into an uncommonly refreshing soup, ajo blanco. It is traditionally made with green grapes, but a lovely rose color and rich flavor can be obtained with red grapes.

¼ cup blanched almonds
2 pounds seedless red grapes
1 or 2 cloves garlic, minced (1 or 2 teaspoons)
2 or 3 slices firm white bread, crusts
   removed, diced (about 2 cups)

1 tablespoon Spanish olive oil
1 tablespoon wine vinegar (or to taste)
½ teaspoon almond extract (optional)
salt and freshly ground black pepper
¼ cup nonfat yogurt

Preheat the oven to 350 degrees F. Lightly toast the almonds on a baking sheet (or use a toaster oven) for 10 minutes, or until crisp but not brown. Let the almonds cool.

Purée the almonds, grapes, and garlic in a blender. Add the bread, oil, vinegar, almond extract (if using), salt, and pepper, and purée until smooth. The gazpacho can be eaten right away, but it will taste better if you "ripen" it in the refrigerator for 1 hour. If too thick, stir in a few tablespoons of cold water.

Just before serving, correct the seasoning, adding vinegar and salt to taste. The sweetness of the grapes should be balanced by the piquancy of the vinegar and pungency of the garlic. Whisk the yogurt in a small bowl until smooth and creamy. Ladle the gazpacho into serving bowls and garnish each with a dollop of yogurt. If you like, marble the yogurt into the soup with the tip of a knife.

Serves 4.

272 CALORIES PER SERVING: 5 G PROTEIN, 9 G FAT, 49 G CARBOHYDRATE; 75 MG SODIUM; 0 MG CHOLESTEROL.

CHILLED PLUM SOUP

I first tasted this refreshing soup at Chillingsworth, a restaurant in Brewster on Cape Cod. Owner/chef Nitzy Rabin favors large, fleshy Friar plums, but any ripe plum will do.

2 pounds ripe plums, pitted and chopped (about 4 cups)
1 cup dry white wine
1 cup cranberry juice cocktail
1 cup water
½ teaspoon ground ginger

½–⅔ cup sugar (or to taste)
1 tablespoon cornstarch
½ cup port wine
½ cup nonfat yogurt
sprigs of fresh mint, for garnish

Place the plums, white wine, cranberry juice, water, ginger, and ½ cup sugar in a large saucepan and bring to a boil. Reduce the heat and cook for 6 to 8 minutes, or until very soft. Skim off any foam or impurities that rise to the surface.

Dissolve the cornstarch in the port. Stir this mixture into the soup and boil for 1 minute. Taste the soup for sweetness, adding sugar as necessary. Cool the soup, then purée it in a blender. Chill for at least 4 hours.

Ladle the soup into chilled bowls and swirl in the yogurt. To create a marbled effect, whisk the yogurt until smooth, spoon it onto the soup, and drag the tip of a knife through it. Garnish each bowl with a sprig of mint and serve at once.

Serves 4 to 6.

329 CALORIES PER SERVING: 4 G PROTEIN, 1 G FAT, 64 G CARBOHYDRATE; 41 MG SODIUM; 1 MG CHOLESTEROL.

CINNAMON PEACH SOUP

Here's another great cold soup for a hot summer day. For the best results, use peaches that are ripe to the point of being squishy soft. A similar soup could be made with nectarines or apricots.

2 pounds ripe peaches
3 whole cloves
3 allspice berries
3 cardamom pods
2 cups freshly squeezed orange juice
3 tablespoons fresh lime juice (or to taste)
3–4 tablespoons honey or brown sugar
(or to taste)

1 teaspoon ground cinnamon
1 teaspoon ground ginger
1 cup nonfat yogurt
1 tablespoon diced candied ginger
sprigs of fresh mint, for garnish

Drop the peaches in a pot of boiling water and boil for 30 seconds. Rinse them under cold water and slip off the skins. Pit the peaches and coarsely chop them. Tie the cloves, allspice, and cardamom in cheesecloth (or wrap in foil and pierce with a fork).

Combine the peaches, spice bundle, orange juice, lime juice, honey, cinnamon, and ginger in a heavy saucepan. (The amount of honey needed will depend on the sweetness of the peaches.) Simmer for 5 to 10 minutes, or until the fruit is very soft.

Remove the spice bundle and let the soup cool to room temperature. Purée the soup in a blender and chill. Just before serving, whisk in the yogurt and candied ginger. Correct the seasoning, adding honey and lime juice to taste. Serve in glass bowls or wine goblets, garnishing each with a sprig of mint.

Serves 4 to 6.

215 CALORIES PER SERVING: 5 G PROTEIN, 1 G FAT, 51 G CARBOHYDRATE; 46 MG SODIUM; 1 MG CHOLESTEROL.

ESCAROLE, PARSNIP, AND WHITE BEAN SOUP

Escarole is a broad-leafed green with a pleasantly bitter flavor.
It mellows when paired with parsnips, which are surprisingly sweet.

1 head escarole
1½ tablespoons olive oil
1 onion, finely chopped
2 cloves garlic, minced (2 teaspoons)
1 leek, finely chopped (about 1 cup)
7 cups chicken stock (page 237)
½ cup dry white beans, soaked overnight
   (or 1 cup cooked beans)

1 bouquet garni of bay leaf, thyme, and
   parsley
salt and freshly ground black pepper
2 parsnips, peeled and diced
3 tablespoons freshly grated Parmigiano
   Reggiano, or other Parmesan-style
   cheese (optional)
1–2 teaspoons hot red pepper flakes,
   for garnish

Break the escarole into leaves and thoroughly wash. Cut the leaves widthwise into ½" strips, or dice them. Heat the olive oil in a large saucepan. Add the onion, garlic, and leek, and cook over medium heat for 3 minutes, or until soft but not brown. Add the stock, beans, bouquet garni, salt, and pepper. Simmer the soup for 6 to 8 minutes, or until the beans are almost tender.

Add the parsnips and escarole, and continue simmering for 5 minutes, or until the parsnips and beans are tender and the escarole is soft. Correct the seasoning, adding salt and pepper to taste. Ladle the soup into bowls and sprinkle cheese (if using) and hot pepper flakes over each.
Serves 6.

160 CALORIES PER SERVING: 7 G PROTEIN, 5 G FAT, 24 G CARBOHYDRATE; 434 MG SODIUM; 1 MG CHOLESTEROL.

COLLARD GREEN AND POTATO SOUP

This soup is modeled on Portugal's caldo verde, *or "green broth," made with a leafy cabbage similar to collard greens. In Portugal, you can buy a device that looks like a meat slicer for cutting collards into paper-thin shreds. Lacking this, roll the greens lengthwise into a tight bundle, then slice them widthwise as finely as possible, using a sharp chef's knife.*

1½ tablespoons Spanish or Portuguese
  olive oil
1 onion, finely chopped
3 cloves garlic, minced (1 tablespoon)
2 large potatoes, peeled and finely diced
3 cups chicken stock

3 cups water
2 bay leaves
salt and freshly ground black pepper
1½ pounds collard greens, stemmed and
  sliced paper-thin (8 cups)

Heat the oil in a large saucepan. Cook the onion and garlic over medium heat for 3 minutes, or until soft but not brown. Add the potatoes, stock, water, bay leaves, salt, and pepper. Bring the soup to a boil, reduce the heat, and simmer for 10 minutes, or until the potatoes are tender.

Stir in the collard greens and simmer for 1 to 2 minutes, or until just tender. Correct the seasoning, adding salt and pepper to taste. Ladle the soup into large bowls and serve with crusty bread.

Serves 6 as an appetizer, 4 as an entrée.

Note: The Portuguese like their greens stringier than most North Americans do. You may wish to cut the shredded greens a few times with a chef's knife.

191 CALORIES PER SERVING: 6 G PROTEIN, 6 G FAT, 31 G CARBOHYDRATE; 82 MG SODIUM; 0 MG CHOLESTEROL.

CURRIED SQUASH SOUP WITH CHUTNEY AND YOGURT

Most squash soups are sweet enough to be classed as liquid pumpkin pie. Not this one, which enlivens the earthy flavor of squash with curry. (Be sure to allow enough time to cook the squash and sweet potato.) To complete the Indian mood, the soup is garnished with dollops of yogurt and chutney.

1 small acorn or butternut squash (about
  1 pound)
1 sweet potato
1 tablespoon olive oil
2 cloves garlic, minced (2 teaspoons)
1 large onion, finely chopped
2 stalks celery, finely chopped
2 teaspoons minced fresh ginger

2 teaspoons curry powder
¼ teaspoon ground cardamom
5 cups chicken stock
salt and freshly ground black pepper
½ cup nonfat yogurt
2 tablespoons chutney
2 tablespoons chopped fresh chives or
  scallions, for garnish

Preheat the oven to 325 degrees F. Place the squash and sweet potato in a roasting pan and bake for 1 hour, or until soft. Let cool. Peel the squash, cut it in half, and scrape out the seeds. Peel the sweet potato. Cut the squash and sweet potato into 1" pieces.

Heat the olive oil in a large pot. Add the garlic, onion, celery, ginger, curry powder, and cardamom, and cook over medium heat, stirring frequently, for 4 to 6 minutes, or until golden brown.

Add the squash, sweet potato, stock, salt, and pepper. Simmer the soup for 20 minutes, or until the vegetables are very soft. Purée the soup in a blender and return it to the pot. If too thick, thin with a little water or stock. Correct the seasoning, adding salt and curry powder to taste.

To serve, ladle the soup into bowls and place a tablespoon of yogurt in the center of each. Place a teaspoon of chutney in the center of each dollop of yogurt. Sprinkle the soup with chives and serve at once.

Serves 6 to 8.

138 CALORIES PER SERVING: 7 G PROTEIN, 4 G FAT, 20 G CARBOHYDRATE; 680 MG SODIUM; 0 MG CHOLESTEROL.

BRAZILIAN CHICKEN RICE SOUP

Every nation has a version of chicken soup. One of the most satisfying is Brazil's canja. This recipe includes instructions for making the broth. If you're in a hurry, use premade stock (page 237) and start with adding the rice in paragraph 3.

1 3-pound chicken
1 bay leaf
1 medium-sized onion, quartered
1 whole clove
2 ripe tomatoes, quartered
1 carrot, cut into 1" pieces
¼ cup chopped celery leaves

20 black peppercorns, tied in a piece of cheesecloth
½ cup uncooked white rice
salt and freshly ground black pepper
3 carrots, thinly sliced on the diagonal
3 stalks celery, thinly sliced on the diagonal
¼ cup finely chopped flat-leaf parsley

Wash the chicken thoroughly. Remove the skin and any pieces of fat. Pin the bay leaf to 1 onion quarter with the clove. Place the chicken in a large pot with the tomatoes, onion quarters, 1 carrot, celery leaves, and peppercorn bundle. Add 10 cups cold water and bring to a boil. Using a ladle, skim off the fat and foam that rise to the surface. Reduce the heat and simmer for 1 hour, skimming often to remove the fat.

Remove the chicken from the broth and let cool. Strain the broth into a large saucepan, pressing the vegetables to extract the juices.

(There should be about 8 cups of broth.) Pull the chicken meat off the bones and shred or finely dice it.

Add the rice, salt, and pepper to the broth and simmer for 10 minutes. Add the thinly sliced carrots and celery to the soup with the shredded chicken and half the parsley. Simmer the soup for another 10 minutes, or until the rice is tender. Correct the seasoning, adding salt and pepper to taste. Sprinkle with the remaining parsley and serve at once.

Serves 8 as an appetizer, 4 to 6 as an entrée.

293 CALORIES PER SERVING: 33 G PROTEIN, 8 G FAT, 22 G CARBOHYDRATE; 131 MG SODIUM; 92 MG CHOLESTEROL.

THAI HOT AND SOUR SOUP

This soup is easy to make, but it requires a few special ingredients that are explained in Cook's Notes. This recipe can also be made with chicken, pork, or squid.

4 or 5 stalks fresh lemongrass (or 3 tablespoons dried), or 4 strips lemon zest
1 tablespoon minced galangal (see Cook's Notes) or fresh ginger (about 1" fresh or frozen galangal, or 3 or 4 dried slices)
4 cups chicken stock
3 tablespoons fish sauce (or to taste)
½–1 teaspoon Thai chili paste or other hot sauce (or to taste)
1 ripe tomato, cut into 8 wedges

1 medium-sized onion, thinly sliced
1 or 2 Thai, serrano, or jalapeño chilies, thinly sliced on the diagonal
4 ounces fresh straw, button, or oyster mushrooms, halved or quartered (about 1 cup)
8 ounces small shrimp
¼ cup fresh lime juice
2 tablespoons thinly sliced scallions
⅓ cup fresh cilantro leaves

Cut the top ⅔ off each lemongrass stalk, trim off the outside leaves and roots, and cut the core into ½" slices on the diagonal. If using dried lemongrass, soak the pieces in warm water for 20 minutes, then mince. If using lemon zest, remove it from the fruit in thin strips with a vegetable peeler and mince. If using dried galangal, soak it in warm water for 20 minutes.

Combine the lemongrass, galangal, chicken stock, fish sauce, and chili paste in a saucepan and bring to a boil. Gently simmer for 5 minutes. Add the tomato, onion, chilies, mushrooms, and shrimp, and simmer for 1 minute, or until the shrimp are firm and pink. The soup can be prepared ahead to this stage.

Just before serving, stir in the lime juice, scallions, and cilantro. Bring the soup just to a boil. It should be spicy and quite sour. If more salt is needed, add more fish sauce. If more tartness or hotness is desired, add more lime juice or chili paste. Suggest to your guests that they eat around the lemongrass pieces.

Serves 4.

104 CALORIES PER SERVING: 14 G PROTEIN, 2 G FAT, 9 G CARBOHYDRATE; 272 MG SODIUM; 90 MG CHOLESTEROL.

VIETNAMESE BEEF NOODLE SOUP

Rice noodle soup is a popular street food throughout Southeast Asia. This version, redolent with star anise and ginger, takes only 15 minutes to make. It even includes its own salad: the platter of bean sprouts and mint sprigs traditionally served with a Vietnamese meal. Asians like long noodles, and it is their custom to slurp them noisily. North Americans may prefer to cut the rice sticks into more manageable lengths.

8 ounces rice sticks, preferably ⅛" wide (see Cook's Notes)
4 scallions, whites minced, greens finely chopped for garnish
6 cups beef or chicken stock (pages 237, 238)
6 thin slices fresh ginger
3 star anise
¼ cup fish sauce
6 ounces beef tenderloin or sirloin, partially frozen

1 large white onion
12–15 fresh basil or mint leaves
2 cups fresh mung bean sprouts
12 sprigs fresh mint or basil
1 or 2 jalapeño or serrano chilies, thinly sliced
2 limes, cut into wedges

Soak the rice sticks in cold water for 30 minutes, or until soft. Combine the scallion whites, stock, ginger, star anise, and fish sauce in a large pot and gently simmer for 10 minutes, or until well flavored. Remove the ginger and star anise with a slotted spoon and discard.

Meanwhile, slice the beef across the grain as thinly as possible. (It's easier if you have a meat slicer.) Thinly slice the onion. Thinly sliver the basil leaves. Arrange the bean sprouts, mint sprigs, sliced chilies, and lime wedges on a platter.

Just before serving, bring the broth to a boil.

Add the rice sticks and simmer for 15 to 30 seconds, or until soft. Stir in the beef and remove the pan from the heat. (The heat of the broth should be sufficient to cook the meat. If not, simmer it for a few seconds.) Stir in the onion slices and ladle the soup into bowls. Garnish each bowl with the slivered basil and chopped scallion greens, and serve at once, with the bean sprout platter on the side. Let each person add bean sprouts, mint sprigs, chilies, and lime juice to the soup to taste.

Serves 6 as an appetizer, 4 as an entrée.

341 CALORIES PER SERVING: 24 G PROTEIN, 5 G FAT, 49 G CARBOHYDRATE; 2671 MG SODIUM; 32 MG CHOLESTEROL.

GRANDMA RAICHLEN'S CABBAGE BORSCHT

To most people, borscht means beets, but this soulful soup can be made with a multitude of vegetables. My great-grandmother brought the recipe from her native Riga to America. To make the broth, she always used flanken, a cheap, flavorful cut of meat similar to skirt steak. For a vegetarian version, you could use water instead of broth. I dedicate this recipe to my Aunt Vivian, who loved cabbage borscht more than anything.

1 head green or savoy cabbage
1½ tablespoons olive oil
2 leeks, finely chopped
1 large onion, finely chopped
2 carrots, peeled and finely chopped
2 stalks celery, finely chopped
1 large parsnip, peeled and finely chopped
3 cloves garlic, minced (1 tablespoon)
4 or 5 ripe tomatoes (about 2 pounds), peeled, seeded, and finely chopped, or 1 28-ounce can imported plum tomatoes

2 quarts beef stock, chicken stock, or water
5 whole cloves (or ¼ teaspoon ground cloves)
2 teaspoons caraway seeds (optional)
salt and freshly ground black pepper
¼ cup brown sugar (or to taste)
¼ cup red wine vinegar (or to taste)
½ cup finely chopped scallions (4 whole scallions), for garnish
¼ cup chopped flat-leaf parsley, for garnish

Cut the cabbage in half lengthwise. Remove the core and cut the leaves widthwise into ¼" strips. Heat the oil in a large saucepan. Add the leeks, onion, carrots, celery, parsnip, and garlic, and cook over medium heat for 3 minutes. Stir in the cabbage and cook, stirring often, for 6 to 8 minutes, or until soft. Stir in the tomatoes, stock, cloves, caraway seeds (if using), salt, and pepper. Bring the soup to a boil, reduce the heat, and simmer for 30 to 40 minutes, or until the vegetables are very tender.

Ten minutes before the end, stir in the brown sugar and vinegar. The soup should be a little sweet and a little sour. Correct the seasoning, adding salt, sugar, and vinegar to taste. Ladle into bowls and garnish with chopped scallions and parsley.

Serves 8 to 10.

160 CALORIES PER SERVING: 6 G PROTEIN, 4 G FAT, 29 G CARBOHYDRATE; 832 MG SODIUM; 0 MG CHOLESTEROL.

....

SALADS

....

WATERCRESS SALAD WITH ENDIVE AND ORANGE
....

This offbeat salad may be the oldest recipe in the book. It was inspired by a "sallet" I tasted at Plimoth Plantation, a museum devoted to the life of the 17th-century New England Pilgrims. The contrast of sweet (oranges and currants) and salty (capers and salt) has characterized New England cooking since the 1600s.

1 bunch watercress
2 Belgian endives
2 oranges
1 tablespoon balsamic vinegar

1 tablespoon extra-virgin olive oil
salt and freshly ground black pepper
2 tablespoons currants
1 tablespoon capers

Wash the watercress, spin dry, and tear into bite-sized sprigs. Cut the endives widthwise into ¼" strips. Cut the rind (both zest and white pith) off the oranges to expose the flesh. Make **V**-shaped cuts to remove the individual segments from the membranes, working over a large salad bowl to catch the juice. (There should be 1 to 2 tablespoons juice.)

Add the vinegar, oil, salt, and pepper to the orange juice in the bowl and whisk until blended. Add the currants and capers. Just before serving, add the watercress, endives, and orange segments. Gently toss to mix and serve at once.

Serves 4.

85 CALORIES PER SERVING: 2 G PROTEIN, 4 G FAT, 13 G CARBOHYDRATE; 47 MG SODIUM; 0 MG CHOLESTEROL.

....

Watercress Salad with Endive and Orange

FRANCO'S BITTER GREEN SALAD

Franco Spalvieri is a dear friend and owner of the restaurant Il Campidolio in Florence. His house salad is prepared with great ceremony in the dining room and is chock-full of the bitter greens so beloved by Italians. It's just the ticket for people who are bored with simple green salads. If any of the ingredients called for below are unavailable, feel free to substitute others.

4–5 cups torn bitter greens (radicchio, escarole, arugula, young dandelions, chicory, and/or others)
1 carrot
1 stalk celery
½ cup thinly sliced fennel
¼ cup thinly sliced green onions or scallions
1 large ripe tomato, cut into wedges

3 tablespoons chopped fresh herbs (tarragon, oregano, and/or basil)
1½ tablespoons extra-virgin olive oil
1½ tablespoons balsamic vinegar
1 tablespoon fresh lemon juice
salt and freshly ground black pepper
3 tablespoons freshly grated Parmigiano Reggiano, or other Parmesan-style cheese (optional)

Wash and dry the greens. Shave the carrot into thin strips using a vegetable peeler. Thinly slice the celery on the diagonal. Place the greens, vegetables, and herbs in a mixing bowl. Sprinkle with the oil, vinegar, lemon juice, salt, pepper, and cheese (if using), and toss well. Serve at once.

Serves 4.

88 CALORIES PER SERVING: 2 G PROTEIN, 5 G FAT, 9 G CARBOHYDRATE; 36 MG SODIUM; 0 MG CHOLESTEROL.

Arugula and Jerusalem Artichoke Salad

This is my wife's favorite salad, especially when we have fresh arugula in the garden. It combines the peppery flavor of arugula with the deliciously crisp, earthy taste of Jerusalem artichokes. The latter are small, lumpy tubers in the sunflower family that taste a little like artichokes. When buying them, choose the largest tubers with the fewest possible knobby protuberances, as these are the easiest to peel.

1 bunch arugula (about 1–1½ cups leaves)
3 or 4 Jerusalem artichokes, peeled and thinly sliced or cut into julienne strips
2 tablespoons minced fresh herbs (tarragon, oregano, parsley, and/or chives)

2 teaspoons extra-virgin olive oil
1 teaspoon sherry or wine vinegar (or to taste)
salt and freshly ground black pepper

Stem the arugula and wash thoroughly by gently agitating the leaves in a large bowl of cold water. Transfer the leaves to a strainer and pour off the sandy water. Refill the bowl and repeat until the leaves are clean. Dry in a salad spinner.

Combine the arugula, artichokes, and herbs in a mixing bowl. Sprinkle the oil, vinegar, salt, and pepper on top and toss gently. Correct the seasoning and serve at once.

Serves 2.

84 CALORIES PER SERVING: 1 G PROTEIN, 5 G FAT, 10 G CARBOHYDRATE; 5 MG SODIUM; 0 MG CHOLESTEROL.

BEET, AVOCADO, AND WATERCRESS SALAD

This colorful salad was invented by macrobiotic baker Michael Evans. The raw beets are wonderfully crunchy, but wear rubber gloves when preparing them to avoid staining your fingers.

FOR THE DRESSING
1 or 2 cloves garlic
salt and freshly ground black pepper
1 tablespoon Dijon-style mustard
2 tablespoons olive oil
3 tablespoons balsamic vinegar

1 ripe avocado, peeled, pitted, and diced
juice of 1 lemon

1 pound fresh beets, peeled and diced
2 bunches watercress, torn or cut into
   1" sprigs, with stems
2 red bell peppers, cored, seeded, and diced
1 red onion, diced
1 cup fresh or slightly thawed frozen peas
2 bunches stemmed and finely chopped
   cilantro and/or parsley

To make the dressing, combine the garlic with the salt and pepper in the bottom of a large salad bowl and mash to a smooth paste. Work in the mustard. Whisk in the oil and vinegar. Correct the seasoning, adding salt and pepper; the dressing should be highly seasoned.

Not more than 10 minutes before serving, add the salad ingredients to the dressing and toss well.

Serves 6 to 8.

156 CALORIES PER SERVING: 4 G PROTEIN, 10 G FAT, 15 G CARBOHYDRATE; 72 MG SODIUM; 0 MG CHOLESTEROL.

TOMATO AND HEARTS OF PALM SALAD

This recipe comes from my Brazilian friend Sheila Thomson. Brazil is the world's largest producer of hearts of palm, which combine beautifully with fresh tomatoes.

2 large, ripe, juicy beefsteak tomatoes
1 14-ounce can hearts of palm
1 teaspoon Dijon-style mustard
2 teaspoons red wine vinegar
2 teaspoons fresh lime juice

salt and freshly ground black pepper
1½ tablespoons extra-virgin olive oil
¼ cup chopped flat-leaf parsley, for garnish
2 tablespoons chopped chives or scallions, for garnish

Cut the peel off one of the tomatoes to make a tomato rose (see Eggplant Cake on page 15). Remove the stems from both tomatoes and thinly slice the tomatoes. Drain the hearts of palm and cut the thick ones lengthwise in quarters, the thin ones lengthwise in half. Combine the mustard, vinegar, lime juice, salt, and pepper in a mixing bowl and whisk until the salt is dissolved. Whisk in the oil in a thin stream. Correct the seasoning, adding salt and vinegar to taste.

Arrange the tomatoes around the edge of a round platter and arrange the hearts of palm in the middle, extending from the center like the spokes of a wheel. Spoon the dressing over the tomatoes and hearts of palm, and sprinkle with the parsley and chives. Place the tomato rose in the center and serve at once.

Serves 4.

114 CALORIES PER SERVING: 4 G PROTEIN, 6 G FAT, 15 G CARBOHYDRATE; 119 MG SODIUM; 0 MG CHOLESTEROL.

CUCUMBER SALAD WITH DILL

Every nation in Central and Eastern Europe has a version of cucumber salad. This one takes about 2 minutes to make, which is why it's a perennial favorite at my house.

1 seedless European cucumber, or
  2 American cucumbers
3 tablespoons cider or white vinegar
1 tablespoon sugar

salt and freshly ground black pepper
1 small red onion, sliced and broken into
  rings
3 tablespoons finely chopped fresh dill

Wash the cucumber(s) and partially remove the peel in lengthwise strips using a vegetable peeler or fork and leaving a little skin between each strip. Thinly slice the cucumber widthwise.

Place the vinegar, sugar, salt, and pepper in a bowl and whisk until the sugar is dissolved. Add the cucumber, onion, and dill, and toss well. The salad can be served at once, but it will improve in flavor if you let the ingredients marinate for 5 minutes.

Serves 4.

38 CALORIES PER SERVING: 1 G PROTEIN, 0 G FAT, 10 G CARBOHYDRATE; 5 MG SODIUM; 0 MG CHOLESTEROL.

CUCUMBER SALAD WITH SPICY WASABI DRESSING

Here's a Japanese version of cucumber salad made with a spicy horseradishlike condiment called wasabi (see Cook's Notes). Rice wine vinegar is milder than most Western vinegars. If unavailable, mix 2 parts distilled white vinegar with 1 part water.

1½ teaspoons dry wasabi (or to taste)
2 cucumbers
2 tablespoons rice wine vinegar
2 teaspoons sugar
1 teaspoon sesame oil

salt and freshly ground black pepper
1 green onion or 2 scallions, thinly sliced
1 tablespoon black or toasted white
  sesame seeds

Mix the wasabi with ½ teaspoon warm water in the bottom of a mixing bowl and let it stand for 5 minutes. Peel the cucumbers, cut each one in half lengthwise, and use a melon baller or spoon to scoop out the seeds. Cut the cucumbers widthwise into ¼" crescents.

Add the vinegar and sugar to the wasabi and whisk until smooth. Whisk in the sesame oil, salt, and pepper. Just before serving, add the cucumbers, green onion, and sesame seeds to the dressing and mix well.

Serves 4.

51 CALORIES PER SERVING: 1 G PROTEIN, 2 G FAT, 7 G CARBOHYDRATE; 25 MG SODIUM; 0 MG CHOLESTEROL.

Cucumber, Yogurt, and Spearmint Salad

This salad is a popular item on a mezza platter, a salad sampler served at the start of a Middle Eastern meal. The mint of choice is spearmint, but any fresh mint will work.

2 cups nonfat yogurt
2 cucumbers
1 or 2 cloves garlic, minced (1 or 2
   teaspoons)
salt
freshly ground black pepper

⅓ cup chopped fresh mint (preferably
   spearmint)
⅓ cup chopped flat-leaf parsley
½ teaspoon sugar (optional)
2 teaspoons extra-virgin olive oil
pita bread

Drain the yogurt in a yogurt funnel (see Mail-Order Sources) or cheesecloth-lined colander for 1 hour. Peel the cucumbers, cut each one in half lengthwise, and use a melon baller or spoon to scoop out the seeds. Cut the cucumbers into ¼" dice. Mash the garlic and salt to a paste in a mixing bowl.

Stir the drained yogurt into the garlic paste. Add the cucumbers, pepper, mint, parsley, and sugar, and toss to mix. Correct the seasoning, adding salt and pepper to taste. Just before serving, drizzle the salad with olive oil. Tear off pieces of pita bread and use them to scoop up the salad.

Serves 4 to 6.

147 CALORIES PER SERVING: 10 G PROTEIN, 5 G FAT, 16 G CARBOHYDRATE; 107 MG SODIUM; 12 MG CHOLESTEROL.

Clockwise from left: Lebanese Yogurt Dip (page 25), Cucumber, Yogurt, and Spearmint Salad (this page), Scallion Salad (page 54)

SCALLION SALAD
....

I first tasted this salad as part of a mezza platter at a harborside restaurant in Acho, Israel. You might think that a forkful of scallions would leave you with bad breath, but the parsley and lemon juice act as a natural mouthwash. Sumac is a purplish berry with a tart, lemony flavor. Look for it at Middle Eastern markets. Serve with grilled meat or fish.

3 bunches scallions, finely chopped
1 large bunch flat-leaf parsley, chopped (about 1 cup)
2 cloves garlic, minced (2 teaspoons)

¼ cup fresh lemon juice (or to taste)
1½ tablespoons olive oil
2 teaspoons ground sumac (optional)
salt and freshly ground black pepper

Combine all the ingredients in a bowl and toss well. Correct the seasoning, adding salt and lemon juice to taste. (The salad should be highly seasoned.) Serve within 1 hour of dressing.

Note: For the best results, chop all ingredients by hand. (A food processor tends to make the greens mushy.)

Serves 4.

82 CALORIES PER SERVING: 1 G PROTEIN, 7 G FAT, 6 G CARBOHYDRATE; 10 MG SODIUM; 0 MG CHOLESTEROL.

SPICY CABBAGE SALAD
....

This zesty salad could be thought of as Korean coleslaw. The recipe calls for nappa (Chinese cabbage), but you could also make it with savoy cabbage.

1 small head nappa (about 4 cups shredded)
3 scallions, minced
2 cloves garlic, minced (2 teaspoons)
1 tablespoon minced fresh ginger
1 or 2 hot chilies, preferably red, seeded and minced (optional)
¼ cup rice wine vinegar or distilled white vinegar

2 tablespoons fresh lime juice
1½ tablespoons sesame oil
salt and freshly ground white pepper
1½ tablespoons sugar
¼ cup sesame seeds
1 red bell pepper, cored, seeded, and thinly sliced

Cut the nappa widthwise into the thinnest possible strips. Combine the scallions, garlic, ginger, chilies (if using), vinegar, lime juice, sesame oil, salt, white pepper, and sugar in a large bowl. Stir until the sugar is dissolved. Lightly toast the sesame seeds in a dry skillet.

Add the nappa and red pepper to the vinegar mixture and mix thoroughly. Sprinkle the salad with toasted sesame seeds. The salad can be served at once, but it will be better if you let it stand for 15 to 20 minutes to let the flavors blend. Toss and correct the seasoning just before serving.

Serves 4 to 6.

133 CALORIES PER SERVING: 4 G PROTEIN, 10 G FAT, 11 G CARBOHYDRATE; 50 MG SODIUM; 0 MG CHOLESTEROL.

THAI EGGPLANT AND SHRIMP SALAD

This fragrant salad comes from the restaurant Bahn Thai in Bangkok. The eggplants were roasted over charcoal to give them a rich smoky flavor. Oriental eggplants are purple or lavender in color and are more slender than the Western kind. If they are unavailable, use the skinniest Western eggplants you can find.

4–6 Oriental eggplants (about 1½ pounds), or 2 Western eggplants
2 tablespoons fish sauce
2 tablespoons fresh lime juice
1 tablespoon sugar
½ teaspoon Thai chili paste (or to taste)
1½ tablespoons canola oil
1–3 Thai chilies or other hot peppers (or to taste), seeded and thinly sliced

3 cloves garlic, thinly sliced
3 shallots, thinly sliced
1 pound fresh shrimp, peeled and deveined
½ cup fresh mint leaves
4 whole lettuce leaves

Grill the eggplants on all sides over a high flame, or roast them under the broiler. The skin should be completely charred. Let cool, then scrape off the burnt skin with a knife. Cut the eggplants into ½" chunks. Combine the fish sauce, lime juice, sugar, and chili paste in a small bowl and whisk until mixed.

Heat a wok until almost smoking and swirl in the oil. Add the chilies, garlic, and shallots, and stir-fry for 15 seconds, or until fragrant. Add the shrimp and cook for 1 minute. Stir in the fish sauce mixture and cook for 1 minute, or until the shrimp are cooked.

Remove the wok from the heat and stir in the eggplant and half the mint leaves. Correct the seasoning, adding lime juice and sugar to taste. Line salad plates with the lettuce leaves and spoon the salad on top. Garnish with the remaining mint leaves and serve at once.

Serves 4.

207 CALORIES PER SERVING: 21 G PROTEIN, 7 G FAT, 17 G CARBOHYDRATE; 291 MG SODIUM; 176 MG CHOLESTEROL.

ONION SALAD

This salad — from Brazil's cattle country — is not for the fainthearted. The onions lose some of their nose-jarring pungency, however, when soaked in ice water. Choose the mildest onions you can find, such as Vidalias or Maui onions.

2 large onions
2 teaspoons Dijon-style mustard
1 tablespoon red wine vinegar (or to taste)
1 tablespoon fresh lemon juice

salt and freshly ground black pepper
2 tablespoons olive oil
3 tablespoons chicken stock
⅓ cup chopped flat-leaf parsley, for garnish

Peel the onions and slice them widthwise as thinly as possible. Separate the slices into rings. Place the onions in a shallow bowl with 2 cups ice cubes and cold water to cover. Refrigerate for 2 hours.

Combine the mustard, vinegar, lemon juice, salt, and pepper in a bowl and whisk until the salt is dissolved. Whisk in the oil and stock in a thin stream. Correct the seasoning.

Drain the onions and rinse under cold water.

Drain again, blot dry, and arrange in a shallow bowl. Whisk the sauce and pour it over the onions. Sprinkle the salad with parsley and serve at once.

Serves 6 to 8.

Note: Warn your guests to cut the onions with a knife and fork. It is difficult to eat the rings whole.

54 CALORIES PER SERVING: 1 G PROTEIN, 5 G FAT, 3 G CARBOHYDRATE; 204 MG SODIUM; 0 MG CHOLESTEROL.

PITA BREAD SALAD

Fattoush, *a pita bread salad popular throughout the Middle East, delights thrifty cooks who love to transform yesterday's leftovers into tomorrow's dish of distinction. As in many recipes in this book, I've reduced the amount of oil by using chicken stock to moisten the pita.*

2 large or 4 small stale (or fresh) pita breads, torn or cut into bite-sized wedges
1 ripe tomato, seeded and diced
3 scallions, finely chopped (⅓ cup)
1 cup finely chopped flat-leaf parsley
¼ cup finely chopped fresh spearmint or other mint

1½ tablespoons olive oil
2–3 tablespoons chicken stock or water
2 tablespoons fresh lemon juice
2 tablespoons red wine vinegar
salt and freshly ground black pepper
1 pomegranate (optional)

Combine the pita bread wedges, tomato, scallions, parsley, and mint in a salad bowl and toss to mix. Combine the oil, stock, lemon juice, vinegar, salt, and pepper in a small bowl and whisk until smooth. (Or combine the ingredients in a jar with a tight-fitting lid and shake well.) The dressing should be highly seasoned; add salt and lemon juice to taste.

If using the pomegranate, cut it in half lengthwise. Working over a bowl to catch any juice,

break the halves into sections and separate the sections into individual seeds.

Not more than 15 minutes before serving, pour the dressing over the salad and toss to mix, adding half the pomegranate seeds and any pomegranate juice. If the pita bread seems too dry, add a little more stock or water. Sprinkle the salad with the remaining pomegranate seeds and serve at once.

Serves 4.

167 CALORIES PER SERVING: 5 G PROTEIN, 6 G FAT, 25 G CARBOHYDRATE; 250 MG SODIUM; 0 MG CHOLESTEROL.

TUSCAN BREAD SALAD

Here's how cooks on the other side of the Mediterranean keep stale bread from going to waste. In Tuscany, the salad would be made with saltless Tuscan bread. Any dense Italian or country-style loaf will work as well.

1 clove garlic, minced (1 teaspoon)
3–4 tablespoons chicken stock or water
1½ tablespoons olive oil
1½ tablespoons red wine vinegar
1–2 tablespoons fresh lemon juice
salt and freshly ground black pepper
2 or 3 thick slices firm, dense white bread, cut into 1" cubes (about 3 cups)
2 ripe tomatoes, diced or cut into wedges
1 small red onion, cut into rings
1 stalk celery, cut into ½" diagonal slices

1 cucumber, peeled, seeded, and cut into ½" pieces
½ bunch flat-leaf parsley, coarsely chopped
½ bunch fresh basil (about 20 leaves), coarsely chopped, plus a few whole leaves for garnish
3 tablespoons capers
8 black olives (optional)
2 anchovy fillets, diced, plus whole or halved fillets for garnish (optional)

Combine the garlic, stock, oil, vinegar, lemon juice, salt, and pepper in a small bowl and whisk until smooth. (Or combine the ingredients in a jar with a tight-fitting lid and shake well.)

Place the remaining ingredients in a large bowl and toss with the dressing. Let the salad stand for at least 30 minutes before serving to allow

the bread to absorb the juices. Toss again just before serving and correct the seasoning, adding salt and vinegar to taste. (If the bread tastes too dry, add a little more stock or water.) Decorate the salad with whole basil leaves and whole or halved anchovy fillets, if desired.

Serves 4.

147 CALORIES PER SERVING: 4 G PROTEIN, 7 G FAT, 20 G CARBOHYDRATE; 295 MG SODIUM; 2 MG CHOLESTEROL.

BARLEY SALAD WITH LEMON AND MINT

The mere mention of barley makes most people think of a steaming bowl of scotch broth. Here's a barley salad that's as refreshing as it is filling. I like to soak the barley before cooking. This greatly shortens the cooking time and makes the barley easier to digest.

2 cups pearl barley
salt
1 clove garlic, minced (1 teaspoon)
2 teaspoons Dijon-style mustard
freshly ground black pepper
4–5 tablespoons fresh lemon juice
2 tablespoons chicken stock
1½ tablespoons extra-virgin olive oil
2 ripe tomatoes, peeled, seeded, and diced

1 cucumber, peeled, seeded, and diced
½ bunch fresh mint, finely chopped (about ⅓ cup), plus a few sprigs for garnish (or 2 tablespoons dried)
½ bunch flat-leaf parsley or cilantro, finely chopped (about ⅓ cup)
2 whole scallions, finely chopped, or 3 tablespoons chopped fresh chives

Wash the barley and drain. Add cold water to cover by 1" and soak for at least 4 hours. Drain the barley and cook in at least a gallon of rapidly boiling salted water for 20 minutes, or until tender but not soft. (You'll need to boil unsoaked barley for about an hour.) Drain in a colander and rinse under cold water until cool. Drain well. (You may wish to save the barley cooking water. Mixed with sugar and lemon, it makes a refreshing, if gluey, beverage.)

Place the garlic, mustard, pepper, and plenty of salt in the bottom of a large salad bowl. Whisk to a smooth paste. Gradually whisk in the lemon juice, stock, and oil. About 15 minutes before serving, add the barley, tomatoes, cucumber, herbs, and scallions. Toss well. Correct the seasoning, adding salt and lemon juice to taste. Garnish the salad with mint sprigs and serve at once.

Serves 6 to 8.

288 CALORIES PER SERVING: 7 G PROTEIN, 5 G FAT, 57 G CARBOHYDRATE; 230 MG SODIUM; 0 MG CHOLESTEROL.

KASHA SALAD WITH DILL

*Kasha is the Jewish name for buckwheat groats. This gray-brown grain has an earthy,
nutty flavor that is unique. In this recipe, the groats are roasted dry with
egg white to keep the grains fluffy and separate. Kasha can be found
in Jewish markets, natural food stores, and most supermarkets.*

1 cup buckwheat groats
½ egg white, beaten
1 small onion
1 bay leaf
1 whole clove
salt
1 small red bell pepper, cored, seeded, and
  diced
1 small yellow bell pepper, cored, seeded,
  and diced

3 scallions, finely chopped
¼ cup finely chopped fresh dill
2 tablespoons red wine vinegar
1½ tablespoons extra-virgin olive oil
1 tablespoon fresh lemon juice
½ teaspoon ground cumin
freshly ground black pepper

Wash the groats under cold running water, drain well, and blot dry. Combine the groats and egg white in a bowl and stir to mix. Put the groats mixture in a heavy (preferably nonstick) pan and cook over high heat, stirring steadily, for 2 to 3 minutes, or until the individual grains are dry.

Cut the onion in half and pin the bay leaf to one half with the clove. Add the onion, 2 cups water, and salt to the groats. Bring to a boil, stirring well. Reduce the heat and simmer for 15 to 18 minutes, or until the groats are tender but not too soft. Transfer the groats to a colander and let cool. Discard the onion.

Place the groats and the remaining ingredients in a large mixing bowl and toss well. Correct the seasoning, adding salt and lemon juice to taste.
Serves 4.

Note: If the groats stick to the pan, soak it and then scour it with oven cleaner.

207 CALORIES PER SERVING: 6 G PROTEIN, 6 G FAT, 35 G CARBOHYDRATE; 22 MG SODIUM; 0 MG CHOLESTEROL.

WILD RICE SALAD

When we tested the recipes in this chapter, this colorful wild rice salad was the unanimous favorite. I can't think of a better dish for a picnic, since you don't need to worry about it wilting. Presoaking the rice shortens the cooking time and improves the final texture.

1 cup wild rice
2 large oranges
¼ cup sultanas (yellow raisins)
2 scallions, finely chopped
½ bunch flat-leaf parsley, finely chopped
  (about ½ cup), plus a few sprigs for
  garnish

1½ tablespoons olive oil
1½ tablespoons balsamic vinegar (or to taste)
1½ tablespoons fresh lemon juice
  (or to taste)
1 or 2 dashes hot sauce
salt and freshly ground black pepper

Rinse the rice thoroughly in cold water in a strainer. Soak it for at least 4 hours in a large bowl with water to cover.

Place the rice in a large pot with 6 cups cold water. Bring to a boil, reduce the heat, and simmer for 30 minutes, or until tender. Meanwhile, cut the rind (both zest and white pith) off the oranges to expose the flesh. Make V-shaped cuts to remove the individual segments from the membranes, working over a bowl to catch the juice. Soak the sultanas in the orange juice for at least 5 minutes.

Combine the rice, orange segments, sultanas, and remaining ingredients in a large bowl, reserving a few of the orange segments for garnish. Toss the salad, adding salt, vinegar, and orange juice to taste. Mound the salad on a platter or in a bowl and decorate the top with the reserved orange segments and parsley sprigs.

Serves 6.

164 CALORIES PER SERVING: 5 G PROTEIN, 4 G FAT, 30 G CARBOHYDRATE; 6 MG SODIUM; 0 MG CHOLESTEROL.

BROWN RICE SALAD WITH PICKLED PLUM DRESSING

Brown rice adds an earthy flavor to salads and creates a great vegetarian main course or hearty side dish. Here it is mixed with umeboshi (Japanese pickled) plum paste in a recipe inspired by the Massachusetts-based Bread & Circus Wholefood Supermarkets. Look for plum paste in Japanese markets and at natural food stores. As in other grain salads, I presoak the brown rice and boil it like pasta to avoid a gluey consistency.

1 cup brown rice
1 clove garlic, peeled
2 bay leaves
salt and freshly ground black pepper
1 small nappa (Chinese cabbage), shredded
    (about 2 cups)
4 scallions, finely chopped
1½ cups red radishes, cut into julienne
    strips
2 carrots, cut into julienne strips

FOR THE DRESSING
3–4 tablespoons umeboshi plum paste
2 tablespoons rice wine vinegar or white
    wine vinegar
2 tablespoons chicken stock or water
1½ tablespoons olive oil
salt and freshly ground black pepper

Wash and drain the rice. Soak the rice in a large bowl with cold water to cover for at least 4 hours. Place the rice, garlic, bay leaves, salt, and pepper in a large, heavy saucepan with 8 cups water. Bring the water to a boil, reduce the heat, and simmer for 30 minutes, or until the rice is tender but not soft. Drain in a colander and refresh under cold water. Discard the garlic and bay leaves. Drain the rice well and blot dry. (If you prefer, you can steam the rice the traditional way.)

To make the dressing, combine the plum paste and vinegar in a large bowl and whisk to a smooth paste. Whisk in the stock, olive oil, salt, and pepper. (Go easy on the salt, as the plum paste is already quite salty.) Add the cooked rice and toss to mix. Let the mixture cool to room temperature.

Gently toss the vegetables with the rice. Correct the seasoning, adding plum paste and vinegar to taste. The salad should be highly seasoned.

Serves 8.

130 CALORIES PER SERVING: 3 G PROTEIN, 3 G FAT, 23 G CARBOHYDRATE; 261 MG SODIUM; 0 MG CHOLESTEROL.

BLACK BEAN SALAD WITH FETA CHEESE AND MINT

This salad offers a striking contrast between the inky darkness of black beans (also known as turtle beans) and the snowy white of feta cheese. Feta isn't a low-fat cheese, but because it has such a sharp flavor, you need only a little. A similar salad could be made using tofu instead of cheese.

2 cups dry black beans (or 4 cups cooked beans)
1 small red onion, finely chopped (about ½ cup)
½ cup tightly packed, finely chopped fresh mint, plus a few sprigs for garnish (or 2 tablespoons dried)

2 ounces drained feta cheese, crumbled
2 tablespoons extra-virgin olive oil
3–4 tablespoons fresh lemon juice
salt and freshly ground black pepper

Wash the beans and soak them in cold water to cover overnight. The next day, drain the beans and place them in a pot with cold water to cover. Bring to a boil, reduce the heat, and simmer for 20 to 25 minutes, or until tender. Refresh under cold water and drain. (For extra flavor, add onion, carrot, celery, and garlic to the beans. See instructions on page 230.)

Combine the beans, onion, mint, and most of the cheese in a bowl. Add the olive oil, lemon juice, salt, and pepper, and mix well. Let the beans marinate for 10 minutes and toss again. Correct the seasoning before serving, adding salt and lemon juice to taste. Garnish the salad with mint sprigs and the remaining cheese.

Serves 4 to 6.

333 CALORIES PER SERVING: 18 G PROTEIN, 11 G FAT, 44 G CARBOHYDRATE; 162 MG SODIUM; 12 MG CHOLESTEROL.

Black Bean Salad with Feta Cheese and Mint

BREADS

ONION DILL BREAD

This recipe uses a sponge (starter) to give the bread an extra lift. The kneading can be done by hand, in a food processor, or in a mixer fitted with a dough hook. If fresh dill is unavailable, substitute any other fresh herb.

1 tablespoon (1 envelope) dry yeast, or
  ½ ounce compressed yeast
2 teaspoons sugar
3 cups warm water
5–7 cups unbleached white flour
3 tablespoons honey

1 tablespoon sea salt
1 bunch dill, finely chopped
1 medium-sized onion, minced
1 cup whole wheat flour
2 tablespoons cornmeal (optional)
1 egg white, beaten

Combine the yeast, sugar, and 2 tablespoons of the warm water in a small bowl and stir to mix. Let stand for 3 to 5 minutes, or until foamy.

Stir 3 tablespoons of the warm water into the yeast mixture. Stir in 1 cup white flour, or enough to obtain a moist but workable dough. Roll the dough into a ball and drop it in a deep bowl filled with warm water. It will sink to the bottom. After 15 to 30 minutes, it will rise to the surface. The sponge is now activated and ready to use.

Transfer the sponge to a large mixing bowl. Use a wooden spoon to stir in the remaining warm water and the honey, salt, dill, and onion. Stir in the whole wheat flour, then the remaining white flour, 1 cup at a time. Continue adding flour until the dough becomes too stiff to stir. It should be dry enough to come away from the sides of the bowl but soft enough to knead. Turn the dough out onto a lightly floured work surface. Wash and lightly oil the bowl.

Knead the dough for 6 to 8 minutes, or until smooth and elastic. If the dough is too sticky to knead, work in a little more flour. When you press the dough with your finger, the depression should spring back.

Return the dough to the oiled bowl and cover with plastic wrap and a dish towel. Place in a warm, draft-free spot and let rise for 1½ to 2 hours, or until doubled in bulk. (The dough will rise at lower temperatures, even in the refrigerator, but the rising time will be longer.)

Lightly oil two 9" loaf pans. Punch the dough down and form the loaves. To make rectangular loaves, cut the dough in half, pat each half into an 8"-long oval, plump the ovals in the center, and drop them into the pans, seam side down. To make free-form round loaves, roll each half into a ball. Liberally sprinkle a baker's peel (or 2 tart pan bottoms) with cornmeal, if desired, and place the balls on top.

Cover the loaves with dish towels and let the dough rise again until doubled in bulk. Preheat the oven to 375 degrees F. Brush the top of each loaf with beaten egg white. Using a razor blade, make a series of diagonal slashes, ¼ to ½" deep, in each loaf. (Slashing allows the steam to escape and the bread to expand without cracking.) Bring 2 cups water to a boil in an ovenproof pan.

Place the loaf pans in the oven next to the pan of boiling water. (The water helps create a crisp crust.) If baking free-form loaves, slide them onto the baking stone. Bake the loaves for about 40 minutes, or until firm and browned on all sides. Tap the bottom of the loaf; if it sounds hollow, the bread is done. You can also test for doneness with an instant-read thermometer. The internal temperature should be about 190 degrees F.

Let the loaves cool for 5 minutes in the loaf pans, then turn them out onto a wire rack to cool slightly before slicing. Bread piping hot out of the oven is very hard to slice.

Makes 2 loaves.

126 CALORIES PER SERVING: 4 G PROTEIN, 0 G FAT, 27 G CARBOHYDRATE; 270 MG SODIUM; 0 MG CHOLESTEROL.

LEMON PEPPER POPOVERS

These delicious popovers take advantage of lemon's strong affinity with freshly grated black pepper. They rise best if baked in deep molds in a very hot oven. One of the best ways to grate lemon peel is to remove the zest in strips using a vegetable peeler, then grind it to a fine powder in a spice mill.

1 cup unbleached white flour
1 cup skim milk, at room temperature
1 tablespoon extra-virgin olive oil
¼ teaspoon salt (or to taste)

½ teaspoon cracked or coarsely ground black pepper
2 teaspoons freshly grated lemon zest
3 egg whites, lightly beaten

Preheat the oven to 450 degrees F. Sift the flour into a mixing bowl and gradually whisk in the milk. Add the remaining ingredients, whisking just to mix. The mixture should be the consistency of heavy cream. If necessary, add more milk.

Grease popover molds or muffin cups with vegetable oil spray or a little olive oil. Fill each mold ½ full. Bake for 15 minutes without opening the oven door. Reduce the heat to 375 degrees F and continue baking for 20 to 25 minutes, or until the popovers are puffed and well browned. Unmold and serve at once.

Makes 6 to 8 large popovers.

119 CALORIES PER SERVING: 5 G PROTEIN, 3 G FAT, 18 G CARBOHYDRATE; 166 MG SODIUM; 1 MG CHOLESTEROL.

BURGUNDIAN SPICE BREAD

....

Pain d'épices (spice bread) is an ancient Burgundian delicacy. This recipe comes from a beekeeper in the village of Looze in northern Burgundy. Rye flour and honey give it a moistness usually achieved by eggs in these sorts of breads. Tightly wrapped, Burgundian spice bread will keep for several days. It also freezes well and is good toasted.

¾ cup honey
½ cup sugar
½ cup sultanas
½ cup warm water
1½ teaspoons aniseed
1½ teaspoons ground ginger

½ teaspoon ground cinnamon
1½ teaspoons freshly grated orange zest
¼ teaspoon salt
1½ cups unbleached white flour
½ cup rye flour
1 tablespoon baking powder

Warm the honey jar in a pan of hot water. (This will make it easier to pour and measure.) Combine the honey, sugar, and sultanas in a large mixing bowl. Stir in the water, spices, zest, and salt.

Sift the flours and baking powder into the honey mixture. Mix with a wooden spoon to obtain a thick batter. Cover the bowl with a dish towel and let the batter rest for 1 hour. Meanwhile, spray a 9-by-4" loaf pan with vegetable oil spray and line it with parchment paper. Lightly spray the parchment paper with vegetable oil spray. Preheat the oven to 300 degrees F.

Check the consistency of the batter. It should fall from a raised spoon in a thick, silky ribbon. Thin it, if necessary, with a little water. Spoon the batter into the pan and bake for 1½ hours, or until a skewer inserted in the center comes out clean. Cool the bread in the pan for 15 minutes, then turn it out onto a wire rack and let cool to room temperature. Slice for serving.

Serves 8 to 10.

281 CALORIES PER SERVING: 3 G PROTEIN, 0 G FAT, 68 G CARBOHYDRATE; 193 MG SODIUM; 0 MG CHOLESTEROL.

....

Burgundian Spice Bread with A Nice Jewish Compote (page 200)

BROWN BREAD

Brown bread is one of oldest recipes in North America, belonging to a great tradition that includes Indian pudding and other steamed desserts. It was traditionally cooked by steaming (often in an old coffee can) and was always served with baked beans (see Healthy Baked Beans, page 87). It also makes a fine breakfast bread, thinly sliced and toasted. For speed and convenience, this recipe calls for the bread to be baked in a loaf pan.

1 cup graham or whole wheat flour
1 cup rye flour
1 cup yellow cornmeal
2 teaspoons baking soda
1 teaspoon salt

¾ cup molasses
2 cups low-fat buttermilk
1 cup sultanas or raisins, tossed with a little flour (optional)

Preheat the oven to 350 degrees F. Sift the dry ingredients into a large mixing bowl. Combine the molasses and buttermilk in another bowl and whisk until smooth. Add the dry ingredients to the molasses mixture and stir with a wooden spoon to form a smooth batter. Stir in the sultanas (if using) and pour the batter into a loaf pan. Cover the pan with a lightly oiled piece of foil.

Bake for 1¼ to 1½ hours, or until a skewer inserted in the center comes out clean. Uncover the bread for the last 30 minutes to brown the top. Turn the bread out onto a wire rack and let it cool slightly. For a real treat, serve the brown bread warm, slathered with honey.

Serves 8 to 10.

259 CALORIES PER SERVING: 7 G PROTEIN, 1 G FAT, 57 G CARBOHYDRATE; 337 MG SODIUM; 2 MG CHOLESTEROL.

BANANA SULTANA MUFFINS

*Unlike most banana breads, which are made with mashed fruit,
this one features whole chunks of banana and sultanas (yellow raisins).*

½ cup sultanas
¼ cup apple juice or orange juice
½ cup low-fat buttermilk
2 egg whites (or 1 whole egg)
1 tablespoon canola oil
3 tablespoons honey
1½ cups unbleached white flour

⅓ cup stone-ground white cornmeal
2 teaspoons baking powder
1 teaspoon baking soda
¼ cup brown sugar
½ teaspoon ground ginger
¼ teaspoon ground cardamom
2 ripe bananas, diced

Preheat the oven to 375 degrees F. Combine the sultanas and apple juice in a large bowl and let stand for 5 minutes. Add the buttermilk, egg whites, oil, and honey, and whisk until smooth.

Sift the flour, cornmeal, baking powder, and baking soda into another large bowl. Whisk in the brown sugar, ginger, and cardamom. Add the bananas and toss lightly. Add the dry ingredients to the buttermilk mixture and stir just to mix with a wooden spoon. (Stir as little as possible, or the muffins will be tough. Ten to 12 strokes should do it.)

Line the muffin cups with parchment paper or paper liners or lightly grease with vegetable oil spray. Spoon the batter into the cups, filling each ⅔ full. Bake for 20 to 30 minutes, or until puffed and lightly browned. A skewer inserted in the center should come out clean. Turn the muffins out onto a wire rack and let cool for 5 to 10 minutes before serving.

Makes 12 muffins.

160 CALORIES PER SERVING: 3 G PROTEIN, 2 G FAT, 34 G CARBOHYDRATE; 145 MG SODIUM; 1 MG CHOLESTEROL.

HOMEMADE BREADSTICKS
....

If you dine at virtually any restaurant in Italy (and many Italian restaurants in North America), you'll be offered a slender bag of grissini, *audibly crisp breadsticks from Turin. Delectable as they are, I prefer homemade breadsticks, which are quick and easy to prepare and can be stretched to any length you desire. These breadsticks can be served with any of the dips in the Appetizers and Dips chapter or with Low-Fat Cheese Fondue (page 20).*

1 tablespoon (1 envelope) dry yeast, or ½ ounce compressed yeast
1 tablespoon sugar
2 tablespoons warm water
4 cups unbleached white flour (or 3 cups unbleached white flour and 1 cup whole wheat flour)

1½ teaspoons salt
1–1¼ cups cold water
1 tablespoon extra-virgin olive oil
1 whole egg or egg white, beaten
sesame seeds, poppy seeds, caraway seeds, aniseed, and/or coarse salt

Combine the yeast with the sugar and 2 tablespoons warm water in a small bowl and let stand for 5 minutes, or until frothy.

Place the flour and salt in the bowl of a food processor. With the machine running, add the dissolved yeast, cold water, and oil. Process for 1 minute, or until the dough comes together in a smooth ball. (If the dough is too dry, add a little more water.) Knead the dough for 2 to 3 minutes in the food processor or for 4 to 5 minutes by hand. (The dough can also be made in a heavy-duty mixer fitted with a dough hook.) Place the dough in a lightly oiled bowl and cover with plastic wrap. Let rise in a warm, draft-free spot for 1 hour, or until doubled.

Preheat the oven to 400 degrees F. Punch the dough down and cut it in half. On a lightly floured board, roll each half into a 14-by-10" rectangle. Cut each rectangle widthwise into ½" strips. Stretch the strips to the desired length by taking an end in each hand and gently pulling and twirling. Arrange the breadsticks, 1" apart, on nonstick or lightly oiled baking sheets. Lightly brush the tops of the breadsticks with the beaten egg, taking care not to drip any on the baking sheet. Sprinkle the breadsticks with sesame seeds, poppy seeds, caraway seeds, aniseed, and/or coarse salt.

Bake for 16 to 20 minutes, or until a deep golden brown. Transfer to wire racks to cool. Serve upright in a jar.

Makes about 3 dozen.

60 CALORIES PER SERVING: 2 G PROTEIN, 1 G FAT, 12 G CARBOHYDRATE; 91 MG SODIUM; 6 MG CHOLESTEROL.

🐌

ROASTED CORN AND CHILI CORN BREAD
....

The best corn bread I ever tasted was baked in a cast-iron skillet slathered with bacon fat. The flavor was sensational, but eating a single slice put one at risk for cardiac arrest! The grilled corn in the following recipe provides the smokiness associated with bacon. (If you don't have time to grill the corn, use canned or frozen kernels.) Additional flavor comes from the cilantro and chilies. For the best results, use an organic stone-ground cornmeal.

2 ears fresh corn (1 cup kernels)
½ teaspoon plus 2 tablespoons olive oil (or to taste)
salt and freshly ground black pepper
3 egg whites (or 1 whole egg and 1 white)
¾–1 cup low-fat buttermilk
1⅓ cups unbleached white flour
1 tablespoon baking powder
3 tablespoons sugar

1 teaspoon salt
⅔ cup yellow cornmeal
½ poblano chili or 1 or 2 fresh jalapeño chilies, cored, seeded, and minced
1 or 2 pickled jalapeño chilies, minced (optional)
¼ cup finely chopped cilantro or parsley
2 scallions, finely chopped

Preheat the grill or broiler. Shuck the corn, brush lightly with the ½ teaspoon olive oil, and season with salt and pepper. Grill the corn over high heat for 4 to 5 minutes per side, or until well browned. Let the corn cool, then cut the kernels off the ears. (The easiest way to do this is to lay the corn on a cutting board and make longitudinal cuts on the cob with a long knife.)

Preheat the oven to 350 degrees F. Brush a 9" cast-iron skillet or baking pan with a little olive oil and place it in the oven to preheat. Combine the egg whites, ¾ cup buttermilk, and remaining oil in a large bowl and whisk until well mixed. Sift the flour, baking powder, sugar, and 1 teaspoon salt into the liquid ingredients. Add the

cornmeal and gently stir with a wooden spoon until the ingredients are just mixed. (This will take about 30 seconds. Don't overmix, or the corn bread will be tough.) Stir in the grilled corn, chilies, cilantro, and scallions. If the batter is too dry, add the remaining buttermilk. Spoon the batter into the hot skillet.

Bake for 35 to 40 minutes, or until golden brown. (The corn bread should be firm but yielding when pressed. A skewer inserted in the center should come out clean.) Loosen the edges with a slender knife and invert the skillet onto a round platter to unmold the corn bread. Cut into wedges and serve with honey.

Serves 6.

276 CALORIES PER SERVING: 8 G PROTEIN, 6 G FAT, 49 G CARBOHYDRATE; 630 MG SODIUM; 2 MG CHOLESTEROL.

SESAME GARLIC FOCACCIA

Focaccia is a cousin of pizza, a flat yeasted bread baked in the oven. (The term comes from the Latin word focus, *meaning "hearth.") Instead of being topped with tomato sauce, focaccia is brushed with olive oil and sprinkled with sesame seeds, chopped nuts, or herbs. Here, too, the dough can be kneaded in a food processor or heavy-duty mixer.*

1 tablespoon (1 envelope) dry yeast, or
½ ounce compressed yeast
1 teaspoon sugar
2 tablespoons plus 1⅓ cups warm water
1 teaspoon sea salt
¼ cup chopped fresh basil, rosemary,
   oregano, thyme, and/or parsley (optional)

3 cloves garlic, minced (1 tablespoon)
2 tablespoons minced shallots
3½–4 cups unbleached white flour
cornmeal
2–3 teaspoons extra-virgin olive oil
2 tablespoons sesame seeds
1 teaspoon coarse salt

Combine the yeast, sugar, and 2 tablespoons water in the bottom of a large mixing bowl. Let stand for 5 minutes, or until the mixture is foamy. Stir in the remaining water, sea salt, herbs (if using), half the garlic, and half the shallots. Stir in the flour, adding a cup at a time, until the dough comes away from the sides of the bowl. Turn it out onto a lightly floured work surface. Wash and lightly oil the bowl.

Knead the dough for 6 to 8 minutes, or until smooth and elastic. Place the dough in the oiled bowl, cover with plastic wrap and a dish towel, and let rise in a warm place for 1½ hours, or until doubled in bulk.

Punch the dough down, then roll it into 1 large or 2 small ovals, each ½" thick. Transfer the oval to a baker's peel or a tart pan bottom liberally sprinkled with cornmeal. Let rise for 30 minutes, or until doubled in bulk. Preheat the oven to 375 degrees F.

Poke your fingers in the surface of the focaccia to give it a dimpled appearance. Brush the top with 1 teaspoon olive oil and sprinkle with the remaining minced garlic and shallots, the sesame seeds, and the coarse salt. Bake for 25 to 35 minutes, or until crisp and golden brown. Let cool slightly. Just before serving, drizzle with the remaining olive oil. Cut into wedges and serve.

Serves 8.

237 CALORIES PER SERVING: 7 G PROTEIN, 3 G FAT, 45 G CARBOHYDRATE; 535 MG SODIUM; 0 MG CHOLESTEROL.

GRILLED BREAD

You don't need a degree in restaurant-going to know that grill fever has reached epidemic proportions. The latest manifestation of this delectable malady is grilled bread. I first tasted it at the restaurant 798 Main Street in Cambridge, Massachusetts.

½ tablespoon (½ package) dry yeast, or
  ¼ ounce compressed yeast
2 tablespoons molasses
⅔ cup warm water
½ teaspoon salt
½ cup whole wheat flour

½ cup fine stone-ground cornmeal
1¼ cups unbleached white flour
  (approximately)
1 tablespoon extra-virgin olive oil
coarse salt and cracked black peppercorns

Combine the yeast, molasses, and 2 tablespoons of the warm water in a large bowl. Stir to mix. Let stand 3 to 5 minutes, or until foamy. Stir in the remaining water and the ½ teaspoon salt, whole wheat flour, cornmeal, and white flour. Add enough white flour to obtain a dough that is stiff enough to come away from the sides of the bowl but soft enough to knead. Turn the dough onto a lightly floured work surface. Wash and lightly oil the bowl.

Knead the dough for 6 to 8 minutes, or until smooth and elastic. The dough can be prepared in a food processor (mix the dry ingredients first, then add the water and yeast mixture), but finish the kneading by hand.

Return the dough to the bowl and cover with plastic wrap and a dish towel. Let the dough rise in a warm place for 1 to 2 hours, or until doubled in bulk. Punch it down and let rise for ½ to 1 hour, or until doubled in bulk again. Light the grill.

Punch down the dough and cut it into 6 pieces. Using a rolling pin or a pasta machine, roll the pieces into circles ¼" thick. Place the circles on a platter, separated by floured sheets of wax or parchment paper.

Just before serving, brush the tops of the circles with oil and sprinkle with coarse salt and cracked pepper. Place the circles, oiled side down, on the grill and cook over medium-high heat for 1 to 2 minutes, or until the bottom is blistered and browned. Meanwhile, brush the tops with oil and sprinkle with salt and pepper. Turn the circles and cook 1 to 2 minutes more, or until both sides are puffed and golden brown. Serve at once.

Serves 6.

209 CALORIES PER SERVING: 5 G PROTEIN, 3 G FAT, 41 G CARBOHYDRATE; 181 MG SODIUM; 0 MG CHOLESTEROL.

VEGETABLES

SWEET AND SOUR PEPPERS

This colorful stir-fry makes a great accompaniment to seafood or grilled meats.
You can add thinly sliced beef, chicken, or tofu (about 1 pound for the
proportions below) and turn it into a full-fledged entrée.

¼ cup fresh lemon juice

3 tablespoons tamari or soy sauce

2 tablespoons honey

1 teaspoon Thai hot sauce, chili oil, or other hot sauce (optional)

1½ tablespoons canola oil

3 cloves garlic, minced (1 tablespoon)

1 tablespoon minced fresh ginger

1 jalapeño chili, seeded and minced

3 scallions, whites minced, greens thinly sliced on the diagonal

2 red bell peppers, cored, seeded, and cut into 1½" squares

2 green bell peppers, cored, seeded, and cut into 1½" squares

2 yellow bell peppers, cored, seeded, and cut into 1½" squares

1 tablespoon black or toasted white sesame seeds

1½ teaspoons cornstarch dissolved in 1 tablespoon cold water

Combine the lemon juice, tamari, honey, and hot sauce (if using) in a bowl and whisk until smooth.

Just before serving, heat a wok over high heat. Swirl in the oil. Add the garlic, ginger, chili, and scallion whites, and stir-fry over high heat for 15 seconds, or until fragrant but not brown. Add the peppers and stir-fry for 1 minute, or until the peppers begin to soften. Stir in half the scallion greens, half the sesame seeds, and the sauce, and bring to a boil. Stir in the dissolved cornstarch and stir-fry for 30 seconds. Transfer to a platter and garnish with the remaining scallion greens and sesame seeds.

Serves 6.

94 CALORIES PER SERVING: 2 G PROTEIN, 4 G FAT, 13 G CARBOHYDRATE; 505 MG SODIUM; 0 MG CHOLESTEROL.

Sweet and Sour Peppers

VENETIAN SWEET AND SOUR SQUASH

You've probably never tasted the likes of zucca in agro-dolce, Venetian-style sweet and sour squash. Chocolate may seem like a strange ingredient, but used in tiny amounts, it brings out the natural sweetness of pumpkins and squashes. This recipe was inspired by Washington, D.C., chef Roberto Donna.

3 tablespoons raisins
1 tablespoon olive oil
2 cloves garlic, peeled and cut in half
1 pound winter squash (such as butternut or Hubbard), peeled and cut into ½" dice (about 3 cups)
2 tablespoons honey

1 teaspoon finely chopped semisweet chocolate
2 tablespoons balsamic vinegar (or to taste)
2 tablespoons pine nuts, lightly toasted
4 fresh basil leaves
4 fresh mint leaves (or more basil)
salt

Place the raisins in hot water to cover for 5 minutes, then drain. Heat the oil in a nonstick frying pan. Add the garlic and cook over medium heat for 2 to 3 minutes, or until tender and lightly browned. Discard the garlic. Add the squash and sauté for 4 to 6 minutes, or until lightly browned and tender.

Stir in the honey and bring to a boil. Add the chocolate and vinegar, and stir until the chocolate melts. Add the raisins and pine nuts, and cook for 1 minute more, or until the sauce forms a syrupy glaze. Just before serving, finely chop the basil and mint, and stir them into the squash with salt to taste. Serve warm or at room temperature.

Serves 4 to 6.

171 CALORIES PER SERVING: 3 G PROTEIN, 7 G FAT, 27 G CARBOHYDRATE; 7 MG SODIUM; 0 MG CHOLESTEROL.

BRAZILIAN-STYLE COLLARD GREENS
. . . .

Brazilians have developed one of the best ways to prepare collard greens:
they slice them paper-thin and sauté them in garlicky olive oil. The roll-cut
method outlined here works well for thinly slicing any leafy green vegetable.

1 bunch collard greens (about 1½ pounds)
1½ tablespoons olive oil
2 cloves garlic, minced (2 teaspoons)

2 shallots, minced
salt and freshly ground black pepper

Wash the collard greens well. Remove the stems and roll up the leaves lengthwise into a tight tube. Cut the greens widthwise into the thinnest possible slices. Fluff the slices in a large bowl and sprinkle with a little water.

Just before serving, heat the oil in a large, heavy skillet over high heat. Add the garlic and shallots, and cook for 20 seconds, or until fragrant but

not brown. Add the collard greens, salt, and pepper. Cook the greens for 1 to 2 minutes, or until just tender, stirring well. If the greens look too dry, add a tablespoon or so of water. Do not overcook; the collards should remain bright green. Correct the seasoning and serve at once.

Serves 4.

107 CALORIES PER SERVING: 3 G PROTEIN, 5 G FAT, 14 G CARBOHYDRATE; 33 MG SODIUM; 0 MG CHOLESTEROL.

CIDER-GLAZED TURNIPS
. . . .

This is a good dish for people who don't think they like turnips. The cider sweetens the root
and neutralizes its radishy aftertaste. For the best results, use tiny new turnips or choose the
smallest ones you can buy. Rutabagas, those giant yellow cousins, can be prepared the same way.

1½ pounds turnips
1½ cups fresh apple cider (approximately)
salt and freshly ground black pepper

1 tablespoon extra-virgin olive oil (optional)
2 tablespoons chopped fresh tarragon
and/or chives

Peel the turnips. Quarter the larger ones and cut the smaller ones in half to obtain uniform-sized pieces. Place the turnips in a heavy saucepan with cider to cover. Add the salt, pepper, and olive oil (if using).

Cook the turnips, uncovered, over high heat for 10 minutes, or until tender, stirring from time to time. The cider should be reduced to a syrupy

glaze. If the liquid evaporates before the turnips are completely cooked, add more cider. If the turnips are soft before the cider forms a glaze, remove them with a slotted spoon. Boil the cider down to a glaze, then return the turnips to the pan. Sprinkle the turnips with the chopped herbs and serve at once.

Serves 4 to 6.

101 CALORIES PER SERVING: 1 G PROTEIN, 4 G FAT, 18 G CARBOHYDRATE; 87 MG SODIUM; 0 MG CHOLESTEROL.

BLUE CABBAGE

*My Austrian-born friend Trudy Cutrone, co-owner of New Hampshire's Snowville Inn,
introduced me to* blaukraut *("blue cabbage"). The cabbage isn't so much blue as pale
lavender—a color that results when you add the vinegar. The Old World
version is made with bacon fat, which I've replaced with olive oil.*

1 tablespoon olive oil
1 onion, finely chopped
3 tablespoons sugar (or to taste)
¼ cup red wine vinegar
¼ cup plus 1 tablespoon dry red wine
1 head red cabbage (about 2 pounds), cored
   and thinly sliced
salt and freshly ground black pepper

¼ teaspoon ground cinnamon
⅛ teaspoon ground cloves
1½ cups water (approximately)
2 tart apples, peeled, cored, and coarsely
   grated
1 teaspoon freshly grated lemon zest
3–4 tablespoons bread crumbs

Heat the oil in a large, nonreactive sauté pan (not aluminum or cast iron). Cook the onion over medium heat for 3 to 4 minutes, or until soft. Stir in the sugar and cook for 2 to 3 minutes, or until lightly caramelized.

Stir in the vinegar and ¼ cup wine, and bring the mixture to a boil. Add the cabbage, salt, pepper, spices, and water (barely to cover). Bring the cabbage to a boil, reduce the heat, and gently simmer, covered, for 20 minutes, or until the cabbage is tender-crisp.

Add the apples and simmer, uncovered, for 5 to 10 minutes or until most of the liquid is absorbed and the cabbage is tender but not mushy. Stir in the zest, remaining 1 tablespoon wine, and enough bread crumbs to absorb any excess liquid. Correct the seasoning, adding salt, vinegar, and sugar to taste. The cabbage should be a little sweet and a little sour.

Serves 6 to 8.

135 CALORIES PER SERVING: 2 G PROTEIN, 3 G FAT, 26 G CARBOHYDRATE; 15 MG SODIUM; 0 MG CHOLESTEROL.

A QUICK SAUTÉ OF YELLOW PEPPERS AND SUGAR SNAP PEAS

*This recipe is simplicity itself, but the colors are breathtaking. Sugar snap peas are
sweet enough to eat pods and all. You can also use snow peas, substitute
sliced jicama for the peppers, or add thinly sliced shiitake mushrooms.*

1 pound sugar snap peas, strung
1½ tablespoons extra-virgin olive oil
1 large clove garlic, minced (1 teaspoon)
½ teaspoon freshly grated lemon zest
2 yellow or red bell peppers, cored, seeded,
   and cut into pea pod–sized strips

1 tablespoon chopped fresh tarragon,
   thyme, or basil (or 1 teaspoon dried)
salt and freshly ground black pepper

Blanch the peas in 1 quart boiling salted water for 30 seconds. Drain in a colander and refresh under cold water. Drain and blot dry.

Just before serving, heat the oil in a large sauté pan. Add the garlic and zest, and cook over medium heat for 30 seconds, or until fragrant. Add the peppers and sauté for 30 seconds. Add the peas, tarragon, salt, and pepper. Cook just long enough to heat the peas. Serve at once.

Serves 4.

87 CALORIES PER SERVING: 4 G PROTEIN, 4 G FAT, 10 G CARBOHYDRATE; 5 MG SODIUM; 0 MG CHOLESTEROL.

WINTER VEGETABLE PURÉE

This purée calls for parsnips and celeriacs (celery root), but you can substitute any starchy root vegetable, even winter squash. Serve with Herb-Roasted Game Hens (page 127) or Braised Brisket with Dried Fruits (page 143).

1 or 2 celeriacs (1 pound)
1 tablespoon lemon juice
1 pound parsnips or turnips, peeled and cut
  into ½" dice
salt
1 tablespoon extra-virgin olive oil (optional)

¼–½ cup skim milk, warmed
salt and freshly ground white pepper
pinch of cayenne pepper
freshly grated nutmeg
2 tablespoons chopped fresh chives or
  scallion greens, for garnish

Peel the celeriacs with a paring knife and cut into ½" dice. Toss the celeriacs with the lemon juice to prevent browning. Place the celeriacs and parsnips in a saucepan with cold salted water or stock to cover. (For extra flavor, but a bit more fat, use part or all chicken stock instead of water.)

Boil the vegetables for 6 to 8 minutes, or until very tender. Drain well (save the liquid for soup), then purée in a food processor or food mill (or mash with a potato masher right in the pot). Work in the oil (if using) and enough warm milk to obtain a creamy purée. Correct the seasoning, adding salt, white pepper, cayenne, and nutmeg to taste. Sprinkle the purée with chives and serve at once.

Serves 4 to 6.

145 CALORIES PER SERVING: 4 G PROTEIN, 4 G FAT, 26 G CARBOHYDRATE; 129 MG SODIUM; 0 MG CHOLESTEROL.

RAPINI WITH GARLIC AND OYSTER SAUCE

*Here's a great street dish I encountered on my culinary peregrinations through Thailand.
In Asia, it is made with Chinese broccoli (gai lan). In this country,
it's easier to find a related vegetable, a leafy cousin of broccoli called rapini
(also known as broccoli rabe, brocoletto, and brocoletti de rape).*

1 pound rapini
1½ tablespoons canola oil
1 tablespoon minced fresh ginger
8 cloves garlic, peeled
½ pound fresh shiitake, straw, or button
mushrooms, stemmed and thinly sliced

4 teaspoons oyster sauce (or to taste)
2 teaspoons fish sauce (or to taste)
freshly ground white pepper

Wash the rapini well and dry. Trim off the ends and cut into 2" pieces.

Just before serving, heat a wok over high heat. Swirl in the oil. Add the ginger and garlic, and cook for 20 seconds, or until fragrant. Add the rapini and mushrooms, and stir-fry for 1 minute. Add the oyster sauce, fish sauce, and white pepper, and stir-fry for 1 minute more, or until the greens are tender-crisp. Correct the seasoning, adding oyster sauce and fish sauce to taste, and serve at once. (You're not supposed to eat the garlic cloves, but you certainly can if you want to. I do!)

Serves 4.

79 CALORIES PER SERVING: 5 G PROTEIN, 4 G FAT, 9 G CARBOHYDRATE; 475 MG SODIUM; 1 MG CHOLESTEROL.

HEALTHY BAKED BEANS

This traditional New England dish is usually made with artery-clogging doses of bacon or salt pork. I've reworked the recipe using smoked turkey for flavor and apple cider instead of pork fat for moistness. My favorite bean for baking is the anasazi, a handsome red-and-white-speckled bean that is high in minerals and protein. (See Mail-Order Sources.) Serve with Brown Bread (page 73) or Roasted Corn and Chili Corn Bread (page 76).

1 pound anasazi or other dried beans
1 pound skinless smoked turkey or chicken
1 tablespoon olive oil
1 large onion, finely chopped
2 cloves garlic, minced (2 teaspoons)
1 tablespoon minced fresh ginger
1 or 2 jalapeño chilies, seeded and minced
2 cups apple cider
1 cup cider vinegar
1 cup water

¼ cup molasses (or to taste)
¼ cup brown sugar
1 tablespoon dry mustard
1 tablespoon Dijon-style mustard
2 bay leaves
1 teaspoon dried thyme
¼ teaspoon ground allspice
⅛ teaspoon ground cloves
salt and freshly ground black pepper

Pick through the beans, removing any twigs or stones. Wash the beans well and soak them overnight in a large bowl with cold water to cover.

The next day, cut the turkey into ½" dice. Heat the oil in a frying pan and cook the onion, garlic, ginger, and chilies over medium heat for 4 to 5 minutes, or until golden brown. Preheat the oven to 300 degrees F.

Transfer the onion mixture to a bean pot or casserole dish. Drain the beans and add them to the pot. Stir in the remaining ingredients.

Tightly cover the pot and bake for 3 hours, or until the beans are very tender. Stir the beans from time to time, adding liquid as necessary to keep them covered. Leave the pot uncovered for the last 30 minutes to allow the beans to brown and excess liquid to evaporate. Baked beans should be moist but not soupy.

Just before serving, correct the seasoning. The beans should be a little sweet, a tiny bit sour, and faintly spicy. Add brown sugar, vinegar, mustard, salt, and pepper to taste.

Serves 8 to 10.

396 CALORIES PER SERVING: 22 G PROTEIN, 9 G FAT, 62 G CARBOHYDRATE; 35 MG SODIUM; 0 MG CHOLESTEROL.

BAKER'S-STYLE POTATOES

In trying to come up with a low-fat gratin, I remembered a recipe I had learned at the La Varenne cooking school in Paris. The potatoes were simmered in veal stock, which made them rich and meltingly tender. The dish was called pommes boulangère, *"baker's-style potatoes," after a practice popular in the rural France of yesteryear: housewives would drop their casseroles at the local bakery to be cooked while they attended church. Sautéed onions provide as much flavor as the cheese used in traditional gratins. You can make this dish with a variety of root vegetables, including yams and sweet potatoes. It's a great party dish.*

1½ tablespoons extra-virgin olive oil
2 onions, thinly sliced (about 2 cups)
4 large potatoes (about 2 pounds)
salt and freshly ground black pepper

2–3 cups chicken or veal stock
  (approximately)
¼ cup bread crumbs

Preheat the broiler. Heat the olive oil in a 10" nonstick frying pan with a metal (not plastic) handle. Add the onions and cook, stirring often, over medium heat for 4 to 6 minutes, or until golden brown.

Meanwhile, peel the potatoes and cut into ¼" slices. Stir the potatoes into the onions and season with salt and pepper. Add enough stock to cover the potatoes and bring to a boil. Reduce the heat and simmer for 15 minutes, or until soft. Flatten the potatoes with a fork and sprinkle with bread crumbs. Place the pan under the broiler. Broil for 1 minute, or until the top is crusty and golden brown.

Serves 4.

303 CALORIES PER SERVING: 7 G PROTEIN, 6 G FAT, 57 G CARBOHYDRATE; 87 MG SODIUM; 0 MG CHOLESTEROL.

Vampire Spuds (Mashed Potatoes with Garlic and Saffron)

....

*Traditionally loaded with butter and cream, mashed potatoes may seem an unlikely
candidate for a low-fat make-over. By boosting the flavor with garlic and saffron,
you can eliminate most of the fat without sacrificing the taste. Don't be
alarmed by the amount of garlic; the boiling reduces its potency.*

4 baking potatoes (about 2 pounds)
1 head garlic, broken into cloves and peeled
salt
¼ teaspoon saffron threads

¾ cup skim milk (approximately)
**1½ tablespoons extra-virgin olive oil
   (optional)**
freshly ground white or black pepper

Peel the potatoes and cut them into ½" pieces. Place them and the garlic in a large, heavy pot with cold salted water to cover. Bring to a boil, reduce the heat, and simmer 8 to 10 minutes, or until the potatoes are soft. Drain in a colander. Meanwhile, soak the saffron threads in 1 tablespoon warm water.

Return the potatoes to the pan and cook over medium heat for a minute or so, stirring with a wooden spoon, to evaporate any water. Heat the milk over a double boiler. Mash the potatoes with a masher or put them through a food mill. (Do not mash the potatoes in a food processor, or they'll be gummy.) Stir the saffron with its soaking liquid into the mashed potatoes. Add the oil (if using) and enough milk to make the potatoes fluffy and creamy. Season with salt and pepper. Transfer the potatoes to plates or a bowl, and serve at once.

Serves 4 to 6.

151 CALORIES PER SERVING: 4 G PROTEIN, 1 G FAT, 31 G CARBOHYDRATE; 298 MG SODIUM; 1 MG CHOLESTEROL.

LACY POTATO PANCAKE

....

This crisp potato pancake was one of my first ventures into low-fat cooking, so it's on the higher end of the fat register. Instead of deep-frying, I bake it in a nonstick frying pan to reduce the fat. Shred the potato on a mandoline, or use the julienne disk of a food processor. (You can use a hand grater, but the pancake won't be as delicate.)

1 large baking potato
2 scallions, chopped

2 tablespoons olive or canola oil
salt and freshly ground black pepper

Preheat the oven to 400 degrees F. Peel the potato and shred it into a fine julienne. Gently squeeze the shredded potato in your hands to wring out as much liquid as possible. Stir the scallions into the potato.

Pour half the oil into a 9" nonstick frying pan and spread it around with a pastry brush. Heat the pan over medium heat. Spread the potato over the bottom of the pan. Season with salt and pepper. Cook the pancake for 2 to 3 minutes, or until the bottom is lightly browned. Shake the pan often to prevent the pancake from sticking.

Flip the pancake with a flick of the wrist; if this gesture seems too daunting, place a plate on top of the pan and invert the pancake onto it. Slide the pancake back into the pan and add the remaining 1 tablespoon oil at the edges of the pancake. Season with salt and pepper, and cook for 2 to 3 minutes more to brown the bottom of the pancake.

Place the pan in the oven and bake for 10 to 12 minutes, or until crisp. Transfer to a platter and cut into wedges for serving.

Serves 2 to 4.

177 CALORIES PER SERVING: 2 G PROTEIN, 9 G FAT, 23 G CARBOHYDRATE; 5 MG SODIUM; 0 MG CHOLESTEROL.

PASTAS AND GRAINS

SPAGHETTI WITH RED-HOT TOMATO SAUCE

Does the world really need another recipe for tomato sauce? If it's this thick, spicy red sauce, pepped up with olives, capers, and pepper flakes, the answer is unequivocally yes! This recipe is loosely modeled on my friend Myrna Mirow's putanesca sauce.

FOR THE SAUCE
2½ pounds fresh ripe tomatoes (4 to 6 regular tomatoes, or 12 to 16 plum tomatoes), or 1½ 28-ounce cans
1 tablespoon olive oil
5 shallots, minced (⅓ cup)
5 cloves garlic, minced (5 teaspoons)
1 tablespoon tomato paste
3 tablespoons finely chopped capers
3 tablespoons finely chopped pimiento-stuffed green olives

1 teaspoon hot red pepper flakes (or to taste)
⅓ cup finely chopped fresh herbs (basil, oregano, tarragon, chervil, parsley, and/or chives); reserve 2 tablespoons for garnish
salt and freshly ground black pepper

salt
1 pound spaghetti or dried bucatini, or 1½ pounds fresh
3–4 tablespoons freshly grated Parmigiano Reggiano (or other Parmesan-style cheese)

To make the sauce, peel, seed, and finely chop the tomatoes, working over a strainer and bowl to collect the juice. Heat the oil in a large saucepan. Cook the shallots and garlic over medium heat for 2 to 3 minutes, or until soft but not brown.

Stir in the tomatoes, 3 to 4 tablespoons reserved tomato juice, tomato paste, capers, olives, and pepper flakes, and cook over medium-low heat for 10 minutes, or until reduced to a thick sauce.

If the mixture seems too dry, add a little reserved tomato juice or water. Stir in the herbs. Season with salt and pepper.

Just before serving, bring at least 4 quarts water to a boil in a large pot. Add salt to taste. Boil the pasta for 6 to 8 minutes, or until cooked but still al dente. Drain and transfer it to a large bowl. Spoon the sauce over it and sprinkle with the reserved herbs. Serve the cheese on the side.

Serves 4 to 6.

605 CALORIES PER SERVING: 21 G PROTEIN, 9 G FAT, 112 G CARBOHYDRATE; 357 MG SODIUM; 4 MG CHOLESTEROL.

Spaghetti with Red-Hot Tomato Sauce

SPAGHETTI WITH ANCHOVIES

....

*One of the most famous restaurants in Liguria—indeed, on the whole Adriatic coast—
is Puny in Portofino. Since 1880, a cosmopolitan clientele has flocked to this harborside
eatery to see and be seen, while enjoying gutsy Ligurian specialties such as this spaghetti
with anchovies. To reduce the fat in the original recipe, I've replaced some of the
olive oil with clam broth. One of the best brands of dried pasta is De Ceccho.*

1 2-ounce can anchovy fillets
1½ tablespoons olive oil
3 cloves garlic, minced (1 tablespoon)
½ teaspoon cracked black peppercorns
1 cup bottled clam broth
salt

½ pound (8 ounces) imported spaghetti
⅔ cup finely chopped flat-leaf parsley
3-4 tablespoons freshly grated Parmigiano
   Reggiano, or other Parmesan-style cheese
   (optional)

Drain the anchovy fillets in a strainer, blot dry with paper towels, and coarsely chop them. Heat the oil in a small saucepan. Add the anchovies, garlic, and cracked pepper, and cook over medium heat for 2 minutes, or until the garlic just begins to color. Add the clam broth and bring to a boil. Simmer the sauce for 2 to 3 minutes, or until reduced to about 1 cup.

Just before serving, bring at least 4 quarts water to a boil in a large pot. Add salt to taste. Boil the spaghetti for 6 to 8 minutes, or until cooked but still al dente. Drain the pasta and transfer it to a large bowl. Pour the sauce over it and stir in the parsley. Serve the cheese on the side (if using).

Serves 4.

330 CALORIES PER SERVING: 12 G PROTEIN, 7 G FAT, 54 G CARBOHYDRATE; 768 MG SODIUM; 12 MG CHOLESTEROL.

FUSILLI WITH MINTED TOMATO SAUCE

....

*This dish should be made only at the height of tomato season, when the
gardens and farm stands are brimming with lucious, vine-ripened
tomatoes. The virtue of this sauce lies in its simplicity: it isn't even cooked!*

FOR THE SAUCE
4 fresh ripe tomatoes, seeded and coarsely
   chopped
1 clove garlic, minced (1 teaspoon)
3 scallions, whites minced, greens finely
   chopped
1-3 jalapeño chilies (or to taste), seeded and
   minced or thinly sliced
1 cup finely chopped fresh mint or cilantro

½ teaspoon ground cumin
3 tablespoons fresh lime juice
1½ tablespoons extra-virgin olive oil
salt and freshly ground black pepper

salt
½ pound dried fusilli
2-3 tablespoons thinly sliced black olives,
   for garnish (optional)

To make the sauce, place the tomatoes, garlic, scallions, chilies, mint, cumin, lime juice, and oil in a food processor and grind to a coarse purée. Correct the seasoning, adding salt, pepper, and lime juice to taste.

Just before serving, bring at least 4 quarts water to a boil in a large pot. Add salt to taste. Boil the fusilli for 6 to 8 minutes, or until cooked but still al dente. Drain the pasta and transfer it to a large bowl. Stir in the sauce. Sprinkle the olive slices (if using) on top and serve at once.

Serves 4.

306 CALORIES PER SERVING: 9 G PROTEIN, 7 G FAT, 53 G CARBOHYDRATE; 15 MG SODIUM; 0 MG CHOLESTEROL.

PENNE WITH ROASTED PEPPERS

The peppers used in this recipe are completely charred on the outside to give them an inimitable smoky flavor and to facilitate removing the skin. I usually serve this dish at room temperature as a salad, but it can also be served hot. Penne are quill-shaped pasta tubes.

salt
3 cups (⅔ pound) imported penne

FOR THE SAUCE
3 large bell peppers (ideally, 1 red, 1 yellow, and 1 green)
1 small clove garlic, minced (½ teaspoon)
2 scallions, whites minced, greens finely chopped

¼ cup finely chopped fresh herbs (basil, oregano, summer savory, parsley, and/or chives), plus a few sprigs for garnish
3 tablespoons capers
3 tablespoons balsamic vinegar (or to taste)
2 teaspoons extra-virgin olive oil
2 tablespoons chicken stock (optional)
salt, freshly ground black pepper, and cayenne pepper

Bring at least 4 quarts lightly salted water to a boil in a large pot. Boil the penne for 6 to 8 minutes, or until cooked but still al dente. Drain the pasta in a colander and rinse well with cold water. Let drain.

To make the sauce, roast the peppers over a high flame or directly on an electric burner (set on high) until black and charred on all sides. Transfer to a bowl, cover, and let cool. Scrape the skin off the peppers using a paring knife.

(Rinse under cold water if necessary to remove any bits of charred skin.) Core and seed the peppers and cut into penne-sized pieces.

Combine the garlic, scallions, and herbs in a large bowl. Add the peppers, capers, vinegar, olive oil, stock (if using), salt, pepper, and cayenne. Stir in the penne. Correct the seasoning, adding salt and vinegar to taste. Garnish with sprigs of fresh herbs.

Serves 4 to 6.

347 CALORIES PER SERVING: 11 G PROTEIN, 4 G FAT, 66 G CARBOHYDRATE; 80 MG SODIUM; 0 MG CHOLESTEROL.

FETTUCCINE WITH WILD MUSHROOM SAUCE

You can use any type of exotic mushroom for this dish, a mixture of them, or even plain button mushrooms. But nothing beats the earthy taste of shiitakes. For the best results, use a dark stock, like the Brown Bone Stock on page 238.

1 tablespoon olive oil
2 cloves garlic, minced (2 teaspoons)
2 shallots, minced
12 ounces shiitake or other exotic mushrooms, thinly sliced
1 cup chicken or veal stock
2 ounces thinly sliced prosciutto, cut into ¼" slivers

½ cup finely chopped flat-leaf parsley
salt, freshly ground black pepper, and cayenne pepper
12 ounces fresh fettuccine
3–4 tablespoons freshly grated Parmigiano Reggiano (or other Parmesan-style cheese)

Heat the oil in a large saucepan. Cook the garlic and shallots over medium heat for 30 seconds, or until soft and fragrant but not brown. Add the mushrooms and cook for 3 to 4 minutes, or until dry. Stir in the stock and prosciutto, and simmer for 2 minutes. Stir in half the parsley and the salt, pepper, and cayenne.

Bring at least 4 quarts water to a boil in a large pot. Add salt to taste. Boil the fettuccine for 1 to 2 minutes, or until cooked to taste. Drain the pasta and divide it among 4 deep dishes or shallow bowls. Ladle the sauce on top and garnish with the remaining parsley. Serve the cheese sprinkled on top.

Serves 4 as an appetizer, 2 to 3 as an entrée.

400 CALORIES PER SERVING: 21 G PROTEIN, 8 G FAT, 63 G CARBOHYDRATE; 561 MG SODIUM; 81 MG CHOLESTEROL.

RICE STICKS WITH BARBECUED PORK

Rice noodle stews are as popular in Southeast Asia as hamburgers are in the West. My favorite meat for this dish is the sweet barbecued pork tenderloin found at Chinese markets, but any cooked meat or seafood will do. Dried shrimp can be found at Asian and Hispanic markets.

8 ounces rice sticks, ideally ¼" wide
(see Cook's Notes)
2 teaspoons canola oil
2 cloves garlic, thinly sliced
5 cups chicken stock
¼ cup fish sauce
1–3 teaspoons Thai chili paste or hot sauce
3 tablespoons sugar
1 tablespoon fresh lime juice (or to taste)
2 cups bean sprouts

6–8 ounces Chinese barbecued pork or
cooked chicken, beef, shrimp, or scallops,
thinly sliced
½ cup finely chopped cilantro
3 tablespoons finely chopped dried shrimp
(optional)
3 tablespoons finely chopped dry-roasted
peanuts
1 lime, quartered

Soak the rice sticks in cold water to cover for 30 minutes, or until pliable. Heat the oil in a large saucepan and cook the garlic until golden brown. Add the stock and bring to a boil. Stir in the fish sauce, chili paste, sugar, and lime juice. Correct the seasoning, adding chili paste and lime juice to taste.

Bring 2 quarts water to a boil in a large pot. Just before serving, drain the rice sticks and cook in boiling water for 1 minute, or until tender. Add the bean sprouts and cook for 10 seconds. Drain the noodles and sprouts, and transfer them to 4 large bowls or soup plates. Arrange the barbecued pork slices on top. Fill each bowl with broth and sprinkle with cilantro, dried shrimp (if using), and chopped peanuts. Serve at once, with lime wedges and hot sauce on the side.

Serves 4.

478 CALORIES PER SERVING: 28 G PROTEIN, 9 G FAT, 71 G CARBOHYDRATE; 627 MG SODIUM; 43 MG CHOLESTEROL.

SINGAPORE-STYLE NOODLES

This popular noodle dish reflects the cosmopolitan cuisine of Singapore: the Indian passion for curry powder, the Thai fondness for chili paste, and the Indonesian use of a sweet soy sauce called kejap maris. *To simplify the recipe, I've substituted regular soy sauce and molasses.*

8 ounces rice vermicelli or very thin Chinese wheat noodles
¼ cup soy sauce
½–1 teaspoon sambal ulek (Indonesian chili paste), Thai chili paste, or hot sauce
2 tablespoons molasses
2 tablespoons rice wine vinegar or lemon juice
1½ tablespoons canola oil
1 tablespoon curry powder
1 tablespoon minced fresh ginger

2 cloves garlic, minced (2 teaspoons)
4 scallions, whites minced, greens cut into 1" pieces
6 ounces lean pork loin (partially frozen), thinly sliced across the grain and cut into ¼" strips
6 ounces shrimp, peeled and deveined
1 red bell pepper, cored, seeded, and cut into ¼" strips
2 cups bean sprouts
salt and freshly ground black pepper

Soak the rice vermicelli in cold water to cover for 20 minutes or until pliable. (If using wheat noodles, cook in 3 quarts boiling water for 2 to 4 minutes, or until tender. Drain in a colander, refresh under cold water, and drain well.)

Combine the soy sauce, sambal ulek, molasses, and vinegar in a small bowl and stir to mix.

Drain the rice vermicelli. Heat a wok over high heat. Swirl in the oil. Stir-fry the curry powder, ginger, garlic, and scallion whites for 20 seconds, or until fragrant but not brown. Add the pork, shrimp, and pepper, and stir-fry for 1 to 2 minutes, or until cooked. Stir in the vermicelli, soy sauce mixture, scallion greens, and bean sprouts. Stir-fry for 1 to 2 minutes, or until the noodles are soft. Add salt and pepper to taste. Serve at once.

Serves 4.

412 CALORIES PER SERVING: 23 G PROTEIN, 10 G FAT, 59 G CARBOHYDRATE; 620 MG SODIUM; 84 MG CHOLESTEROL.

BUCKWHEAT NOODLES WITH SPICY SESAME SAUCE

This refreshing dish, made with soba (chewy buckwheat noodles from Japan), is one of my favorite warm-weather lunches. (Look for soba in Japanese markets, natural food stores, and the Oriental food sections of most supermarkets.) It can also be made with spaghetti or linguine.

8 ounces soba
salt
1 teaspoon sesame oil
1 red bell pepper, cored, seeded, and cut into strips
1 yellow bell pepper, cored, seeded, and cut into strips
1 small cucumber, peeled, halved, seeded, and cut into strips

FOR THE SAUCE
¼ cup sesame seeds
1 tablespoon minced fresh ginger
2 cloves garlic, minced (2 teaspoons)
3 scallions, whites minced, greens cut into ½" pieces for garnish
¼ cup peanut butter
3–4 tablespoons warm water
3 tablespoons soy sauce
2 tablespoons rice or cider vinegar
1 teaspoon Thai or other hot sauce (or to taste)
1 tablespoon sugar

Cook the soba in 4 quarts rapidly boiling salted water for 4 to 6 minutes, or until tender. Drain in a colander, refresh under cold water, and drain well. Transfer to a large bowl and toss with the sesame oil.

To make the sauce, lightly toast the sesame seeds in a dry skillet over medium heat. Transfer to a mixing bowl to cool. Reserve 2 tablespoons for garnish.

Add the remaining sauce ingredients (except the scallion greens) and whisk until smooth. Correct the seasoning, adding sugar, vinegar, soy sauce, and hot sauce to taste. The sauce should be sweet-tart, salty, and spicy. If it's too thick, add a little water. The recipe can be prepared ahead to this stage.

Just before serving, toss the noodles with half the peppers, cucumber, and sauce. Arrange on a platter. Spoon the remaining sauce on top. Decorate the noodles with the remaining peppers and cucumber, the scallion greens, and the reserved sesame seeds.

Serves 4.

383 CALORIES PER SERVING: 16 G PROTEIN, 14 G FAT, 56 G CARBOHYDRATE; 1309 MG SODIUM; 0 MG CHOLESTEROL.

KOREAN SESAME NOODLES WITH BEEF
....

This dish, called chap chae, *could be thought of as Korean chop suey. It's traditionally made with a silvery gray sweet potato starch noodle called* dang myun *(available in Asian markets), but you can use 8 ounces of any thin cooked noodle.*

8 ounces dang myun
½ teaspoon plus 1 tablespoon sesame oil
5 Chinese dried black mushrooms
3 tablespoons sesame seeds
3 cloves garlic, minced (1 tablespoon)
1 onion, thinly sliced
1 large carrot, peeled and cut into julienne strips

6 ounces beef tenderloin or sirloin (partially frozen), thinly sliced across the grain and cut into ½" strips
5 ounces fresh spinach
4–5 tablespoons soy sauce
2–3 tablespoons sugar
salt and freshly ground black pepper

Cook the dang myun in 3 quarts boiling water for 3 to 4 minutes, or until tender. Drain in a colander, refresh under cold water, and drain well. Cut the dang myun 3 or 4 times with scissors and toss with ½ teaspoon oil. Soak the mushrooms in hot water to cover for 20 minutes.

Lightly toast the sesame seeds in a dry skillet over medium heat. Stem the mushrooms and cut into thin slivers.

Heat the 1 tablespoon oil in a wok or skillet over medium heat. Add the garlic, onion, carrot, and mushrooms, and stir-fry for 2 minutes, or until soft but not brown. Increase the heat to high and add the beef. Stir-fry for 1 minute, or until cooked. Transfer the beef mixture to a platter with a slotted spoon and keep warm.

Add the spinach, soy sauce, and sugar to the wok and cook for 2 minutes, or until the spinach is wilted. Stir in the dang myun and the beef mixture. Cook for 1 to 2 minutes, or until the noodles are soft. Correct the seasoning, adding salt, pepper, soy sauce, and sugar to taste. The mixture should be a little sweet and a little salty. Sprinkle with sesame seeds and serve at once.

Serves 4.

416 CALORIES PER SERVING: 13 G PROTEIN, 10 G FAT, 69 G CARBOHYDRATE; 590 MG SODIUM; 24 MG CHOLESTEROL.

PAD THAI

Pad thai, or stir-fried noodles, is one of the national dishes of Thailand. My version uses less oil than the original, but it's tasty enough to have become a once-a-week special at our house.

8 ounces rice sticks, ideally ⅛" wide (see Cook's Notes)
4 tablespoons fresh lime juice
3 tablespoons fish sauce
1 tablespoon soy sauce
1 tablespoon sugar
1–2 teaspoons Thai hot sauce (or to taste)
1½ tablespoons canola oil
3 cloves garlic, minced (1 tablespoon)
1 tablespoon minced fresh ginger or galangal (see Cook's Notes)
4 scallions, whites minced, greens cut into ½" pieces for garnish

1 or 2 hot chilies, seeded and minced
4 ounces skinless, boneless chicken breast, thinly sliced across the grain
4 ounces shrimp, peeled, deveined, and cut into 1" pieces
1 red or yellow bell pepper, cored, seeded, and diced
1 medium-sized onion, thinly sliced
2 carrots, peeled and thinly sliced
2 cups mung bean sprouts
3 tablespoons chopped dry-roasted peanuts, for garnish

Soak the rice sticks in cold water to cover for 30 minutes, or until pliable. Combine the lime juice, fish sauce, soy sauce, sugar, and hot sauce in a small bowl and whisk to mix.

Just before serving, drain the rice sticks. Heat a wok over high heat. Swirl in the oil. Add the garlic, ginger, scallion whites, and chilies, and stir-fry for 15 seconds, or until fragrant. Add the chicken, shrimp, pepper, onion, and carrots, and stir-fry for 1 to 2 minutes, or until the chicken is cooked.

Stir in the rice sticks and bean sprouts, and cook for 30 seconds. Stir in the sauce and cook for 30 seconds, or until the rice sticks are tender.

Correct the seasoning, adding fish sauce, lime juice, and sugar to taste. The dish should be a little sweet, a little sour, and a little salty. Transfer the pad thai to a platter or plates. Sprinkle with the scallion greens and peanuts, and serve at once.
Serves 4.

434 CALORIES PER SERVING: 22 G PROTEIN, 11 G FAT, 64 G CARBOHYDRATE; 508 MG SODIUM; 58 MG CHOLESTEROL.

QUINOA PILAF

Quinoa (pronounced KEEN-wa) is a grain native to the Andes Mountains, where it has been cultivated for 5,000 years. It contains more protein than wheat, oats, millet, rye, and barley. Unlike most grains, it is rich in lysine, an essential amino acid seldom found in the vegetable kingdom.

1 cup quinoa
1 tablespoon olive oil
1 small onion, finely chopped
1 stalk celery, finely chopped

2 tablespoons pine nuts (optional)
2 cups chicken stock or water
salt and freshly ground black pepper

Place the quinoa in a strainer, rinse with cold water, and drain. Heat the oil in a saucepan or sauté pan. Add the onion, celery, and pine nuts, and cook over medium heat for 2 to 3 minutes, or until the onion is soft but not brown. Add the quinoa and toast for 30 seconds.

Add the stock, salt, and pepper, and bring to a boil. Reduce the heat to a low simmer and cover the pan. Cook the quinoa for 15 to 20 minutes, or until all the liquid is absorbed and the grain is tender. Fluff with a fork and correct the seasoning. Serve at once.

Serves 4 to 6.

277 CALORIES PER SERVING: 11 G PROTEIN, 7 G FAT, 42 G CARBOHYDRATE; 542 MG SODIUM; 0 MG CHOLESTEROL.

HERB RISOTTO

Risotto is the rice dish that thinks it's pasta. My low-fat risotto calls for less butter and cheese than the traditional recipe. To boost the flavor, I add chopped fresh herbs or saffron. Arborio rice is a starchy, short-grain rice that has the unique ability to absorb 5 times its volume in liquid without becoming mushy. It is widely available at gourmet shops and Italian markets. You can also use short-grain Valencia, which is found at Hispanic markets.

1 tablespoon olive oil
1 onion or 2 leeks, finely chopped
    (about 1 cup)
1 clove garlic, minced (1 teaspoon)
1½ cups arborio rice
½ cup dry white wine
5–6 cups chicken stock (page 237),
    heated to simmering

¼ cup chopped fresh herbs (or ¼ teaspoon
    saffron threads soaked in 1 tablespoon
    warm water)
¼–½ cup freshly grated Parmigiano
    Reggiano (or other Parmesan-style
    cheese)
salt and freshly ground black pepper

Heat the oil in a large saucepan over medium heat. Cook the onion and garlic for 3 to 4 minutes, or until soft but not brown, stirring well. Stir in the rice and cook for 1 minute, or until all the grains are shiny. (Do not wash arborio rice. You need the starch to thicken the sauce.)

Add the wine and bring to a boil, stirring steadily. When most of the wine is absorbed, add ½ cup stock. Cook the rice at a gentle simmer, stirring steadily. When most of the liquid is absorbed, add another ½ cup stock. Continue add-

ing the stock, ½ cup at a time, until 5 cups are used up. If the rice is still hard, add ½ to 1 cup more stock. Add the herbs or saffron during the last 3 minutes of cooking. The whole process should take 18 to 20 minutes. Properly prepared risotto will be soft and creamy, but you should still be able to taste the individual grains of rice.

Remove the pan from the heat and stir in the cheese, salt, and pepper. Serve immediately. Guests may wait for risotto, but risotto does not wait for the guests!

Serves 4.

400 CALORIES PER SERVING: 14 G PROTEIN, 7 G FAT, 62 G CARBOHYDRATE; 1094 MG SODIUM; 5 MG CHOLESTEROL.

BLACK-EYED PEAS AND BASMATI RICE
....

Beans and rice are a staple throughout the Caribbean and Central and South America. The reason is simple: the combination produces a cheap but complete form of protein. This recipe features Indian basmati rice, which has a distinctive, milky-nutty flavor, not to mention the unusual property of doubling in length, not width, when cooked. Look for basmati in Indian and Pakistani markets, natural food stores, and major supermarkets. I use the cooking method recommended by Indian cooking authority Julie Sahni.

1 cup basmati rice
1 tablespoon olive oil
1 onion, finely chopped

1 cup cooked black-eyed peas
salt and freshly ground black pepper

Wash the rice. Place it in a bowl with cold water to cover. Swirl it around with your fingers until the water becomes cloudy, then drain. Continue rinsing, swirling, and draining the rice until the water runs clear. Drain the rice, return it to the bowl, and add 2 cups water. Let stand for 30 minutes.

Drain the rice in a colander over a large, heavy pot. Bring the soaking water to a boil. Stir in the rice and bring it to a boil. Reduce the heat and gently simmer the rice, loosely covered, for 10 to 12 minutes, or until the surface is riddled with steamy holes.

Reduce the heat to the lowest setting and raise the pan 1" above the burner. (This can be done by placing it on a wok ring.) Tightly cover the pan and let the rice steam for 10 minutes.

Heat the oil in a large skillet. Cook the onion over medium heat for 4 to 5 minutes, or until golden brown. Stir in the black-eyed peas and cook for 2 minutes, or until heated. Stir in the rice and cook for 1 minute. Season with salt and pepper.

Serves 4 to 6.

279 CALORIES PER SERVING: 6 G PROTEIN, 4 G FAT, 54 G CARBOHYDRATE; 6 MG SODIUM; 0 MG CHOLESTEROL.

WILD RICE STUFFING

Wild rice is something of a culinary misnomer, being neither wild (it's cultivated in paddies) nor rice (botanically speaking, it's an aquatic grass seed). Nevertheless, it's a uniquely American food — it was first harvested by the Indians of Minnesota. I like to presoak the rice to shorten the cooking time. You can omit this step and lengthen the cooking time, but you'll have to add more water.

2 cups wild rice
1 firm apple (such as a Granny Smith), peeled and finely diced
1 teaspoon lemon juice
2 ears fresh corn (1 cup kernels)
1½ tablespoons olive oil
1 large onion, finely chopped (1 cup)
3 stalks celery, finely chopped
3 cloves garlic, minced (1 tablespoon)
4–5 cups water or chicken stock (approximately)
1 small green bell pepper, cored, seeded, and cut into ½" dice

1 small red bell pepper, cored, seeded, and cut into ½" dice
1 small yellow bell pepper, cored, seeded, and cut into ½" dice (optional)
2 tablespoons finely chopped fresh herbs (sage, thyme, basil, oregano, parsley, and/or chives)
2 tablespoons freshly grated Parmigiano Reggiano, or other Parmesan-style cheese (optional)
salt and freshly ground black pepper

Rinse the wild rice in a strainer with cold water and drain. Soak the rice in cold water to cover for at least 4 hours. Drain again.

Toss the apple pieces with the lemon juice to prevent browning. If using fresh corn, cut the kernels off the cobs.

Heat the oil in a large, heavy saucepan. Add the onion, celery, and garlic, and cook over medium heat for 3 to 4 minutes, or until soft but not brown. Stir in the rice and 4 cups water, and bring to a boil. Reduce the heat and simmer for 20 minutes.

Stir in the peppers, apple, and corn, and continue simmering, uncovered, for 10 minutes, or until the rice is tender but not too soft. If the rice begins to dry out, add more water. If the rice is too wet, increase the heat to high to evaporate the excess water.

Just before serving, stir in the herbs, cheese (if using), salt, and pepper. The stuffing should be highly seasoned.

Serves 6 to 8.

Note: This stuffing can be simmered until done and then baked inside a turkey, chicken, or game hens, but I usually prepare it ahead of time and warm it in a baking dish on the side.

216 CALORIES PER SERVING: 7 G PROTEIN, 3 G FAT, 42 G CARBOHYDRATE; 25 MG SODIUM; 0 MG CHOLESTEROL.

KASHA WITH BOW TIES

Kasha may lack the cachet of wild rice, but thanks to a renewed interest in whole foods, this dark, nutty grain is making a comeback. This recipe takes its inspiration from a traditional Jewish dish called kasha varniskes *(buckwheat groats with pasta bow ties). Use just about any type of fresh mushrooms—button mushrooms, shiitakes, porcini (boletus)—the more exotic, the better!*

1 cup buckwheat groats
1 cup small pasta bow ties
salt
1 tablespoon olive oil
1 medium-sized onion, finely chopped
1½ cups thinly sliced button mushrooms, shiitakes, or porcini

½ egg white, beaten
2 cups chicken stock or water, heated to boiling
freshly ground black pepper

Wash the groats under cold running water, drain well, and blot dry. Cook the bow ties in boiling salted water for 5 minutes, or until al dente. Drain in a colander, refresh under cold water, and drain.

Heat the oil in a large, heavy saucepan. Add the onion and mushrooms, and cook over high heat for 2 to 3 minutes, or until the onion is golden brown and the mushrooms have lost most of their liquid. Transfer the onion and mushrooms to a bowl and let the pan cool.

Combine the groats and egg white in a bowl. Stir to mix. Transfer to the pan and cook over high heat, stirring steadily, for 2 to 3 minutes, or until the individual grains are dry. Stir in the onion, mushrooms, stock, salt, and pepper. Simmer the mixture, covered, for 15 to 18 minutes, or until the grains are tender and all the liquid has been absorbed. Stir in the bow ties and correct the seasoning, adding salt and pepper to taste. Serve at once.

Serves 4 to 6.

289 CALORIES PER SERVING: 10 G PROTEIN, 5 G FAT, 53 G CARBOHYDRATE; 174 MG SODIUM; 0 MG CHOLESTEROL.

HERB SPAETZLE

Spaetzle are tiny dumplings. The name literally means "little sparrow" in German, and with a bit of imagination, these pea-sized dumplings do, indeed, look like tiny birds. The traditional recipe for spaetzle is loaded with eggs and butter. This low-fat version omits the yolks and generously uses fresh herbs for flavor and richness. It goes particularly well with meat and poultry dishes made with sauces.

2 egg whites
1 whole egg (or 2 more whites)
1 cup skim milk
½ cup minced fresh herbs (basil, oregano, tarragon, thyme, chervil, chives, and/or flat-leaf parsley)

salt and freshly ground black pepper
freshly grated nutmeg
2 cups flour (approximately)
2 teaspoons olive oil (optional)

Combine the egg whites, egg, milk, 6 tablespoons herbs, salt (I use 1 scant teaspoon), pepper, and nutmeg in a large bowl and whisk until smooth. Sift in the flour. Mix with a wooden spoon to obtain a loose, sticky batter. (It should be the consistency of apple sauce. If it's too thin, add a little flour.)

Bring at least 2 quarts water to a rolling boil in a large, deep saucepan. Add 1 teaspoon salt. Place a spaetzle maker over the pan, load it with dough, and cut tiny droplets into the water. Cook for 1 minute, or until the water returns to a boil and the spaetzle rise to the surface. Remove the spaetzle with a skimmer or slotted spoon and transfer to a colander to drain. Continue cooking the spaetzle in this fashion until all the batter is used up.

Transfer the spaetzle to a bowl and toss with the olive oil (if using). Sprinkle with the remaining herbs and serve at once.

Serves 6 to 8.

Note: The easiest way to make spaetzle is to use a spaetzle maker, a metal rectangle with holes in it surmounted by a movable, open-topped box. As the box slides back and forth over the metal plate, tiny droplets of dough fall through the holes in the bottom. These cook into tiny dumplings. This probably sounds more complicated than it is, for spaetzle can be made from start to finish in less than 15 minutes. Spaetzle makers can be purchased at most cookware shops.

190 CALORIES PER SERVING: 8 G PROTEIN, 2 G FAT, 34 G CARBOHYDRATE; 319 MG SODIUM; 36 MG CHOLESTEROL.

QUICK-COOK COUSCOUS

Couscous is often described as a grain, but it's actually a type of pasta made by mixing flour and water and forcing the dough through a sieve. The tiny pellets that result make a delectable, light, healthy starch. This is the quickest, easiest way to cook couscous, and although the individual grains aren't quite as light as when they are steamed (see the next recipe), the overall convenience of this method makes up for it. Most recipes call for lots of butter, but here celery, currants, and pine nuts bolster the flavor without the fat.

1 tablespoon olive oil
1 small onion, finely chopped (½ cup)
1 stalk celery, finely chopped
3 tablespoons currants

2 tablespoons pine nuts
1 cup couscous
1½ cups chicken stock or water
salt and freshly ground black pepper

Heat the oil in a heavy saucepan. Add the onion, celery, currants, and pine nuts, and cook over medium heat for 3 to 4 minutes, or until the onion is soft but not brown. Stir in the couscous and cook for 1 minute, or until lightly toasted.

Add the stock, salt, and pepper. Bring the mixture to a boil, stirring gently. Cover the pan, remove it from the heat, and let the couscous stand for 5 minutes. Just before serving, fluff the couscous with a fork and correct the seasoning. Serve at once.

Serves 4.

353 CALORIES PER SERVING: 12 G PROTEIN, 8 G FAT, 58 G CARBOHYDRATE; 407 MG SODIUM; 0 MG CHOLESTEROL.

Couscous — Traditional Method

If you want to experience couscous in all its glory, try this method, which uses a series of steamings and soakings to swell the grains to four times their original size. This recipe is loosely modeled on Paula Wolfert's method for preparing Moroccan-style couscous. It tastes similar to Quick-Cook Couscous (see previous recipe) but is much lighter. A couscousiere is a large pot bowed out in the middle like a barrel, with a steamer that fits in the top. Calphalon makes one; other models are available at cookware shops. Alternatively, you can rig up a steamer using 2 large saucepans and 2 large strainers or colanders. Serve with Chicken Tagine (page 131).

3 cups couscous (1½ pounds)
salt and freshly ground black pepper

2 cups skim milk
2 cups cold water

Start 4 to 5 hours or even a day before you plan to serve the dish. Place the couscous in a strainer and rinse thoroughly under cold water. Spread it out in a large roasting pan and let it dry for 10 minutes. Gently rake the couscous with your fingers, lifting and sifting, to break up any lumps.

In the bottom of a couscousiere or in 2 large saucepans, bring 3" salted water to a boil over high heat. Set the steamer or colanders on top; the fit should be snug. (To guarantee a tight fit, wrap the base of the steamer with wet, rolled paper towels.) Add the couscous and steam for 15 minutes, or until hot and moist. Remove the couscousiere from the heat (leave the water in it) and dump the couscous back into the roasting pan.

Spread out the couscous using a long-pronged fork. Sprinkle it with salt, pepper, and 1 cup milk. Gently rake the couscous with the fork, stirring and sifting to break up any lumps. Sprinkle on the remaining milk and rake again. Let the couscous stand for 1 hour, or until no longer wet to the touch, raking occasionally to break up lumps.

Replenish the water in the couscousiere or saucepans.

Return the couscous to the couscousiere or colanders, and steam for another 15 minutes. Dump it back into the roasting pan and gradually rake in 1 cup cold water. Sprinkle on the remaining water and rake again.

Let the couscous dry for 1 hour, or until no longer wet to the touch. Rake it occasionally to break up any lumps. The couscous can be prepared to this point up to 24 hours in advance. Cover it with a dish towel and set it aside at room temperature. (For longer than 6 hours, cover and refrigerate.)

About 20 minutes before serving, wet your hands and rake the couscous again to break up any lumps. Return it to the couscousiere and steam for 20 minutes. Some people like to do the third steaming over a stew.

Serves 8 to 10.

Note: This couscous may be softer than what you're accustomed to. Unlike other pasta, it isn't supposed to be eaten al dente. It's also extremely mild; the flavor comes from the stew served on top of it.

281 CALORIES PER SERVING: 11 G PROTEIN, .6 G FAT, 56 G CARBOHYDRATE; 305 MG SODIUM; 1 MG CHOLESTEROL.

....

FISH AND SHELLFISH

....

SHRIMP KEBABS WITH SUN-DRIED TOMATOES AND BASIL

....

These kebabs are as delectable as they are easy to make. Sun-dried tomatoes are a sort of vegetarian prosciutto. They're made by slicing, salting, and drying tomatoes, sometimes in the sun, more often in a food drier. Look for them in gourmet shops, natural food stores, and most supermarkets.

1 tablespoon extra-virgin olive oil
½ teaspoon freshly grated lemon zest
2 tablespoons fresh lemon juice
2 teaspoons chopped fresh thyme
   (or 2 teaspoons dried)
salt and freshly ground black pepper

24 large shrimp (about 1½ pounds), peeled
   and deveined
1 bunch basil (24 large leaves)
twenty-four 1" pieces of sun-dried tomato,
   drained and blotted dry

Combine the oil, zest, lemon juice, thyme, salt, and pepper in a bowl. Add the shrimp and marinate for 15 to 20 minutes. Thread the marinated shrimp onto skewers, placing a basil leaf and a piece of sun-dried tomato between each (as pictured on the cover of this book).

Season with salt and pepper. Preheat the grill. Just before serving, grill the kebabs, basting with marinade, for 1 to 2 minutes per side, or until the shrimp are cooked.

Serves 4 to 6.

207 CALORIES PER SERVING: 30 G PROTEIN, 5 G FAT, 11 G CARBOHYDRATE; 319 MG SODIUM; 261 MG CHOLESTEROL.

Shrimp Kebabs with Sun-Dried Tomatoes and Basil

SHRIMP SAAG

Saag is a mild Indian curry made with spinach. Indians tend to cook spinach much longer than we do, so frozen spinach will work fine for this recipe. Serve with Black-Eyed Peas and Basmati Rice (page 105).

1 tablespoon olive or canola oil
1 onion, finely chopped
2 teaspoons minced fresh ginger
2 cloves garlic, minced (2 teaspoons)
½ teaspoon cumin seeds
½ teaspoon ground coriander
½ teaspoon ground turmeric
¼ teaspoon ground cinnamon
¼ teaspoon ground cardamom
pinch of ground cloves

1 bay leaf
1 cup clam broth or fish stock
   (approximately)
2 12-ounce bags fresh spinach, finely
   chopped (or 2 packages frozen)
1½ pounds large shrimp, peeled and
   deveined
salt and freshly ground black pepper
3 tablespoons finely chopped cilantro or
   parsley, for garnish

Heat the oil in a sauté pan. Add the onion, ginger, garlic, spices, and bay leaf, and cook over medium heat for 3 minutes, or until soft but not brown. Add the clam broth and bring to a boil. Stir in the spinach and cook for 10 to 15 minutes, or until the spinach is soft and mushy. If the mixture dries out too much, add more clam broth.

Stir in the shrimp and simmer for 1 to 2 minutes, or until cooked. Remove and discard the bay leaf. Season with salt and pepper. Transfer to a serving dish, garnish with the cilantro, and serve at once.

Serves 4.

198 CALORIES PER SERVING: 34 G PROTEIN, 3 G FAT, 9 G CARBOHYDRATE; 414 MG SODIUM; 261 MG CHOLESTEROL.

SALMON WITH YOGURT-TAHINI SAUCE

This recipe, loosely inspired by a Lebanese sauce called taratoor, *calls for the fish to be baked, but it can also be grilled. (If you grill it, spread the sauce on the fish after you've turned it.) Tahini (sesame paste) can be found at Middle Eastern markets, natural food stores, and most supermarkets.*

4 6–8-ounce salmon fillets or steaks
salt and freshly ground black pepper
1 small clove garlic, minced (½ teaspoon)
3 tablespoons tahini
3 tablespoons nonfat yogurt
3 tablespoons fresh lemon juice

2 teaspoons soy sauce
2 tablespoons finely chopped fresh chives
   or scallion greens, for garnish
½ cup pomegranate seeds, for garnish
   (optional)

Preheat the oven to 400 degrees F. If using salmon fillets, run your fingers over the fish, feeling for bones. Remove any you find with needle-nose pliers. If using salmon steaks, leave the bones intact—they'll help hold the fish together. Season the fish with salt and pepper, and arrange it in a lightly oiled baking dish just large enough to hold it.

Combine the garlic, tahini, and yogurt in a small bowl and whisk until smooth. Whisk in the lemon juice, soy sauce, salt, and pepper. Spoon the sauce over the fish.

Bake the salmon for 20 minutes, or until a skewer inserted in the center comes out very hot to the touch. (Another test for doneness is to press the fish with your finger. When cooked, it will break into flakes.) Sprinkle the fish with chives and pomegranate seeds (if using), and serve at once.

Serves 4.

234 CALORIES PER SERVING: 27 G PROTEIN, 12 G FAT, 5 G CARBOHYDRATE; 1232 MG SODIUM; 31 MG CHOLESTEROL.

WOK SMOKED SALMON

Smoking salmon is easy. I should know; I do it every weekend for Sunday brunch. This recipe produces a kipper-style salmon to eat with bagels or serve on toast points. To make smoked salmon pâté, purée leftovers with a little low-fat cream cheese or Yogurt Cream Cheese Spread (page 241).

1 1-pound salmon fillet
5 tablespoons brown sugar, honey, molasses, or maple syrup
2½ tablespoons kosher or sea salt

1 teaspoon freshly ground white pepper
2 tablespoons oak, alder, or other hardwood sawdust or small wood chips
¼ teaspoon oil

Skin the salmon fillet (if necessary) and remove any bones, using needle-nose pliers or tweezers. Combine the brown sugar, salt, and white pepper in a shallow bowl and whisk to mix. Marinate the salmon in this mixture for 3 to 4 hours, turning several times. Drain the salmon on a rack, wiping off any crystalized salt with a moist paper towel, and let dry for 30 minutes.

Line a wok with foil and place the sawdust at the bottom. Place a circular wire rack in the wok 2" above the sawdust. Oil the rack and place the salmon, exterior side down, on top.

Place the wok over high heat. When the wood begins to smoke, reduce the heat to medium and tightly cover the wok. Smoke the fish for 20 to 30 minutes, or until cooked. (A skewer inserted in the center will come out hot to the touch.) Do not overcook, or the salmon will be dry.

Transfer the fish to a wire rack to cool. Wrap it in foil and refrigerate overnight.

Serves 4.

117 CALORIES PER SERVING: 16 G PROTEIN, 4 G FAT, 3 G CARBOHYDRATE; 960 MG SODIUM; 20 MG CHOLESTEROL.

RHODE ISLAND RED CHOWDER

*Clams or fish? Tomatoes or cream? Nothing brings out controversy like chowder.
Red chowder contains no cream and (this one at least) no salt pork. Use tiny
cherrystone clams if you can find them. Otherwise, use quahogs (pronounced KO-hogs—
large hard-shell clams), preshucked clam meat, or even canned clams.*

3 dozen tiny cherrystone clams, 16
   quahogs, or 2 cups chopped clam meat
2 cups dry white wine
2–4 cups bottled clam broth, fish stock, or
   water
1½ tablespoons olive oil
1 large onion, finely chopped
2 stalks celery, finely chopped
3 cloves garlic, minced (1 tablespoon)
1 teaspoon minced fresh thyme (or 1
   teaspoon dried)

1 bunch flat-leaf parsley, minced
2 bay leaves
4 ripe tomatoes, peeled, seeded, and
   chopped (or 1 28-ounce can)
1 tablespoon tomato paste
2 large potatoes, peeled, diced, and placed
   in cold water to cover
salt, freshly ground black pepper, and
   cayenne pepper

Scrub the clams and place them in a large pot with the wine. Tightly cover the pot and steam until the shells open. (Cherrystones will need about 6 to 8 minutes steaming, quahogs 12 to 15 minutes.) If using cherrystones, leave the clams in the shells and set aside. If using quahogs, remove the meat from the shells and finely chop, using a meat grinder or food processor. (There should be about 2 cups meat.)

Strain the cooking liquid through a cheesecloth-lined strainer into a large measuring cup. Add enough clam broth to make 6 cups. (If using preshucked or canned clams, omit the steaming and use 2 cups wine and 4 cups clam broth.) Heat the oil in a large pot. Add the onion, celery,

garlic, thyme, half the parsley, and bay leaves. Cook over medium heat for 3 to 4 minutes, or until soft but not brown. Add the tomatoes and tomato paste, and cook for 2 minutes. Add the wine–clam broth mixture, and bring to a boil. Add the potatoes, reduce the heat, and simmer for 8 to 10 minutes, or until the potatoes are tender.

Just before serving, stir in the cooked cherrystones or clam meat and the salt, pepper, and cayenne. Remove and discard the bay leaves. Garnish with the remaining parsley and serve at once.

Serves 6.

252 CALORIES PER SERVING: 13 G PROTEIN, 5 G FAT, 28 G CARBOHYDRATE; 402 MG SODIUM; 26 MG CHOLESTEROL.

Rhode Island Red Chowder

THAI SQUID SALAD
....

Part stir-fry and part salad, this dish is 100 percent delicious. I first tasted it at the streetside restaurant Panawan in the village of Mai Sariang in northwestern Thailand. Scoring the squid helps tenderize it and creates an attractive pattern.

FOR THE SAUCE
1 tablespoon fish sauce (or to taste)
1 tablespoon fresh lime juice (or to taste)
2–3 teaspoons Thai chili paste (or to taste)
1 teaspoon sugar

3 stalks fresh lemongrass, or 2 tablespoons dried (see Cook's Notes)
4 large lettuce leaves
1 large ripe tomato, cut into wedges

1 tablespoon canola oil
2 cloves garlic, minced (2 teaspoons)
1–3 Thai or serrano chilies (or to taste), thinly sliced
1 onion, cut into thin wedges
1 pound squid, cleaned, cut into 1" pieces, and lightly scored in a crosshatch pattern
½ cup fresh mint leaves, for garnish

To make the sauce, combine the fish sauce, lime juice, chili paste, and sugar in a small bowl. Whisk until the sugar is dissolved.

Cut the top ⅔ off each lemongrass stalk, trim off the outside leaves and roots, and thinly slice the cores on the diagonal. If using dried lemongrass, soak it in warm water for 20 minutes. Arrange the lettuce leaves on a platter or salad plates, and place the tomato wedges on top. The dish can be prepared ahead to this stage.

Just before serving, heat a wok over high heat. Swirl in the oil. Add the garlic and chilies, and stir-fry for 10 seconds. Add the onion, squid, and lemongrass, and stir-fry for 1 to 2 minutes, or until the squid is firm and opaque.

Spoon the squid mixture over the tomatoes and lettuce leaves. Sprinkle with mint leaves and spoon the sauce on top. Serve at once.

Serves 4.

172 CALORIES PER SERVING: 19 G PROTEIN, 5 G FAT, 12 G CARBOHYDRATE; 129 MG SODIUM; 265 MG CHOLESTEROL.

SAFFRON STEAMED MUSSELS
....

This fragrant dish is a variation on classic French moules marinière.
Serve it with crusty bread for dunking in the broth.

3 pounds fresh mussels
1 onion, finely chopped
1 leek, trimmed, washed, and
    finely chopped
1 carrot, finely chopped
2 stalks celery, finely chopped
1 small fennel bulb, finely chopped
    (optional)
1 red bell pepper, cored, seeded, and
    finely chopped

3 cloves garlic, minced (1 tablespoon)
½ cup finely chopped flat-leaf parsley
⅛ teaspoon saffron threads soaked in
    1 tablespoon warm water
1½ cups dry white wine
1½ cups clam broth, fish stock, or water
2 bay leaves
1 teaspoon chopped fresh thyme
    (or 1 teaspoon dried)
salt and freshly ground black pepper

Scrub the mussels and discard any with cracked shells or shells that fail to close when tapped. Remove the cluster of threads at the hinge of each mussel. (Pinch it between your thumb and the back of a paring knife and pull.)

Shortly before serving, combine all the ingredients except the mussels in a large pot. Bring to a boil and cook for 5 minutes. Add the mussels, tightly cover the pot, and cook over high heat for 5 minutes, or until the mussels open. Stir the mussels once or twice, so those on the bottom have room to open.

Remove and discard the bay leaves. Serve the mussels with their cooking liquid in bowls, and provide extra bowls to hold the empty shells. When the mussels are finished, use empty half shells to spoon up the broth and vegetables.

Serves 4 as an appetizer, 2 to 3 as an entrée.

262 CALORIES PER SERVING: 22 G PROTEIN, 4 G FAT, 19 G CARBOHYDRATE; 355 MG SODIUM; 48 MG CHOLESTEROL.

SESAME SEARED TUNA

With an investment of a few minutes, you get a dish that looks fabulous and tastes even better. This recipe is a specialty of Mark's Place in North Miami, Florida, where chef Mark Militello serves the tuna blood-rare in the center, like sushi. (Don't try this unless you have access to impeccably fresh tuna.) Japanese pickled ginger would make an appropriate garnish.

4 5–6-ounce tuna steaks
2 teaspoons sesame oil
salt and freshly ground black pepper
3 tablespoons white sesame seeds, lightly toasted

3 tablespoons black sesame seeds
4 teaspoons wasabi (or to taste)
2 teaspoons warm water
small carafe soy sauce

Preheat the oven to 400 degrees F. Brush the tuna steaks on all sides with the sesame oil and season with salt and pepper. Combine the white and black sesame seeds in a shallow bowl. Dip each steak in sesame seeds, thickly encrusting the top, bottom, and sides. Transfer the tuna to a nonstick frying pan or roasting pan. Bake for 20 minutes, or until cooked to taste. (To test for doneness, press the steaks with your finger. At medium-rare, they'll yield gently.)

Combine the wasabi and warm water in a small bowl and stir to form a thick paste. Let stand for 5 minutes. Wet your fingers and shape the paste into 4 balls.

To serve, transfer the tuna to plates. (For a more elaborate presentation, cut the steaks into ¼" slices and fan them out across the plate.) Garnish each with a ball of wasabi. Provide each guest with a small ramekin or saucer, and invite everyone to pour a little soy sauce into the ramekin and stir in wasabi to taste. Dip each bite of tuna into the wasabi soy sauce before eating.

Serves 4.

Note: Wasabi is very hot. Use it sparingly the first time you try it.

318 CALORIES PER SERVING: 39 G PROTEIN, 16 G FAT, 2 G CARBOHYDRATE; 377 MG SODIUM; 59 MG CHOLESTEROL.

BRAISED COD WITH TUNISIAN SPICES

This dish spans two continents: cod is a native of the icy North Atlantic; coriander, caraway, and cumin are ingredients in a popular Tunisian spice mixture called tabil. You can also make this dish with snapper, hake, or bluefish.

1½ pounds cod fillets
½ teaspoon coriander seeds
½ teaspoon cumin seeds
½ teaspoon hot red pepper flakes
½ teaspoon caraway seeds
½ teaspoon salt (or to taste)
3 cloves garlic, thinly sliced

1 medium onion, thinly sliced
2 ripe tomatoes, thinly sliced
1 cup bottled fish stock, clam broth, or chicken stock
juice of ½ lemon (or to taste)
3 tablespoons chopped flat-leaf parsley, for garnish

Run your fingers over the fish, feeling for bones. Remove any you find with tweezers or needle-nose pliers. Cut the fish into 4 pieces.

Combine the coriander seeds, cumin seeds, pepper flakes, caraway seeds, and salt in a small, dry skillet. Roast over medium heat for 2 to 3 minutes, or until the spices are fragrant. Grind the spices in a blender or spice mill. Rub the fish with the spice mixture and let stand for 10 minutes.

Oil a baking dish just large enough to hold the fish and arrange half the garlic, onion, and tomato slices over the bottom. Place the fish pieces in the dish and top with the remaining garlic, onion, and tomato slices. Pour the fish stock and lemon juice over the fish. The recipe can be prepared to this stage up to 2 hours ahead.

Preheat the oven to 400 degrees F. Bake the fish for 20 to 30 minutes, or until cooked to taste. Sprinkle with parsley and serve at once.

Serves 4.

162 CALORIES PER SERVING: 30 G PROTEIN, 2 G FAT, 6 G CARBOHYDRATE; 568 MG SODIUM; 67 MG CHOLESTEROL.

Snapper with Mediterranean Vegetable Sauté

This colorful dish was inspired by one I enjoyed at the restaurant Robuchon in Paris, where chef Joel Robuchon dices the vegetables literally as fine as grains of sand. This version requires far less precision. The fish is browned with the skin on, which creates a crisp crust.

1½ tablespoons olive oil
1 clove garlic, minced (1 teaspoon)
1 red bell pepper, cored, seeded, and minced
1 yellow bell pepper, cored, seeded, and minced
1 small zucchini, cut in half lengthwise, seeded, and minced
1 small yellow squash, cut in half lengthwise, seeded, and minced

¼ teaspoon saffron threads, soaked in 3 tablespoons hot water
1 teaspoon chopped fresh thyme (or 1 teaspoon dried)
salt, freshly ground black pepper, and cayenne pepper
1½ pounds snapper fillets (skin left on)
½ cup flour (approximately)

Heat ½ tablespoon oil in a nonstick frying pan. Add the garlic, peppers, zucchini, and yellow squash, and cook over high heat for 1 minute. Stir in the saffron, thyme, salt, pepper, and cayenne. Lower the heat to medium and cook the vegetables for 3 to 4 minutes, or until tender but not soft. Correct the seasoning, adding salt, pepper, and cayenne to taste. The mixture should be very flavorful.

Preheat the oven to 400 degrees F. Cut the snapper into 4 pieces and season with salt and pepper. Dredge the pieces in flour, shaking off any excess. Heat the remaining 1 tablespoon oil in a nonstick frying pan with a metal handle. Add the fish, skin side down, and cook over medium heat for 3 to 4 minutes, or until the skin is very crisp. Turn the fish and place the pan in the oven. Bake for 10 to 15 minutes, or until cooked. (When done, it will flake easily when pressed.)

To serve, transfer the fish, skin side up, to plates or a platter. Spoon the vegetable mixture around it and serve at once.

Serves 4.

273 CALORIES PER SERVING: 37 G PROTEIN, 8 G FAT, 12 G CARBOHYDRATE; 16 MG SODIUM; 62 MG CHOLESTEROL.

SHARK IN LEMON PARSLEY BROTH

This delicate stew takes its inspiration from Greek avgolemono, egg lemon soup.
You can make it with any delicate white fish, from shark to cod to haddock.
Serve with crusty Italian bread for dipping in the broth.

1½ pounds shark, cod, or haddock fillets
1½ teaspoons olive oil
3 cloves garlic, minced (1 tablespoon)
4 cups water
1 pound baby red potatoes, cut into
   1" chunks

salt and freshly ground black pepper
½ cup finely chopped flat-leaf parsley
3–4 tablespoons freshly grated Parmigiano
   Reggiano (or other Parmesan-style cheese)
2–3 tablespoons fresh lemon juice
   (or to taste)

Cut the shark into ¼" slices. (If using cod or haddock, cut into 2" pieces.)

Heat the oil in a large sauté pan. Cook the garlic over medium heat for 1 minute, or until soft but not brown. Add the water, potatoes, salt, and pepper. Bring to a boil, reduce the heat, and simmer, uncovered, for 6 to 8 minutes, or until almost tender.

Add the shark, parsley, and cheese, and simmer for 2 minutes, or until the fish is just cooked. (It should flake easily when pressed.) Remove the pan from the heat, stir in the lemon juice, and let the stew sit for 2 minutes. Correct the seasoning and ladle the fish and broth into bowls.

Serves 4.

268 CALORIES PER SERVING: 32 G PROTEIN, 4 G FAT, 25 G CARBOHYDRATE; 147 MG SODIUM; 67 MG CHOLESTEROL.

....

POULTRY

....

HERB-ROASTED GAME HENS
....

A platter of game hens makes a dramatic centerpiece for a dinner party, while a single bird is a perfect serving for 1. This recipe features an aromatic paste of garlic and herbs stuffed under the skin of the hens before roasting. It's important to use fresh herbs.

8 large cloves garlic, peeled
½ cup chicken stock
½ cup finely chopped fresh herbs (rosemary, basil, thyme, oregano, chives, and/or parsley)
1 tablespoon fresh lemon juice (or to taste)

1 tablespoon olive oil
salt and freshly ground black pepper
4 Cornish game hens (about 1¼ pounds each)
1 very small onion or shallot, quartered
8 sprigs fresh rosemary or thyme

Combine the garlic and chicken stock in a saucepan and gently simmer, covered, for 20 minutes, or until the garlic is soft. Let cool. Purée the garlic and stock with the herbs in a food mill or blender. Work in the lemon juice, oil, salt, and pepper. The mixture should be highly seasoned.

Remove any lumps of fat from inside the birds. Season the cavities with salt and pepper, and place an onion quarter in each. Starting at the neck of each bird, work your finger under the skin to create a pocket between the skin and the breast meat. Try to loosen the skin over the breast, thighs, and drumsticks. Work carefully so as not to tear the skin. Preheat the oven to 400 degrees F.

Spread 1 tablespoon herb mixture under the skin of each bird. (This is most easily done with a small spoon.) Tightly truss each bird with string, tucking sprigs of rosemary or thyme between the legs. Season the outside of the birds with salt and pepper, and brush with the remaining herb mixture.

Roast the birds on a rack in a roasting pan for 40 minutes, or until golden brown. To test for doneness, insert a trussing needle into the thickest part of the thigh. The juices will run clear when the bird is cooked. Transfer the birds to a platter and let stand for 3 minutes. For a really low-fat dish, remove the skin before serving. Remove the trussing string and serve at once.

Serves 4.

265 CALORIES PER SERVING: 34 G PROTEIN, 12 G FAT, 3 G CARBOHYDRATE; 199 MG SODIUM; 102 MG CHOLESTEROL.

....

QUARTET OF STUFFED CHICKEN BREASTS

A skinless, boneless chicken breast is like a blank painter's canvas: uninteresting by itself but full of promise when the cook adds his or her colors. I love the surprise of cutting into a chicken breast and discovering a tangy layer of sage and prosciutto or a crimson pocket of sun-dried tomato. Here are 4 of my favorite stuffings. Use them as a springboard for your own creations. Each of these recipes can easily be adapted to serve 1, 2, or a multitude.

2 large skinless, boneless chicken breasts (double-sided)
your choice of stuffing (see next page)
salt and freshly ground black pepper

½ cup flour (approximately)
1½ tablespoons olive oil
¼ cup balsamic vinegar
¾ cup chicken stock

Trim the "tenderloins" (the long, thin, cylindrical muscles on the inside of the breast—save them for stir-fries) and any fat off the chicken breasts and cut the breasts in half. Place each half flat on a cutting board and, using the palm of one hand to hold the breast flat, cut a deep horizontal pocket in the side with a slender knife. Make the pocket as large as you can without piercing the top or bottom of the breast.

Choose one of the stuffings given on the next page and stuff the chicken breasts as indicated. Pin the breasts closed with toothpicks and season with salt and pepper. Dredge each breast in flour,

shaking off any excess.

Heat the oil in a nonstick frying pan and brown the breasts on both sides. Add the balsamic vinegar and bring to a boil. Add the stock and bring to a boil. Reduce the heat and gently simmer the chicken breasts for 2 to 3 minutes per side, or until cooked. (A skewer inserted in the center will come out hot to the touch.) Transfer to a platter and remove the toothpicks.

Season the sauce with salt and pepper and spoon it over the chicken. Serve at once.

Serves 4.

PROSCIUTTO AND SAGE STUFFING

4 very thin slices prosciutto (about 1 ounce)   **12 fresh sage leaves**

Place a slice of prosciutto and 3 sage leaves in the pocket of each half breast.

253 CALORIES PER SERVING: 30 G PROTEIN, 9 G FAT, 12 G CARBOHYDRATE; 158 MG SODIUM; 77 MG CHOLESTEROL.

SAUERKRAUT AND SMOKED CHEESE STUFFING

½ cup sauerkraut, drained   **4 thin slices low-fat smoked mozzarella or other smoked cheese**

Place a spoonful of sauerkraut and a slice of cheese in the pocket of each half breast.

279 CALORIES PER SERVING: 34 G PROTEIN, 9 G FAT, 13 G CARBOHYDRATE; 306 MG SODIUM; 77 MG CHOLESTEROL.

BASIL AND SUN-DRIED TOMATO STUFFING

eight 1" pieces sun-dried tomato (drained)   **16 large basil leaves**

Place 2 pieces of sun-dried tomato and 4 basil leaves in the pocket of each half breast.

262 CALORIES PER SERVING: 29 G PROTEIN, 8 G FAT, 16 G CARBOHYDRATE; 81 MG SODIUM; 73 MG CHOLESTEROL.

RICOTTA AND SPINACH STUFFING

5 ounces fresh spinach, washed and stemmed
salt
½ cup low-fat ricotta cheese

½ small clove garlic, minced (¼ teaspoon)
freshly ground black pepper
freshly grated nutmeg

Cook the spinach in ½ cup boiling salted water for 2 minutes, or until limp. Drain, refresh under cold water, and drain again. Squeeze the spinach in your hands to wring out as much water as possible. Finely chop the spinach and mix it with the ricotta, garlic, salt, pepper, and nutmeg in a small bowl. Stuff the ricotta mixture into the pocket of each half breast using a spoon.

291 CALORIES PER SERVING: 32 G PROTEIN, 11 G FAT, 14 G CARBOHYDRATE; 130 MG SODIUM; 83 MG CHOLESTEROL.

CHICKEN TAGINE

Vibrantly spiced with ginger and saffron and chock-full of interesting root vegetables, this dish is modeled on a Moroccan stew called tagine. *Enjoy it as is (it's great on a cold winter day), or add extra broth and serve as part of a traditional couscous (page 111).*

1 tablespoon olive oil
1 large onion, finely chopped
3 cloves garlic, minced (1 tablespoon)
2 tablespoons minced fresh ginger
1½ teaspoons ground turmeric
1½ teaspoons ground cumin
1½ teaspoons ground coriander
1 cinnamon stick
6–8 cups chicken stock (page 237) or water
2 tablespoons fresh lemon juice
½ pound turnips, peeled and cut into ¾" dice
½ pound carrots, peeled and cut into ¾" dice

½ pound parsnips, peeled and cut into ¾" dice
½ pound celeriac, peeled, cut into ¾" dice, and sprinkled with 1 tablespoon lemon juice
1 tablespoon chopped Pickled Lemons, page 189 (optional)
½ cup raisins
salt and freshly ground black pepper
2 pounds skinless, boneless chicken breasts, cut into 2" pieces
½ cup cooked chick-peas (optional)
⅓ cup chopped cilantro or flat-leaf parsley, for garnish

Heat the oil in a large casserole dish. Add the onion, garlic, ginger, turmeric, cumin, coriander, and cinnamon stick. Cook over medium heat for 3 to 4 minutes, or until the onion is soft but not brown. Add 6 cups of the stock and the lemon juice, root vegetables, Pickled Lemons (if using), raisins, salt, and pepper. Simmer for 20 minutes, or until the root vegetables are almost tender. Add stock or water as necessary to keep the stew from drying out.

Just before serving, remove the cinnamon stick and stir in the chicken and chick-peas (if using). Simmer for 2 to 3 minutes, or until cooked. Correct the seasoning, adding salt, pepper, and lemon juice to taste. The stew can be prepared ahead to this stage. (It just gets better with age.) Garnish with cilantro and serve at once.

Serves 6 to 8.

Note: To serve this stew as a couscous, use 10 cups stock. Prepare the couscous (page 111) and mound it on a platter or plates. Ladle the stew on top and serve with *harissa* (North African hot sauce, available at Middle Eastern markets and gourmet shops), Yemenite Hot Sauce (page 187), or even sambal ulek (Indonesian chili paste) or Vietnamese hot sauce.

359 CALORIES PER SERVING: 43 G PROTEIN, 8 G FAT, 29 G CARBOHYDRATE; 942 MG SODIUM; 96 MG CHOLESTEROL.

JAPANESE STEAK HOUSE–STYLE CHICKEN
....

Here's a home version of Japanese teppan (steak house–style) chicken that both kids and adults will enjoy, especially if you cook it at the table in an electric frying pan or large skillet. Serve with steamed white or brown rice.

1½–2 tablespoons canola oil
1 large onion, thinly sliced
8 ounces shiitake or button mushrooms, stemmed and thinly sliced
4 scallions, whites minced, greens thinly sliced
2 cloves garlic, minced (2 teaspoons)
1 tablespoon minced fresh ginger

1–1½ pounds skinless, boneless chicken breasts, thinly sliced
3 tablespoons sesame seeds
2 tablespoons sake (rice wine) or sherry
2 tablespoons soy sauce (or to taste)
2 tablespoons fresh lemon juice
3 cups mung bean sprouts
salt and freshly ground black pepper

Just before serving, heat a large wok over high heat. Swirl in 1 tablespoon of the oil. Add the onion and mushrooms, and cook for 2 minutes, or until the onion is tender-crisp. Transfer the mixture to a platter with a slotted spoon.

Swirl the remaining oil in the wok. Add the scallion whites, garlic, and ginger, and cook for 20 seconds, or until fragrant but not brown. Add the chicken and sesame seeds, and cook for 1 minute, stirring with a wooden spoon. Add the sake and flambé. (If working over a gas burner, simply tilt the pan toward the flame, and the wine will catch fire. If using an electric burner, light the wine with a match.)

When the flame dies down, stir in the soy sauce and lemon juice, and continue cooking for 2 to 3 minutes, or until the chicken is done. Add the bean sprouts and cook over high heat for 30 seconds, or until the sprouts lose their rawness. Stir in the onion, mushrooms, scallion greens, salt, and pepper. Correct the seasoning, adding soy sauce and lemon juice to taste.

Serves 4.

245 CALORIES PER SERVING: 23 G PROTEIN, 11 G FAT, 14 G CARBOHYDRATE; 566 MG SODIUM; 46 MG CHOLESTEROL.

PEKING CHICKEN

Andrew Swersky, owner/chef of the Morada Bar & Grille in Boca Raton, Florida, had the idea of using chicken, instead of fatty duck, in this classic Chinese recipe. I've lightened and simplified his version, using flour tortillas instead of Mandarin pancakes. The result is a great party dish, with scallion brushes providing some of the crunch of the duck skin in the traditional recipe.

5 cloves garlic, minced (5 teaspoons)
2 tablespoons minced fresh ginger
1 cup hoisin sauce
¼ cup soy sauce
¼ cup rice wine vinegar
¼ cup honey

2 pounds skinless, boneless chicken breasts, thinly sliced across the grain
12 scallions
1 tablespoon sesame oil
12 flour tortillas

Combine the garlic, ginger, hoisin sauce, soy sauce, vinegar, and honey in a small bowl. Whisk to mix. Set aside half of this mixture to use as a sauce. Marinate the chicken in the remaining mixture for 1 to 2 hours, stirring several times.

Meanwhile, make the scallion brushes. Cut the roots and greens off the scallions. (Reserve the latter for another recipe in this book.) There should be 3" pieces of scallion white remaining. Make a series of 1" lengthwise cuts in each end, gradually rotating the scallion, to form the individual "bristles" of the brush. Soak the scallions in a bowl of ice water for a couple of hours to swell the ends of the brushes.

Just before serving, heat the oil in a large non-stick frying pan. Cook the chicken over medium heat for 2 minutes, or until done. Set aside and keep warm. Lightly brush each tortilla with water and toast in a nonstick frying pan over high heat (or warm in a steamer). Divide the reserved marinade among 6 small ramekins or dishes.

Mound the chicken in the center of a platter. Arrange the tortillas (fold them in quarters or halves) and scallion brushes around the chicken. Invite guests to use a scallion to brush a tortilla with hoisin sauce. Have them place a spoonful of chicken and the scallion brush in a tortilla and roll it into a cone.

Serves 6 to 8.

436 CALORIES PER SERVING: 42 G PROTEIN, 8 G FAT, 47 G CARBOHYDRATE; 1519 MG SODIUM; 96 MG CHOLESTEROL.

CHICKEN POACHED WITH STAR ANISE

If you think the first chicken poached in this fragrant broth is good, wait until you taste the second. The flavor improves each time you use it. Star anise is a hard, star-shaped spice with a smoky, licorice flavor. Look for it in Asian and Hispanic markets. I first learned of this cooking method from Bruce Cost, owner of the San Francisco restaurant Monsoon. For the lowest possible fat, skin the chicken. For a pretty presentation, truss it.

6 cups water
1¼ cups soy sauce
1¼ cups Chinese rice wine or dry sherry
1 cup honey
2 teaspoons salt
4 star anise
1 cinnamon stick

2 strips orange zest
1 whole 3½–4-pound chicken
5 scallions, whites left whole, greens finely chopped for garnish
¼ cup finely chopped cilantro, for garnish
2 teaspoons sesame oil (optional)

Combine all the ingredients except the chicken, sesame oil, and garnishes in a deep pot just large enough to hold the chicken. Bring to a boil. Add the chicken and simmer for 40 to 50 minutes, or until cooked, turning the bird from time to time to make sure it poaches evenly. Skim the mixture often with a shallow ladle to remove any fat that rises to the surface. To test the chicken for doneness, insert a skewer into the thick part of the thigh; the juices should run clear.

Drain the chicken, remove the trussing string, and carve it or cut it into pieces. Sprinkle it with scallion greens and cilantro. Serve hot, at room temperature, or chilled.

Tasty as this chicken is, it looks rather drab.

To jazz up the presentation, serve it in large, shallow soup bowls with broth ladled over it. Sprinkle with chopped scallions and cilantro. Or brush the chicken pieces with sesame oil and brown them on the grill or under the broiler, then sprinkle with chopped scallions and cilantro.

Serves 4.

Note: The broth can and should be reused. Strain it and let it cool to room temperature. Chill overnight in the refrigerator and skim off any fat that collects on the surface. Freeze until you're ready to use again. To reuse, bring the broth to a boil, adding seasonings and water as necessary.

408 CALORIES PER SERVING: 53 G PROTEIN, 13 G FAT, 14 G CARBOHYDRATE; 758 MG SODIUM; 161 MG CHOLESTEROL.

TURKEY WIENERSCHNITZEL

By substituting turkey for the veal, egg whites for the whole eggs, and olive oil for the butter, I came up with a tasty and healthy remake of this Austrian classic.

1½ pounds turkey cutlets
salt and freshly ground black pepper
½ cup flour (approximately)
2 egg whites

½ cup bread crumbs (approximately)
2 tablespoons olive oil
2 tablespoons capers, for garnish
lemon wedges, for garnish

Place each cutlet between two pieces of plastic wrap and pound with a scaloppine pounder or the side of a cleaver to ¼" thick. Season the cutlets on both sides with salt and pepper.

Place the flour, egg whites, and bread crumbs in three shallow bowls. Dip each turkey cutlet first in flour, shaking off any excess, then in the egg whites, and then in the bread crumbs.

Heat the oil in a nonstick frying pan over high heat. Pan-fry the schnitzel for 30 seconds per side, or until golden brown. Drain on paper towels. Sprinkle the schnitzel with capers and serve with lemon wedges on the side.

Serves 4.

342 CALORIES PER SERVING: 37 G PROTEIN, 11 G FAT, 21 G CARBOHYDRATE; 219 MG SODIUM; 74 MG CHOLESTEROL.

TURKEY TAQUITOS WITH SALSA VERDE

A taquito is a baby taco. This ubiquitous street food is as popular in Mexico as sandwiches are in North America. Unlike our version of tacos, taquitos are always served in soft tortillas, so they're much lower in fat. They feature a piquant green salsa made with tomatillos. A tomatillo is a small, green tomatolike fruit recognizable by its papery skin. There's nothing quite like its tart, perky flavor. If you can't find fresh or canned tomatillos, you can substitute plum tomatoes, but the look and taste will be quite different.

2 teaspoons olive oil
1 onion, finely chopped
2 cloves garlic, minced (2 teaspoons)
1 or 2 serrano or jalapeño chilies (or to taste), seeded and minced
1 pound fresh tomatillos, husked and finely chopped
½ cup chicken stock or water
¼ cup chopped cilantro
¼ teaspoon ground cumin

½ teaspoon sugar (or to taste)
1 tablespoon lime juice (or to taste)
salt and freshly ground black pepper
1 pound skinless, boneless turkey, ground, finely chopped, or cut into slivers
1 cup tightly packed chopped flat-leaf parsley
⅓ cup nonfat yogurt
12 flour or corn tortillas

Heat the oil in a saucepan. Add the onion, garlic, and chilies, and cook over medium heat for 2 to 3 minutes, or until soft but not brown. Add the tomatillos and chicken stock. Simmer, covered, 6 to 8 minutes, or until the tomatillos are soft. Stir in the cilantro, cumin, sugar, lime juice, salt, and pepper. Purée the salsa in a blender or food processor. If the salsa seems too tart, add sugar. If it's too thick, add a little water.

Stir the turkey into the salsa verde and simmer 2 to 3 minutes, or until the turkey is just cooked. Correct the seasoning. Purée the parsley in a spice mill or blender. (A food processor does not work particularly well for this procedure.)

Blend in the yogurt and salt to obtain a bright green sauce. (If you want to get fancy, place the sauce in a plastic squirt bottle for squirting whimsical designs.)

Just before serving, heat a nonstick frying pan over medium-high heat. Very lightly brush each tortilla with water and toast it in the pan. The trick is to brown it slightly without making it brittle. Place spoonfuls of the turkey-tomatillo mixture in each tortilla and fold in quarters (or serve in corn tortillas folded in half, as you would for tacos). Arrange the taquitos on a platter and decorate with squiggles of parsley sauce.

Serves 4.

442 CALORIES PER SERVING: 26 G PROTEIN, 10 G FAT, 63 G CARBOHYDRATE; 150 MG SODIUM; 38 MG CHOLESTEROL.

❧

Turkey Taquitos with Salsa Verde

SMOKED HOLIDAY TURKEY

Smoking adds a wonderful flavor to turkey, and the wet heat keeps the meat—even the breast—succulent and tender. It's also very fast. Using a stovetop smoker, you can cook a 10-pound turkey in less than 2 hours. I do most of my smoking indoors using a stovetop smoker (see Mail-Order Sources). If you have an outdoor smoker, follow the manufacturer's instructions. Or improvise a stovetop smoker using the procedure outlined below. Don't be intimidated by the length of the recipe. This will probably be the easiest holiday turkey you've ever made.

1 10-pound turkey
2 teaspoons garlic salt
2 teaspoons paprika
½ teaspoon freshly ground black pepper
⅓ cup hardwood sawdust (such as alder or maple)

2 cups turkey or chicken stock
½ cup dry vermouth
3 tablespoons soy sauce
1½–2 teaspoons cornstarch
3 tablespoons Madeira

Wash and dry the turkey. Remove the wishbone to facilitate carving. Sprinkle the outside of the turkey with garlic salt, paprika, and pepper. Place the sawdust in the bottom of the smoker. Combine the stock, vermouth, and soy sauce, and pour into the drip pan. Place the turkey on a rack over the liquid. Tightly cover the smoker with a lid or foil tent. Place the smoker over medium heat and smoke the turkey for 1½ hours.

Preheat the oven to 400 degrees F. Uncover the turkey and roast it for 20 minutes, or until the skin is crisp. (This step is optional, but the skin won't be crisp without it.) Whether you roast the turkey or simply smoke it without roasting, cook it until the internal temperature registers 185 degrees F.

To make the gravy, strain the liquid from the drip pan into a heavy saucepan. Skim off any fat. Boil the pan liquid until reduced to about 2 cups. Dissolve the cornstarch in the Madeira.

Whisk into the simmering liquid and bring to a boil. Boil for 1 minute. Correct the seasoning, adding salt and pepper to taste.

Let the turkey stand for 5 minutes before carving. Serve the gravy on the side.

Serves 10 to 12.

Note: To rig up a smoker, you'll need a turkey roaster, Dutch oven, or heavy roasting pan; a smaller pan to catch the drips; two wire racks; lots of heavy-duty foil; and hardwood sawdust or small chips. Place the sawdust on a large piece of foil in the bottom of the roasting pan. Place a wire rack over the wood. Place a smaller pan (or a cake pan) on the rack to hold the steaming liquid and catch any drips. Place a second rack on top of the drip pan to hold the turkey. Place the bird on the rack and cover the roasting pan with a tight-fitting lid or a tent made of heavy-duty foil. Tightly seal the edges of the foil to keep in the smoke and steam.

226 CALORIES PER SERVING: 33 G PROTEIN, 9 G FAT, 1 G CARBOHYDRATE; 390 MG SODIUM; 84 MG CHOLESTEROL.

Watch Points for Stovetop Smoking

• Stovetop smoking generates some stray smoke. Keep the exhaust fan on high. (You may need to disconnect nearby smoke alarms temporarily.)

• Line the roasting pan and drip pan with aluminum foil and coat the drip pan and wire racks with vegetable oil spray to facilitate cleaning.

• When you're finished smoking, let the ash cool completely before discarding it in the trash. (Smoldering wood can set fire to your garbage.)

• Smoked turkey and other meats remain pink at the bone, even when fully cooked. Use an instant-read meat thermometer to make sure that a safe internal temperature—185 degrees F—has been reached.

MEAT

GRILLED VEAL CHOPS WITH BITTER GREENS

*This dish, which combines meat and salad, is all the rage in Miami's Italian restaurants.
The veal chops are pounded so thin that they all but bury the plate. Marinated
in an aromatic mixture of lemon, garlic, and rosemary, they're topped
with a colorful salad of radicchio, arugula, and endives.*

4 10–12-ounce veal chops, with the bone
2 lemons
3 cloves garlic, thinly sliced
3 sprigs fresh rosemary (about 3 tablespoons leaves), stemmed and lightly crushed

1½ tablespoons olive oil
salt and freshly ground black pepper
1 small radicchio, cored
1 bunch arugula, stemmed
2 Belgian endives, ends trimmed

Make a ¼" cut in the rounded edge of each chop opposite the bone. (This prevents the chops from curling during cooking.) Place each chop between 2 sheets of plastic wrap and pound with a scaloppine pounder or the side of a cleaver until ¼ to ⅓" thick. (Better still, have your butcher do it.)

Remove the zest from 1 lemon in broad strips using a vegetable peeler. Juice the peeled lemon (there should be about 3 to 4 tablespoons juice). Cut the second lemon into slices or wedges for garnish. Combine the zest, garlic, rosemary, 1 tablespoon of the oil, and all but 2 teaspoons of the lemon juice in a small bowl. Stir in plenty of salt and pepper. Rub the flattened veal chops

with this mixture and marinate in a shallow pan for 20 minutes.

Slice the greens widthwise into ¼" strips. Place in a bowl with the remaining ½ tablespoon oil, 2 teaspoons lemon juice, and salt and pepper. Do not toss. Preheat the grill.

Grill the veal chops over high heat, basting with marinade, for 2 minutes per side, or until cooked. (Alternatively, cook the chops in a ridged skillet or under the broiler.)

Just before serving, toss the greens with the dressing. Arrange the chops on a platter or plates, and top with the dressed greens. Garnish with lemon slices or wedges, and serve at once.

Serves 4.

230 CALORIES PER SERVING: 28 G PROTEIN, 11 G FAT, 4 G CARBOHYDRATE; 84 MG SODIUM; 100 MG CHOLESTEROL.

Grilled Veal Chops with Bitter Greens

CARDAMOM BEEF WITH CARAMELIZED ONIONS

Cardamom is generally used in desserts in this country, but in India and the Near East, the fragrant spice is often paired with meat. This recipe was inspired by one of my cooking students, Dina Hannah. Think of it as Levantine beef Stroganoff.

1–1½ pounds lean beef (such as tenderloin or sirloin)
2 cloves garlic, minced (2 teaspoons)
½ teaspoon ground cardamom
freshly ground black pepper
1 cup nonfat yogurt
1 tablespoon Dijon-style mustard
1 tablespoon cognac

1½ teaspoons flour
1½ tablespoons olive oil
1 large or 2 medium-sized onions, thinly sliced
½ teaspoon sugar
salt
3 tablespoons chopped fresh chives or scallions, for garnish

Trim any fat or sinew off the meat and cut into thin (2 by ½ by ¼") strips. Place the meat in a mixing bowl with the garlic, cardamom, and pepper, and marinate for 15 minutes. Combine the yogurt, mustard, cognac, and flour in a small bowl and whisk until smooth.

Heat the oil in a large nonstick frying pan. Cook the onions over medium-low heat for 10 minutes, or until a deep golden brown, stirring often. Add the sugar after 5 minutes to help the onions brown.

Just before serving, season the beef with salt and pepper. Increase the heat to high, add the beef to the onions, and sauté for 1 to 2 minutes, or until cooked to taste. Stir in the yogurt mixture and bring to a boil. Correct the seasoning, adding salt and pepper to taste. Sprinkle the beef with the chives and serve at once.

Serves 4.

268 CALORIES PER SERVING: 26 G PROTEIN, 13 G FAT, 10 G CARBOHYDRATE; 144 MG SODIUM; 65 MG CHOLESTEROL.

BRAISED BRISKET WITH DRIED FRUITS

Ask a Jewish person about his favorite meat, and he'll probably name brisket. It is customary to eat this dish at Rosh Hashanah, the Jewish New Year. The fruit symbolizes the promise of sweetness for the coming year. Miami publicist Barbara Seldin taught me how to make this brisket and it's one of the best. I should know. She's my wife!

1 3½–4-pound brisket
salt and freshly ground black pepper
1 tablespoon canola oil
1 large onion, finely chopped
3 carrots, finely chopped
3 stalks celery, finely chopped
2 cloves garlic, minced (2 teaspoons)
½ cup port, kosher concord grape wine, or marsala

3 cups beef stock, chicken stock, or water (approximately)
bouquet garni of bay leaf, thyme, and parsley
8 ounces dried apricots (1½ cups)
1½ cups pitted prunes
1 cup sultanas
¼ cup chopped flat-leaf parsley, for garnish

Trim the fat from the brisket and season with salt and pepper. Preheat the oven to 325 degrees F. Heat the oil in a nonstick frying pan. Cook the onion, carrots, celery, and garlic over medium heat for 4 to 5 minutes, or until golden.

Transfer the vegetables to a large roasting pan. Add the brisket, port, stock, and bouquet garni. Bring the liquid to a boil on the stovetop. Tightly cover the pan and bake the brisket in the oven for 1½ hours.

Transfer the brisket to a cutting board and thinly slice it on the diagonal. (An electric knife works great for slicing.) Return the brisket to the roasting pan and stir in the dried fruit. (Make sure the fruit is submerged in the cooking liquid. Add stock, as necessary, to cover it completely.) Cover the pan and bake for 1 to 2 hours more,

or until the meat is tender. Add stock or water as necessary to keep the meat and fruit moist. If there's too much cooking liquid, uncover the pan for the last half hour to allow some of it to evaporate.

Arrange the meat on a platter. Using a slotted spoon, transfer the fruit to the platter around the meat. Pour the pan juices into the sort of gravy boat that allows you to pour the broth off from the bottom, leaving the fat on top. If you don't have one of these, pour the gravy into a bowl or measuring cup and skim the fat off the top with a ladle. Spoon some of the gravy over the meat and fruit, serving the rest on the side. Garnish with parsley.

Serves 6 to 8.

522 CALORIES PER SERVING: 31 G PROTEIN, 12 G FAT, 74 G CARBOHYDRATE; 492 MG SODIUM; 79 MG CHOLESTEROL.

BRAISED LAMB SHANKS

This recipe, made with lamb shanks instead of veal, might be thought of as a Greek osso buco. The shanks are parboiled to melt off the excess fat. Ask your butcher to cut each shank into 3" pieces. Serve the braised shanks over rice, orzo or other pasta, or another absorbent grain.

4 lamb shanks
1 tablespoon olive oil
1 large onion, finely chopped
2 carrots, finely chopped
2 stalks celery, finely chopped
2 cloves garlic, finely chopped
3 large ripe tomatoes, peeled, seeded, and chopped, or 1 28-ounce can peeled plum tomatoes, drained and chopped

1 tablespoon flour
1 cup dry white wine
3 cups chicken or veal stock or water
1 tablespoon tomato paste
bouquet garni of bay leaf, thyme, and parsley
salt and freshly ground black pepper
½ cup minced flat-leaf parsley, for garnish
freshly grated zest of 1 lemon, for garnish

Place the shanks in a large pot with cold water. Bring to a boil and cook for 3 minutes. Rinse under cold water and drain. Using a paring knife, cut off any pieces of fat. Preheat the oven to 350 degrees F.

Heat the oil in a large sauté pan. Add the onion, carrots, celery, and garlic, and cook over medium heat for 4 to 5 minutes, or until lightly browned. Stir in the tomatoes and cook for 1 minute. Stir in the flour.

Add the lamb shanks and wine, and bring to a boil, stirring with a wooden spoon. Add the stock, tomato paste, bouquet garni, salt, and pepper, and bring back to a boil. Tightly cover the pan and place it in the oven. Combine the parsley and zest in a small bowl.

Bake the lamb shanks, stirring occasionally, for 1½ to 2 hours, or until the meat is fall-off-the-bone tender. Uncover the pan for the last 45 minutes to allow the excess liquid to evaporate. (There should be about 2 cups sauce.) Correct the seasoning, adding salt and pepper to taste. Sprinkle each shank with the parsley-zest mixture and serve at once.

Serves 4.

Note: A whole lamb shank will weigh about 1 pound and be 6 to 8" long. Some butchers sell foreshanks—the bottom half of the shank—which weighs about ½ pound. If you use foreshanks, you'll need 8 for this recipe. There is no need to cut them in half.

292 CALORIES PER SERVING: 26 G PROTEIN, 10 G FAT, 16 G CARBOHYDRATE; 140 MG SODIUM; 74 MG CHOLESTEROL.

Braised Lamb Shanks

RACK OF LAMB WITH INDIAN SPICES

This spicy dish makes a nice change from the usual rack of lamb served at French restaurants. Loosely modeled on Indian tandoori, it's marinated in an aromatic mixture of yogurt and spices, then smokily charred on the grill. Rack of lamb is a relatively expensive and fatty cut of meat. It's more a dish for splurging than for everyday eating. A more economical version could be made with lamb chops.

1 8-rib rack of lamb
1 small onion
3 cloves garlic, minced (1 tablespoon)
1 tablespoon minced fresh ginger
¼ cup finely chopped cilantro, plus ¼ cup for garnish
1 cup nonfat yogurt
3 tablespoons fresh lemon juice

2 teaspoons ground turmeric
2 teaspoons paprika
2 teaspoons ground cumin
2 teaspoons ground coriander
1 teaspoon salt (or to taste)
freshly ground black pepper and cayenne pepper
1 lemon cut into wedges, for garnish

Trim as much of the exterior fat off the rack as possible and scrape the ribs clean. (Better still, have your butcher do it.) Combine the remaining ingredients (except the cilantro and lemon for garnish) in a large bowl. Whisk to a smooth paste. Add salt and pepper to taste. Marinate the lamb for 8 to 24 hours (the longer the better), turning 3 or 4 times.

Preheat the grill. Grill the lamb over medium-high heat, basting with the marinade, for 4 to 6 minutes per side for medium-rare, or until cooked to taste. The lamb can also be roasted in a 400 degree F oven for 15 to 20 minutes. Medium-rare lamb will register 130 degrees F on an instant-read meat thermometer; medium lamb will register 140 degrees F.

To serve, carve the rack into chops. Sprinkle each with cilantro and serve with lemon wedges.

Serves 2 to 4.

324 CALORIES PER SERVING: 30 G PROTEIN, 14 G FAT, 19 G CARBOHYDRATE; 1224 MG SODIUM; 81 MG CHOLESTEROL.

LEAN ROAST PORK WITH MUSTARD AND APRICOTS

This dish has something for everyone: the spice of mustard, the sweetness of dried apricots, and the crispness of a garlic crumb crust. Wild Rice Stuffing (page 106) would make a nice accompaniment.

1 1–1½-pound lean pork tenderloin
10 large dried apricots
¼ cup minced fresh herbs (oregano, tarragon, thyme, chives, and/or flat-leaf parsley)

3 cloves garlic, minced (1 tablespoon)
1 cup lightly toasted bread crumbs (preferably homemade)
salt and freshly ground black pepper
3 tablespoons Dijon-style mustard

Preheat the oven to 375 degrees F. Trim any fat off the pork. Using a sharpening steel, boning knife, or other long, slender object, poke a hole through the center of the roast from end to end. Insert the apricots in this hole, pushing them in with your finger. (This gives you a pretty patch of orange when you slice the roast.)

Combine the herbs, garlic, and bread crumbs in a shallow bowl. Season the roast all over with salt and pepper, and paint it on all sides with mustard. Dredge the roast in the bread crumb mixture, turning with two forks to coat all sides.

Place the roast on a wire rack over a roasting pan. Bake for 1 hour, or until cooked. Transfer the roast to a cutting board and let stand for 5 minutes. Cut into ½" slices and serve.

Serves 4.

Note: People tend to overcook pork. It's safe to eat when the internal temperature reaches 160 degrees F, a point at which it will still be juicy.

267 CALORIES PER SERVING: 21 G PROTEIN, 9 G FAT, 25 G CARBOHYDRATE; 379 MG SODIUM; 51 MG CHOLESTEROL.

SPICY PORK STIR-FRY WITH CABBAGE

I love the Asian approach to meat eating—combining small amounts of meat with large amounts of vegetables. This colorful stir-fry pairs pork with ginger, chilies, and Chinese cabbage.

1 1-pound pork tenderloin
2 tablespoons soy sauce
2 tablespoons rice wine
2 tablespoons rice wine vinegar
1 tablespoon brown sugar
1½ tablespoons canola oil
3 cloves garlic, minced (1 tablespoon)
1 tablespoon minced fresh ginger
3 scallions, whites minced, greens cut into ½" pieces for garnish

1 or 2 fresh hot chilies, seeded and minced (or ½ teaspoon hot red pepper flakes)
12 ounces nappa (Chinese cabbage) or savoy cabbage, cut widthwise into ½" strips
1 red bell pepper, cored, seeded, and cut into ½" strips
2 carrots, peeled, thinly sliced on the diagonal, and cut into ½" strips
⅓ cup chicken stock
1 teaspoon cornstarch, dissolved in 1 tablespoon rice wine or water

Trim any fat off the pork and thinly slice across the grain. Cut the slices into ½" strips. Combine the soy sauce, wine, vinegar, and brown sugar, and marinate the pork for 30 minutes. Drain, reserving the marinade.

Just before serving, heat a wok over high heat. Swirl in the oil. Add the garlic, ginger, scallion whites, and chilies, and cook for 15 seconds, or until fragrant but not brown. Add the pork and stir-fry for 1 to 2 minutes. Add the nappa, pepper, and carrots, and stir-fry for 1 to 2 minutes more. Stir in the reserved marinade and chicken stock. Bring to a boil and cook for 1 minute, or until the vegetables are tender-crisp. Stir in the dissolved cornstarch and bring to a boil. Sprinkle the stir-fry with scallion greens and serve at once.
Serves 4.

269 CALORIES PER SERVING: 28 G PROTEIN, 10 G FAT, 17 G CARBOHYDRATE; 617 MG SODIUM; 81 MG CHOLESTEROL.

MA PO TOFU (SICHUAN-STYLE BEAN CURD WITH PORK)

Here's a tofu dish for people who are avid meat eaters. It's traditionally prepared with custardlike soft tofu, but you can also use the more readily available firm tofu. Tree ears are a dark, thin, round fungus with a crisp, chewy texture and mild taste. Look for them in Chinese markets and gourmet shops. If they're unavailable, simply omit from the recipe.

1 cup chicken stock or water
3 tablespoons soy sauce
3 tablespoons rice wine vinegar
3 tablespoons rice wine or sherry
1 teaspoon Chinese hot bean paste, Thai chili paste, or hot sauce
1 teaspoon sugar
1½ tablespoons canola oil
1 tablespoon minced fresh ginger
3 cloves garlic, minced (1 tablespoon)
1–3 hot chilies, seeded and minced (optional)

4 scallions, whites minced, greens sliced on the diagonal for garnish
6 ounces pork tenderloin (or other lean cut), finely chopped
1 pound tofu, rinsed, drained, and cut into ½" dice
½ cup dried tree ears, soaked in warm water for 1 hour (optional)
2 teaspoons cornstarch, dissolved in 1 tablespoon water
1 teaspoon Sichuan peppercorns, lightly toasted and crushed, for garnish

Combine the stock, soy sauce, vinegar, wine, bean paste, and sugar in a bowl. Stir to make a smooth sauce.

Heat a wok over high heat and swirl in the oil. Add the ginger, garlic, chilies (if using), and scallion whites, and stir-fry for 15 seconds, or until fragrant. Add the pork and stir-fry for 1 minute, or until the meat changes color. Add the tofu and stir-fry for 30 seconds.

Stir in the sauce and tree ears (if using), and bring to a boil. Reduce the heat and simmer gently for 5 minutes. Stir the dissolved cornstarch into the tofu and cook for 30 seconds. Correct the seasoning, adding soy sauce, vinegar, and bean paste to taste. The mixture should be hot, tart, and salty. Transfer to a deep platter or bowls and sprinkle with the scallion greens and peppercorns.

Serves 4 as an appetizer, 2 as an entrée.

Note: It's best to chop the pork by hand with a cleaver or chef's knife. A food processor tends to mash the meat.

213 CALORIES PER SERVING: 20 G PROTEIN, 12 G FAT, 9 G CARBOHYDRATE; 821 MG SODIUM; 30 MG CHOLESTEROL.

MONGOLIAN HOT POT

China's glorious fondue gets the guests involved with the cooking. Aficionados might argue that the best part of Mongolian Hot Pot is enjoying the broth as soup at the end of the meal. The traditional hot pot is a bundt pan–shaped pot heated over a charcoal brazier. You can use a fondue pot, but you'll need an electric hot plate or a tabletop butane burner to keep the broth boiling. Feel free to substitute other vegetables for the ones listed.

10 cups chicken broth (page 238)
1" piece fresh ginger, thinly sliced
4 scallions
3 star anise
1 1-pound lamb loin, partially frozen
1 1-pound pork loin, partially frozen
1 1-pound beef tenderloin, partially frozen
1 small nappa (Chinese cabbage) or bok choy, broken into leaves and cut widthwise into 1" strips
1 bunch watercress, broken into large sprigs
10 ounces fresh spinach
12 ounces shiitakes or button mushrooms, stemmed and cut into quarters or halves

FOR THE DIPPING SAUCE
½ cup hoisin sauce
2 tablespoons soy sauce
2 tablespoons rice wine vinegar
2 tablespoons honey

FOR THE SOUP (optional)
1 tablespoon cornstarch
2 egg whites (or 1 whole egg), beaten
salt and freshly ground black pepper

Combine the broth, ginger, scallions, and star anise in a large pot. Simmer for 15 minutes and strain.

Trim any fat and sinew off the meat. Cut the lamb, pork, and beef across the grain into the thinnest possible slices. Attractively arrange the slices, overlapping slightly, around the perimeter of a large platter. (If the platter swivels, like a lazy Susan, so much the better.)

Arrange the nappa, watercress, spinach, and mushrooms in the center.

Combine the ingredients for the dipping sauce in a small bowl and whisk until smooth.

Fill the hot pot with the strained broth and bring to a boil over a tabletop gas burner. Invite your guests to dip the meat and vegetables in the simmering broth and cook each to taste. Use chopsticks for dipping the meat slices. Use the small wire baskets sold at Asian markets and natural food stores for dipping fragile ingredients. Dip the ingredients in the sauce before eating. Add broth as necessary.

For an extra treat, at the end of the meal turn the broth into soup. Dissolve the cornstarch in 2 tablespoons cold water. Whisk into the broth and bring to a boil. Whisk in the beaten egg whites in a thin stream and bring to a boil. Correct the seasoning, adding salt and pepper to taste. Ladle the broth into soup bowls for serving.

Serves 8.

366 CALORIES PER SERVING: 43 G PROTEIN, 11 G FAT, 14 G CARBOHYDRATE; 795 MG SODIUM; 87 MG CHOLESTEROL.

VENISON WITH CRANBERRIES

*Leaner than beef, pork, or veal, venison is great for a low-fat diet. Here it is served
with a New England–style fruit sauce flavored with cranberries and maple syrup.
Beef, pork, or veal medallions could be prepared the same way.*

1 1–1½-pound venison loin
3 tablespoons fresh orange juice
3 tablespoons gin
1 12-ounce bag cranberries
⅔ cup dry red wine
⅔ cup maple syrup
3 strips lemon zest
3 strips orange zest

1 cinnamon stick
salt, freshly ground black pepper, and
   cayenne pepper
coarse salt and cracked black peppercorns
1½ tablespoons olive oil
sprigs of fresh tarragon, chervil, or parsley,
   for garnish

Cut the venison into ½"-thick medallions. Marinate in the orange juice and gin in a shallow dish for 20 to 30 minutes.

Pick through the cranberries, removing any stems. Combine the wine, maple syrup, zests, and cinnamon stick in a heavy saucepan and bring to a boil. Add the cranberries, reduce the heat, and gently simmer for 3 to 4 minutes, or until barely cooked. (Remove the pan from the heat the moment the cranberry skins begin to split; they should not be mushy.)

Strain the berries over another heavy saucepan. Discard the zests and cinnamon stick, and boil the sauce until thick and syrupy. (There should be about ¾ cup sauce.) Let it cool slightly and stir in the cranberries. Add salt, pepper, and cayenne pepper to taste. Keep the sauce warm.

Just before serving, drain the venison and thoroughly blot dry. Season each medallion with coarse salt and cracked black pepper. Heat the oil in a nonstick skillet over high heat. Cook the venison for 1 minute per side, or until cooked to taste. (I like the meat charred on the outside and still quite rare inside.) Spoon the cranberry sauce on a platter or plates, and arrange the venison medallions on top. Garnish with herb sprigs and serve at once.

Serves 4.

Note: You can also grill the venison.

414 CALORIES PER SERVING: 25 G PROTEIN, 7 G FAT, 53 G CARBOHYDRATE; 117 MG SODIUM; 0 MG CHOLESTEROL.

STIR-FRIES

ALL ABOUT STIR-FRYING

STIR-FRYING IS A RELATIVELY NEW TECHNIQUE IN the repertoire of American cooks. But in terms of the sheer number of users, it is probably the most popular cooking method in the world. The reasons are simple: It is quick, easy, and efficient and requires little fuel. It also preserves the crisp texture of vegetables and produces intense flavors with a minimum of fat.

The theory of stir-frying is simple. Small pieces of vegetables and/or meat are cooked as quickly as possible over very high heat in a bowl-shaped pot called a wok. The traditional wok has a round bottom, but you can also find flat-bottomed woks designed for use on modern electric stoves.

Buying a wok: You can buy a wok at any Asian market (and pay a good deal less for it there than at a cookware shop). Woks are available in a variety of materials. I prefer the inexpensive spun-steel woks, so called because of the circular striations left in the metal during the manufacturing process. This steel is slightly porous, enabling it to hold a thin sheen of oil that reduces sticking.

The walls of the wok should be thick and heavy to ensure an even spread of heat. Don't waste money on a thin or lightweight wok; you'll burn rather than stir-fry your food. Some woks have U-shaped handles, others a single long wooden handle, like a frying pan. If you can find it, buy a wok that has both. A well-made wok will last a lifetime. I bought mine in college; 20 years later it's better than ever.

You'll also need a wok ring—a metal collar with holes in the side that fits over the stove burner. This ring serves two purposes: it keeps the wok from wobbling and raises the base to the hottest part of the flame. For the best results, set the ring on the burner, wide part up. (If the narrow part doesn't fit over the burner, invert it.) A wok ring enables you to use a round-bottom wok on an electric burner. This is the setup I have at home and it works fine. If you have a gas stove, you can cook directly on the burner.

The other useful utensil is a metal wok spatula with a rounded edge that conforms perfectly to the contour of the wok. In a pinch, use a sturdy metal skimmer or even a wooden spoon.

Seasoning a wok: First scrub a new wok with soap and an abrasive metal pad (like Brillo) to remove any grease from the factory. This should be the last time you use soap and abrasives to clean it. Wipe it dry and place it over high heat. When it's hot enough to evaporate a drop of water in a few seconds, wipe the inside of the wok with a paper towel dipped in oil. Heat until

Thai Basil Stir-Fry (page 155)

the wok smokes and begins to turn black in the center. Wipe out the excess oil with a paper towel and let the wok cool completely. Repeat this procedure 3 or 4 times. You can also heat the wok in a 400 degree F oven before applying the oil. For a complete discussion of seasoning a wok, see Barbara Tropp's *The Modern Art of Cooking* (William Morrow, Inc., 1982).

Having taken the trouble to season your wok, you want to keep it seasoned. To clean it after cooking, rinse it with hot water and scrub it with a soft-bristle brush. (It will be easiest to clean the moment it comes off the stove, when it's still hot.) Place the wok over high heat and heat it until all the moisture has evaporated. Wipe it with a lightly oiled paper towel and let cool.

Organizing your ingredients: Do all your mincing and chopping ahead of time. Measure out and prepare all the sauces. The average stir-fry takes 2 to 3 minutes to cook from start to finish. Once you've begun, you don't have time to run to the other side of the kitchen to fetch an ingredient or measure a sauce. Whenever I stir-fry, I arrange all the ingredients on a tray next to the stove: the aromatics on one plate, the main ingredients on another, the sauce in a small bowl. The prep work can be done ahead of time, but the cooking is strictly last minute. And be sure to work over high heat to sear the ingredients and seal in the flavor. If you stir-fry over low heat, you wind up with mush.

The basic procedure: First, heat the wok over high heat until it just begins to smoke. Swirl in the oil in a circular motion around the top of the wok. It will flow to the bottom, lubricating the sides as it goes. Use canola or peanut oil, which has a high burning point. (In keeping with the dietary guidelines of this book, the recipes in this chapter call for 1½ tablespoons oil; if your diet permits it, use 2 tablespoons oil for easier stir-frying.)

To test the temperature of the oil, add a tiny piece of scallion. If bubbles dance around it, the oil is ready. If it sinks to the bottom, the oil is too cool. If it burns immediately, the oil is too hot. Lower the flame slightly, or if you're using an electric burner, remove the wok from the heat for a few seconds.

When the oil begins to smoke, add the aromatics (ginger, garlic, scallions, chilies, etc.), which flavor the oil. (The Chinese call this step the "exploding of fragrance.") Cook the aromatics for 15 seconds, or until very fragrant, stirring and tossing with the wok spatula.

Next, add the main ingredients in sequence of approximate cooking times. I add the meat first, then hard vegetables such as carrots and cabbage, and then soft vegetables such as squash. Stir-fry these ingredients for 1 to 2 minutes, or until tender-crisp, tossing with a spatula. If the ingredients start to stick, add a little more oil. If you have too many ingredients to stir-fry comfortably in one batch, work in two batches and transfer the first to a bowl.

The last step is to add the sauce (the liquid ingredients). Bring the mixture to a boil and simmer for a minute or so, or until all the ingredients are fully cooked. If using cornstarch to thicken the sauce, dissolve it in water (or other liquid) and add it to the stir-fry. Bring the mixture just to a boil again. Taste the stir-fry before serving to correct the seasoning. Add a splash of soy sauce, a squeeze of lemon, or other flavoring to obtain a balanced and richly flavored dish.

In this chapter, you'll find six general stir-fry recipes that are equally suitable for seafood, poultry, meat, tofu, or vegetables. Once you've mastered the basic process and these classic flavor combinations, you can stir-fry just about anything.

Note: The analyses for the following six recipes apply to the sauces only. The number of servings is based on accompanying the stir-fry with 2 side dishes, including rice.

THAI BASIL STIR-FRY

This fragrant dish is one of the glories of Thai street food. Thai basil has smaller leaves and a more pronounced licorice flavor than Italian-style basil, but regular basil or even fresh mint works fine, too. This stir-fry is wetter than most Chinese stir-fries, and it's never thickened with cornstarch. Serve it over rice.

½ cup chicken stock
1½ tablespoons fish sauce
2 teaspoons soy sauce
1 teaspoon sugar
1½ tablespoons canola oil
3 cloves garlic, minced (1 tablespoon)
2 scallions, whites minced, greens cut into 1" pieces for garnish
3 shallots, thinly sliced

1–3 Thai, serrano, jalapeño, or other fresh hot chilies, thinly sliced
1 pound shrimp, peeled and deveined; or 1 pound chicken, pork, or beef, thinly sliced
2–3 cups diced vegetables (zucchini, summer squash, onions, and/or peppers)
1 bunch fresh basil leaves (2 cups)

Combine the stock, fish sauce, soy sauce, and sugar in a small bowl and stir until the sugar dissolves.

Just before serving, heat a wok over high heat. Swirl in the oil. Add the garlic, scallion whites, shallots, and chilies, and cook for 15 seconds or until fragrant but not brown. Add the shrimp and vegetables, and stir-fry for 1 to 2 minutes.

Add the sauce and most of the basil leaves, and simmer for 1 to 2 minutes, or until the main ingredient is cooked and the vegetables are tender-crisp. Correct the seasoning, adding fish sauce as necessary. Garnish the stir-fry with the scallion greens and remaining basil leaves.

Serves 4.

84 CALORIES PER SERVING: 2 G PROTEIN, 6 G FAT, 8 G CARBOHYDRATE; 249 MG SODIUM; 1 MG CHOLESTEROL.

SWEET AND SOUR STIR-FRY

The first stir-fry most Americans ever tasted was some version of sweet and sour. Food coloring made it orange; excess cornstarch made it gluey. This recipe uses honey and lemon juice, eliminates deep-frying the meat in batter, and greatly reduces the amount of thickener.

2 cloves garlic, minced (2 teaspoons)
1 tablespoon minced fresh ginger
4 scallions, whites minced, greens cut into
   ½" pieces
3 tablespoons honey
3 tablespoons lemon juice
3 tablespoons soy sauce
2 tablespoons ketchup
1 teaspoon cornstarch
1 tablespoon rice wine or sherry

1½ tablespoons canola oil
1 pound shrimp, peeled and deveined;
   1 pound chicken, pork, or beef, thinly
   sliced; or 1 pound tofu, pressed under
   a heavy pot for 15 minutes and cut into
   1" pieces
2–3 cups mixed diced vegetables (bell peppers, carrots, zucchini, water chestnuts,
   and/or bamboo shoots)

Combine the garlic, ginger, and scallion whites in a small bowl. Combine the honey, lemon juice, soy sauce, and ketchup in a second small bowl and stir until smooth. Dissolve the cornstarch in the wine in a third small bowl.

Just before serving, heat a wok over high heat. Swirl in the oil. Add the garlic mixture and cook for 15 seconds, or until fragrant but not brown.

Add the shrimp and stir-fry for 1 to 2 minutes. Add the vegetables and stir-fry for 1 to 2 minutes. Add the sauce and cook for 1 to 2 minutes, or until the main ingredient is cooked. Stir the cornstarch mixture and add it to the stir-fry with the scallion greens. Bring to a boil and serve at once.
Serves 4.

149 CALORIES PER SERVING: 2 G PROTEIN, 5 G FAT, 25 G CARBOHYDRATE; 604 MG SODIUM; 0 MG CHOLESTEROL.

HOT AND SOUR STIR-FRY
....

This recipe combines dishes from several countries in Southeast Asia. Cilantro root tastes like a cross between cilantro and celeriac. Asian and Hispanic markets often sell the whole plant. If you can't find cilantro root, use the leaves, which have plenty of flavor, too.

3 or 4 stalks fresh lemongrass (or 3 table-spoons dried), or 4 strips lemon zest
2½ tablespoons fresh lime juice
2½ tablespoons fish sauce
1 tablespoon sugar
1½ tablespoons canola oil
1 tablespoon minced cilantro root or leaves (optional)
3 cloves garlic, minced (1 tablespoon)
1 tablespoon minced fresh ginger or galangal (see Cook's Notes)

3 shallots, thinly sliced
1–4 hot Thai, serrano, or jalapeño chilies, thinly sliced
1½ pounds seafood; 1½ pounds chicken, pork, or beef, thinly sliced; or 1½ pounds tofu, pressed under a heavy pot for 15 minutes and cut into 1" pieces
1 large onion, cut into 12 wedges
1 cup straw or other mushrooms
2 scallions, cut into 1" pieces

Cut the top ⅔ off each lemongrass stalk, trim off the outside leaves and roots, and mince the core. (If using dried lemongrass, soak for 20 minutes in warm water to cover.)

Combine the lime juice, fish sauce, and sugar in a small bowl. Stir until the sugar dissolves.

Just before serving, heat a wok over high heat. Swirl in the oil. Add the cilantro (if using), garlic, ginger, shallots, and chilies, and cook for 15 seconds, or until fragrant but not brown. Add the seafood, onion, and mushrooms, and stir-fry for 1 to 2 minutes. Add the sauce and cook for 1 to 2 minutes, or until the main ingredient is cooked. Stir in the scallions and serve at once.

Serves 4.

102 CALORIES PER SERVING: 2 G PROTEIN, 6 G FAT, 12 G CARBOHYDRATE; 221 MG SODIUM; 2 MG CHOLESTEROL.

GINGER AND SCALLION STIR-FRY

In most dishes, ginger and scallions play a supporting role, like dancers in a chorus line. In this vibrant stir-fry, they're elevated to the leading role. The thick slices of ginger are for flavor; they're not actually meant to be eaten. This preparation usually features seafood: shrimp, scallops, fish, or even lobster.

6" piece fresh ginger
1 bunch scallions, whites minced, greens
   cut into 2" pieces
3 cloves garlic, minced (1 tablespoon)
¼ cup fish stock, bottled clam broth,
   lobster cooking liquid, or chicken stock
1 teaspoon cornstarch
1½ tablespoons soy sauce

1½ tablespoons oyster sauce
1 tablespoon rice wine or sherry
1 teaspoon sugar
1½–2 tablespoons canola oil
1 pound seafood, cut into 1" pieces
2 cups diced bell peppers or other
   vegetables (optional)

Mince about 2" of ginger—enough to obtain 2 tablespoons. Cut the remaining ginger on the diagonal into ¼" slices and set aside. Combine the minced ginger, scallion whites, and garlic in a small bowl.

Combine 1 tablespoon of the fish stock and the cornstarch in a small bowl. Stir to form a smooth paste. Combine the remaining fish stock, soy sauce, oyster sauce, wine, and sugar in a small bowl and stir until the sugar crystals dissolve.

Just before serving, heat a wok over high heat.

Swirl in the oil. Add the minced ingredients and cook for 15 seconds, or until fragrant but not brown. Add the seafood and peppers (if using), and stir-fry for 1 minute. Add the sauce and cook for 1 to 2 minutes, or until the seafood is cooked and the peppers are tender-crisp. Stir the cornstarch mixture and add it to the stir-fry with the scallion greens. Bring the sauce to a boil and serve at once. (Warn your guests not to eat the ginger slices!)

Serves 4.

77 CALORIES PER SERVING: 1 G PROTEIN, 5 G FAT, 5 G CARBOHYDRATE; 398 MG SODIUM; 3 MG CHOLESTEROL.

Ginger and Scallion Stir-Fry

BLACK BEAN STIR-FRY

....

The black beans in this recipe are Chinese salted black soybeans. Their tangy, cheeselike flavor may remind you of another fermented soybean product, Japanese miso. This preparation is delicious with poultry and meat, as well as seafood.

3 cloves garlic, minced (1 tablespoon)
1 tablespoon minced fresh ginger
1 or 2 fresh hot chilies, minced (or ½ teaspoon hot red pepper flakes)
4 scallions, whites minced, greens cut on the diagonal into ½" pieces
3 tablespoons Chinese salted black beans
¼–½ cup chicken stock (page 237)
2 tablespoons soy sauce
2 teaspoons sugar

½ teaspoon sesame oil
1 teaspoon cornstarch
1 tablespoon rice wine or sherry
2 pounds shellfish (clams, mussels, periwinkles, crabs, and/or lobster), or
1 pound shrimp, fish, poultry, or pork
1½ tablespoons canola oil
2–3 cups thinly sliced vegetables (cabbage, snow peas, and/or carrots)

Combine the garlic, ginger, chilies, scallion whites, and black beans in a small bowl.

Combine the stock, soy sauce, sugar, and sesame oil in a small bowl and stir until the sugar dissolves. (For a wetter stir-fry—useful for steaming open clams—use ½ cup stock; for a drier mixture, use ¼ cup stock.) Dissolve the cornstarch in the wine in a small bowl. Scrub the clams (if using), cut the shellfish into 1" pieces, or thinly slice the poultry or meat.

Just before serving, heat a wok over high heat.

Swirl in the canola oil. Add the garlic and bean mixture, and cook for 15 seconds, or until fragrant but not brown. Add the seafood and stir-fry for 1 minute. Add the sauce and cook for 2 to 5 minutes, or until the seafood is cooked. (If steaming clams, tightly cover the wok.) Stir the cornstarch mixture and add it to the stir-fry with the scallion greens and diced vegetables. Bring the sauce to a boil and serve at once.

Serves 4.

91 CALORIES PER SERVING: 2 G PROTEIN, 6 G FAT, 6 G CARBOHYDRATE; 564 MG SODIUM; 0 MG CHOLESTEROL.

SICHUAN STIR-FRY

Here's my version of a fiery Sichuan stir-fry. I have a high threshold for chili hellfire, so I use the maximum amount of hot bean paste called for in this recipe. You may wish to start out with less. Sichuan peppercorns are a reddish, peppercorn-shaped spice with a sweet, aromatic flavor. They aren't particularly hot. Both hot bean paste and Sichuan peppercorns can be found at Asian markets and in the Oriental food section of most supermarkets.

6 cloves garlic, minced (2 tablespoons)
1 tablespoon minced fresh ginger
4 scallions, whites minced, greens cut on
   the diagonal into ½" pieces
½ teaspoon Sichuan peppercorns, ground
   or crushed
3 tablespoons soy sauce
3 tablespoons rice or balsamic vinegar
2 tablespoons rice wine or sherry
1–3 teaspoons hot bean paste
   (see Cook's Notes)

1½ teaspoons sugar
1 teaspoon cornstarch
2 cups broccoli florets
salt
1½ tablespoons canola oil
3 dried hot red chilies (optional)
1 pound shrimp, peeled and deveined;
   1 pound chicken, pork, or beef, thinly
   sliced; or 1 pound tofu, pressed under a
   heavy pot for 15 minutes and cut into
   1" pieces

Combine the garlic, ginger, scallion whites, and peppercorns in a small bowl.

Combine the soy sauce, vinegar, 1 tablespoon of the wine, hot bean paste, and sugar in another small bowl and stir until the sugar dissolves. Dissolve the cornstarch in the remaining 1 tablespoon wine in another small bowl. Blanch the broccoli florets in boiling salted water for 30 seconds. Refresh under cold water and drain.

Just before serving, heat a wok over high heat. Swirl in the oil. Add the dried chilies (if using) and cook for 10 seconds, or until dark and fragrant. Remove the chilies with a slotted spoon and discard. Add the minced ingredients and cook for 15 seconds, or until fragrant but not brown.

Add the shrimp and stir-fry for 1 to 2 minutes. Add the sauce and cook for 1 minute, or until the main ingredient is cooked. Stir in the broccoli. Stir the cornstarch mixture and add it to the stir-fry with the scallion greens. Bring the sauce to a boil and serve at once.

Serves 4.

98 CALORIES PER SERVING: 2 G PROTEIN, 5 G FAT, 10 G CARBOHYDRATE; 537 MG SODIUM; 0 MG CHOLESTEROL.

Seasonings and Marinades

S E A S O N I N G S

Garam Masala

Widely used in India, this fragrant blend of roasted spices goes well with everything from grilled meat to salads. Garam masala is ideal for people who don't like turmeric, the predominant spice in curry powder. Roasting the spices in a dry skillet helps bring out their flavor. Salt isn't in the traditional recipe, but I like to add it to make an all-purpose seasoning.

½ cup coriander seeds
¼ cup cumin seeds
2 teaspoons black peppercorns
1 tablespoon fennel seeds or aniseed
1 tablespoon sesame seeds

10 whole cloves
10 black cardamom pods
6 bay leaves
½ teaspoon freshly grated nutmeg
1 teaspoon salt

Combine all the ingredients and cook in a dry skillet over low heat for 5 minutes, or until fragrant and lightly browned. Grind the roasted spices to a fine powder in a spice mill or blender. Sift and store in an opaque airtight container.

Makes 1 cup.

10 CALORIES PER TEASPOON: 0 G PROTEIN, .6 G FAT, 1 G CARBOHYDRATE; 61 MG SODIUM; 0 MG CHOLESTEROL.

CAJUN SPICE

There's nothing revolutionary about pan-blackening these days, but when New Orleans chef Paul Prudhomme introduced the technique in the early 1980s, it sparked a whole movement of regional American cooking. This version of Cajun Spice makes a delicious seasoning for roasts, stews, grilled fare, and, of course, pan-blackened dishes.

2 tablespoons sea salt
1 tablespoon garlic powder
1 tablespoon onion powder
1 tablespoon dried thyme
1 tablespoon dried oregano

1 tablespoon hot paprika
2 teaspoons freshly ground black pepper
2 teaspoons freshly ground white pepper
1 teaspoon paprika

Combine all the ingredients and store in an airtight container.

Makes ½ cup.

Note: To pan-blacken fish, chicken, or steaks, heat a heavy, dry skillet over high heat. Lightly brush the food with olive oil and thickly encrust it with Cajun Spice. Pan-fry for 1 minute per side, or until cooked to taste.

5 CALORIES PER TEASPOON: 0 G PROTEIN, 0 G FAT, 1 G CARBOHYDRATE; 493 MG SODIUM; 0 MG CHOLESTEROL.

HOMEMADE CHILI POWDER

Another uniquely American spice mix is chili powder. This recipe, which features 3 different kinds of dried chilies (see Mail-Order Sources), isn't particularly hot, but it's loaded with flavor. Chipotles (smoked jalapeño chilies) add an interesting dimension. Try this chili powder sprinkled on sliced jicama.

2 ancho chilies
2 pasilla or mulato chilies
4 chipotle chilies

2 teaspoons cumin seeds
2 teaspoons dried oregano
½ teaspoon ground cinnamon

Preheat the oven to 300 degrees F. Stem the chilies and roast them on a baking sheet for 10 minutes, or until crisp. Let cool. Place the cumin seeds in a dry skillet over medium heat and cook for 30 seconds, or until fragrant and lightly toasted.

Break the chilies open and shake out the seeds. (For a hotter chili powder, leave the seeds in.) Combine the chili pieces, cumin seeds, and other spices, and grind to a fine powder in a spice mill or blender.

Makes 1 cup.

5 CALORIES PER TEASPOON: 0 G PROTEIN, .1 G FAT, 1 G CARBOHYDRATE; 13 MG SODIUM; 0 MG CHOLESTEROL.

HERBES DE PROVENCE

Drive through Provence in summer, and your eyes will feast on shimmering fields of purple: fresh lavender. Most of the crop goes into sachets and perfumes, but some is reserved for making this fragrant herb mixture. There's nothing like it for seasoning lamb, chicken, or fish. Lavender can be purchased at health food stores and shops carrying potpourris and dried herbs.

¼ cup dried basil
¼ cup dried rosemary
3 tablespoons dried thyme
3 tablespoons dried oregano or summer savory

1 tablespoon dried lavender
3 bay leaves, pulverized
1 teaspoon freshly ground white pepper
1 teaspoon ground coriander
½ teaspoon ground cloves

Combine all the ingredients in a bowl and mix well with a whisk.

Store in an opaque airtight container.

Makes 1 cup.

4 CALORIES PER TEASPOON: 0 G PROTEIN, 0 G FAT, 1 G CARBOHYDRATE; 1 MG SODIUM; 0 MG CHOLESTEROL.

CHINESE SEASONED SALT

Chinese chefs roast salt and pepper in a dry skillet, creating a distinctive smoky flavor that raises these commonplace spices to the level of art. Traditionally sprinkled on roast squab, chicken, or shrimp cooked in the shell, this seasoning is equally delectable on baked potatoes or popcorn.

6 tablespoons kosher salt
4 tablespoons Sichuan peppercorns

2 tablespoons black peppercorns

Combine the ingredients in a dry wok or heavy skillet. Cook over medium heat, shaking the pan until the peppercorns begin to darken and smoke. (Turn on your oven exhaust fan or use a gas grill outside.) Transfer the mixture to a spice mill or blender, and grind to a coarse powder.

Makes ¾ cup.

Note: The blender works best if tilted at a 30 degree angle.

3 CALORIES PER TEASPOON: 0 G PROTEIN, 0 G FAT, 1 G CARBOHYDRATE; 1066 MG SODIUM; 0 MG CHOLESTEROL.

MADRAS-STYLE CURRY POWDER

This homemade curry powder will make you want to banish mild-mannered commercial blends from your spice shelf. Don't worry if you can't find one of the minor ingredients for this recipe—the powder will still have plenty of flavor. Two teaspoons are enough to spice up 4 cups of soup, 1 pound of vegetables, or 1 cup of dried grains. I make a large batch in December and bottle it for holiday gifts.

3½ tablespoons cumin seeds
3 tablespoons coriander seeds
20 black peppercorns
1 tablespoon cardamom pods
1 teaspoon fennel seeds
10 whole cloves
1 teaspoon mace or freshly grated nutmeg

1 teaspoon black mustard seeds
1 teaspoon poppy seeds
1 teaspoon fenugreek (optional)
1 small cinnamon stick
5 tablespoons ground turmeric
1 tablespoon ground ginger
1 teaspoon cayenne pepper

Combine the first 11 ingredients (the whole spices) in a dry skillet and roast over medium heat for 2 to 3 minutes, or until fragrant. Remove the pan from the heat and stir in the remaining spices.

Grind the mixture to a fine powder in a spice mill or blender. Store the curry powder in an opaque airtight container. For optimum flavor, use within 3 months.

Makes ⅔ cup.

10 CALORIES PER TEASPOON: 0 G PROTEIN, .5 G FAT, 2 G CARBOHYDRATE; 2 MG SODIUM; 0 MG CHOLESTEROL.

MARINADES

INDIAN YOGURT MARINADE

A tandoor is a giant urn-shaped clay oven in which kebabs that have been marinated in a tangy mixture of yogurt and spices are roasted on vertical skewers. Most Indian restaurants add food coloring to give the marinated meat its traditional Mercurochrome color. I prefer a natural, if paler, look. This marinade is particularly well suited to lamb, chicken, and shrimp.

2 cups nonfat yogurt
1½ tablespoons minced fresh ginger
4 cloves garlic, minced (4 teaspoons)
2 jalapeño chilies or other hot chilies, seeded and minced
¼ cup fresh lemon juice
2 bay leaves
2 teaspoons paprika

1½ teaspoons ground cumin
1½ teaspoons ground coriander
1 teaspoon ground turmeric
½ teaspoon ground cinnamon
½ teaspoon freshly ground black pepper
⅛ teaspoon ground cardamom
1–2 teaspoons salt (or to taste)

Drain the yogurt in a yogurt funnel (see Mail-Order Sources) or a cheesecloth-lined colander for 2 hours. Place the ginger, garlic, and chilies in a bowl and whisk in the yogurt, lemon juice, bay leaves, and spices. Add the salt.

Marinate seafood for 2 to 3 hours, poultry for 6 hours, and meat overnight, turning once or twice. Remove and discard the bay leaves before serving.

Makes 2 cups, enough marinade for 1½ to 2 pounds seafood, poultry, or meat.

Note: This marinade also makes a great dressing for grain or pasta salads.

13 CALORIES PER TABLESPOON: 1 G PROTEIN, .4 G FAT, 2 G CARBOHYDRATE; 78 MG SODIUM; 1 MG CHOLESTEROL.

BERBER MARINADE

This thick, spicy paste comes from the nomadic Berbers of North Africa. A little goes a long way! I have used it with great success on tuna, pork tenderloin, and sirloin steak.

1 medium-sized onion, diced (1 cup)
3 cloves garlic, minced (1 tablespoon)
2 tablespoons minced fresh ginger
½ cup imported paprika
1 tablespoon coriander seeds
2 teaspoons cracked black peppercorns
2 teaspoons cardamom pods
1 teaspoon hot red pepper flakes (or to taste)
1 teaspoon fenugreek seeds (optional)

1 teaspoon ground cinnamon
½ teaspoon allspice berries
¼ teaspoon ground cloves
1 tablespoon salt (or to taste)
¼ cup fresh lemon juice
¼ cup olive oil
2 tablespoons chicken stock or water (if needed)

Place the onion, garlic, ginger, spices, and salt in a dry skillet. Cook over medium heat for 2 to 3 minutes, or until the spices are lightly roasted and fragrant.

Combine the spice mixture, lemon juice, and oil in a spice mill or blender, and purée to a smooth paste. (If the mixture is too dry to purée, add a little stock or water.)

Spread the paste on the seafood, poultry, or meat, and marinate overnight.

Makes 1 cup, enough marinade for 1½ to 2 pounds seafood, poultry, or meat.

42 CALORIES PER TABLESPOON: 0 G PROTEIN, 4 G FAT, 3 G CARBOHYDRATE; 402 MG SODIUM; 0 MG CHOLESTEROL.

VIETNAMESE LEMONGRASS MARINADE

Lemongrass is a scallion-shaped herb with a lovely aromatic lemon flavor
(see Cook's Notes). If unavailable, you can use thin strips of lemon zest.

¼ cup chopped fresh lemongrass (4–6
  stalks), ¼ cup dried lemongrass, or
  6 strips lemon zest
3 cloves garlic, minced (1 tablespoon)
2 or 3 shallots, minced (3 tablespoons)
2 serrano, jalapeño, or Thai chilies, minced

2 teaspoons brown sugar (or to taste)
3 tablespoons fish sauce
3 tablespoons fresh lime juice
1 teaspoon Vietnamese or Thai hot sauce,
  chili oil, or Tabasco

Cut off the top ⅔ of each lemongrass stalk, trim off the outside leaves and roots, and slice the core thinly. (If the roots are long enough, they can be resprouted in your garden.)

Place the lemongrass, garlic, shallots, chilies, and brown sugar in a spice mill or mortar and pestle, and purée to a coarse paste. Work in the fish sauce, lime juice, and hot sauce. Marinate fish or thinly sliced beef for 1 to 2 hours, turning once or twice.

Makes ¾ cup, enough marinade for
1½ to 2 pounds seafood, poultry, or meat.

13 CALORIES PER TABLESPOON: 1 G PROTEIN, 0 G FAT, 3 G CARBOHYDRATE; 52 MG SODIUM; 1 MG CHOLESTEROL.

KOREAN SESAME MARINADE

Bool-kogi is to Korea what barbecue is to the American South. To make it, paper-thin
slices of beef are marinated in a sweet-salty mixture of soy sauce, sugar, and sesame
oil. The meat is traditionally cooked at the table on what looks like an inverted
wok, but it can also be grilled on a hibachi or stir-fried in a wok.

¼ cup toasted sesame seeds
3 cloves garlic, minced (1 tablespoon)
1 tablespoon minced fresh ginger
3 scallions, minced
⅓ cup soy sauce

3 tablespoons sugar or honey
1½ tablespoons sesame oil
1 teaspoon hot red pepper flakes
½ teaspoon freshly ground black pepper

Lightly toast the sesame seeds in a dry skillet over medium heat. Combine the sesame seeds and the remaining ingredients in a shallow bowl. Marinate fish for 30 minutes, chicken breasts for 1 hour, and thinly sliced beef for 1 to 2 hours, turning once or twice.

Makes ¾ cup, enough marinade for
1½ to 2 pounds seafood, poultry, or meat.

46 CALORIES PER TABLESPOON: 1 G PROTEIN, 2 G FAT, 6 G CARBOHYDRATE; 342 MG SODIUM; 0 MG CHOLESTEROL.

RED WINE MARINADE

French chefs use this marinade to give tame meats, such as pork and beef, the sourish tang of wild game. It can also be used with poultry, but it's a little strong for fish. Juniper berries are small, blue-black berries that are the predominant flavoring in gin.

1 onion, finely chopped
2 carrots, finely chopped
2 stalks celery, finely chopped
3 shallots, finely chopped
3 cloves garlic, finely chopped
3 cups dry red wine
½ cup red wine vinegar

20 peppercorns
5 whole cloves
10 juniper berries (or ¼ cup gin)
3 sprigs parsley
5 bay leaves
1½ teaspoons dried thyme
2 tablespoons olive oil

Place all the ingredients in a saucepan and bring to a boil. Let cool completely. Place the meat in a glass or nonmetallic dish. Add the marinade and let sit for at least 6 hours, prefer-ably overnight, turning once or twice.

*Makes 4½ cups, enough marinade
for 2 pounds meat.*

16 CALORIES PER TABLESPOON: 0 G PROTEIN, .4 G FAT, 1 G CARBOHYDRATE; 3 MG SODIUM; 0 MG CHOLESTEROL.

FRESH HERB MARINADE FOR SEAFOOD AND POULTRY

This simple marinade is good for fish, shrimp, scallops, and chicken breasts. The particular variety of herbs you use is less important than that the herbs be fresh.

¼ cup fresh lemon juice
¼ cup dry vermouth
salt and freshly ground black pepper
2 tablespoons extra-virgin olive oil
3 shallots or 1 small onion, thinly sliced
2 cloves garlic, thinly sliced

1 green bell pepper, 1 poblano chili, or
   3 jalapeño chilies, thinly sliced
½ cup finely chopped fresh basil, dill, rose-mary, parsley, tarragon, and/or other herbs

Combine the lemon juice, vermouth, salt, and pepper in a small bowl and whisk until all the salt is dissolved. Whisk in the olive oil.

Place half the sliced vegetables, herbs, and lemon juice mixture in a shallow glass dish and cover with the food to be marinated. Add the remaining vegetables, herbs, and lemon juice mixture. Marinate seafood for 2 hours and chicken breasts for 4 hours, turning once or twice.

*Makes 1 cup, enough marinade for
1½ to 2 pounds seafood or poultry.*

67 CALORIES PER TABLESPOON: 1 G PROTEIN, 5 G FAT, 5 G CARBOHYDRATE; 8 MG SODIUM; 0 MG CHOLESTEROL.

GEORGIAN CINNAMON-ORANGE MARINADE

Tabaka is a cinnamon-orange marinade from the Republic of Georgia (formerly part of the Soviet Union) in the Caucasus Mountains. It is often used for poultry, but it goes well with swordfish, too.

4 or 5 oranges (2 cups juice)
2–4 lemons (½ cup juice)
½ cup dry white wine
3 cloves garlic, minced (1 tablespoon)
1 tablespoon minced fresh ginger
1 medium-sized onion, minced (1 cup)
2 cinnamon sticks

3 tablespoons paprika
1 teaspoon cracked black peppercorns
¼ teaspoon freshly grated nutmeg
1–2 teaspoons sugar (or to taste)
½ teaspoon salt (or to taste)
3 tablespoons olive oil

Grate the zest of 1 orange and 1 lemon. Juice the oranges and lemons. Combine the orange juice, lemon juice, and wine in a saucepan and boil until only ½ cup liquid remains. Let cool.

Combine the garlic, ginger, and onion in a bowl. Stir in the juice mixture, grated zest, spices, sugar, salt, and oil. Marinate swordfish steaks and boneless chicken breasts for 1 to 2 hours, whole chickens or game hens overnight, turning once or twice.

Makes 1½ cups, enough marinade for 1½ to 2 pounds seafood, poultry, or meat.

29 CALORIES PER TABLESPOON: 0 G PROTEIN, 2 G FAT, 3 G CARBOHYDRATE; 45 MG SODIUM; 0 MG CHOLESTEROL.

Mexican Smoked Chili Marinade

Chipotles (smoked jalapeño chilies) add character to this fiery seasoning, which is often used with pork. Chipotles are usually sold canned in tomato paste, but you also see them dried. (If you use dried chilies for this recipe, soften them in hot water and add 2 tablespoons tomato paste.)

1 cup fresh orange juice
¼ cup fresh lime juice
5 canned chipotle chilies, minced, plus
   1 tablespoon juice
4 cloves garlic, minced (4 teaspoons)
1 teaspoon freshly grated orange zest

2 teaspoons dried oregano
1 teaspoon cumin seeds
2 tablespoons wine vinegar
½ teaspoon each salt and freshly ground
   black pepper (or to taste)

Combine the orange juice and lime juice in a saucepan and boil until only ½ cup liquid remains. Place this and the remaining ingredients in a blender and purée to a smooth paste.

Spread this paste on the food to be marinated.

Marinate seafood for 2 hours, poultry for 4 to 6 hours, and meat overnight, turning once or twice.

Makes 1 cup, enough marinade for 1½ to 2 pounds seafood, poultry, or meat.

6 CALORIES PER TABLESPOON: 0 G PROTEIN, 0 G FAT, 2 G CARBOHYDRATE; 117 MG SODIUM; 0 MG CHOLESTEROL.

Teriyaki Marinade

Teriyaki could be called the national marinade of Japan. It is equally at home on seafood, poultry, and meat. The traditional sweetener for teriyaki is mirin (sweet rice wine), but if it is unavailable, use sake, sherry, or white wine, and increase the sugar slightly.

1 tablespoon minced fresh ginger
3 cloves garlic, minced (1 tablespoon)
1 or 2 jalapeño chilies, seeded and minced
   (optional)
3 scallions, finely chopped

¼ cup soy sauce
¼ cup mirin or white wine
1½ tablespoons sesame oil
2 tablespoons maple syrup or brown sugar
   (or to taste)

Place the ginger, garlic, chilies (if using), and scallions in a bowl and whisk in the soy sauce, mirin, sesame oil, and maple syrup.

Marinate seafood for 2 hours, poultry for 4

hours, and meat overnight, turning once or twice.

Makes 1 cup, enough marinade for 1½ to 2 pounds seafood, poultry, or meat.

36 CALORIES PER TABLESPOON: 0 G PROTEIN, 3 G FAT, 3 G CARBOHYDRATE; 260 MG SODIUM; 0 MG CHOLESTEROL.

CUBAN LIME MARINADE

Cubans use this simple marinade on just about everything. It can be made with limes or sour oranges, and it goes especially well with grilled fish.

6 cloves garlic, minced (2 tablespoons)
1½ teaspoons salt (or to taste)
2 teaspoons ground cumin

1 tablespoon chopped fresh oregano
 (or 1 teaspoon dried)
½ teaspoon freshly ground black pepper
½ cup fresh lime juice or sour orange juice

Place the garlic in a mortar and pestle with the salt, and mash to a smooth paste. (Or mash these ingredients in a shallow bowl with a fork.) Work in the cumin, oregano, pepper, and lime juice.

Cut small pockets in the food to be marinated and stuff half the marinade inside. Spread the remaining marinade on top. Let marinate for at least 6 hours (meat overnight), turning once or twice. Use any leftover marinade for basting.

Makes ½ cup, enough marinade for 1 to 1½ pounds seafood, poultry, or meat.

16 CALORIES PER TABLESPOON: 1 G PROTEIN, .2 G FAT, 4 G CARBOHYDRATE; 402 MG SODIUM; 0 MG CHOLESTEROL.

SAUCES AND CONDIMENTS

PINEAPPLE SALSA

Here's a fruit salsa that's great with grilled fish or poultry. (It's also great by itself as a salad.) For a jazzy presentation, serve it in a pineapple shell.

1 small pineapple
1 red bell pepper, cored, seeded, and cut into 1" pieces
1 yellow bell pepper, cored, seeded, and cut into 1" pieces
1 green bell pepper, cored, seeded, and cut into 1" pieces

1 fresh poblano chili or 2 or 3 jalapeño or serrano chilis, cored, seeded, and finely chopped
1 small red onion, finely diced
½ cup chopped fresh mint or cilantro
3–4 tablespoons fresh lime juice
salt and freshly ground black pepper
1 tablespoon brown sugar (optional)

Cut the pineapple in half lengthwise, leaving the leaves intact. Using a grapefruit knife, cut out the pineapple flesh, leaving the shell intact. Core the pineapple and cut the flesh into 1" pieces.

Combine the pineapple with the remaining in-gredients in a mixing bowl and gently toss. Correct the seasoning, adding lime juice, salt, and sugar to taste. This salsa tastes best served within 1 hour of being made.

Makes 3 to 4 cups.

6 CALORIES PER TABLESPOON: 0 G PROTEIN, 0 G FAT, 1 G CARBOHYDRATE; 0 MG SODIUM; 0 MG CHOLESTEROL.

Clockwise from left: Melon Salsa (page 178),
Pineapple Salsa (this page), Cranberry Salsa (page 178)

MELON SALSA

This is one of my favorite warm-weather salsas. It's light enough to accompany seafood and interesting enough to eat by itself as a salad. It can be made with any one melon if you don't have cantaloupe, honeydew, and watermelon.

1 quart mixed fresh melon balls (cantaloupe, honeydew, and/or watermelon), drained
1 small cucumber, peeled, seeded, and cut into ½" dice
2 scallions, finely chopped

1 or 2 serrano chilies or ½ scotch bonnet chili, seeded and minced
¼ cup chopped fresh mint or cilantro
3–4 tablespoons fresh lime juice (or to taste)
1 tablespoon brown sugar (or to taste)
salt and freshly ground black pepper

Combine all the ingredients in a mixing bowl and gently toss to mix. Correct the seasoning, adding sugar, lime juice, and salt to taste. The salsa should be a little sweet and a little sour.

This salsa tastes best served within 1 hour of being made.

Serves 8.

40 CALORIES PER SERVING: 1 G PROTEIN, 0 G FAT, 10 G CARBOHYDRATE; 10 MG SODIUM; 0 MG CHOLESTEROL.

CRANBERRY SALSA

New England meets New Mexico in this unusual salsa. It makes a perfect accompaniment to Smoked Holiday Turkey (page 138).

1 12-ounce bag cranberries
¾ cup sugar
1 clove garlic, minced (1 teaspoon)
1 or 2 jalapeño chilies, seeded and minced
⅓ cup finely chopped cilantro

3 scallions, minced
¼ cup fresh lime juice
splash or two of hot sauce
salt and freshly ground black pepper

Pick through the cranberries, removing any stems, and wash thoroughly. Bring 2 cups water and ½ cup of the sugar to a boil. Reduce the heat, add the cranberries, and simmer for 2 to 3 minutes, or until cooked but still firm. Do not overcook; the cranberries should keep their shape. Drain in a colander. Refresh under cold water and drain thoroughly.

Combine the cranberries with the remaining ingredients in a bowl and mix with a wooden spoon. Correct the seasoning, adding sugar and lime juice to taste. The salsa should be sweet, sour, and spicy.

Makes 2 cups.

23 CALORIES PER TABLESPOON: 0 G PROTEIN, 0 G FAT, 6 G CARBOHYDRATE; 8 MG SODIUM; 0 MG CHOLESTEROL.

SICILIAN SALSA

What would salsa be like if it had been invented in the Mediterranean region instead of Mexico? I added capers, olives, and basil to the traditional recipe to find out. This salsa makes a great accompaniment to grilled seafood and roast chicken. You could also eat it on crostini toasts (page 18) or scooped up with wedges of pita bread.

2 ripe tomatoes, peeled, seeded, and cut into ½" dice
½ yellow bell pepper, diced (¼ cup)
½ bunch flat-leaf parsley, chopped (¼ cup)
2–3 tablespoons chopped fresh basil
6 pitted black olives, halved

3 tablespoons capers, drained
1 tablespoon olive oil
1 tablespoon fresh lemon or lime juice
2 teaspoons balsamic vinegar
¼ teaspoon hot red pepper flakes
salt and freshly ground black pepper

Combine all the ingredients in a large bowl and gently toss to mix. (You probably won't need much salt, as the olives and capers are already quite salty.) Correct the seasoning, adding lemon juice and vinegar to taste.

Makes 2 cups.

8 CALORIES PER TABLESPOON: 0 G PROTEIN, .6 G FAT, 1 G CARBOHYDRATE; 16 MG SODIUM; 0 MG CHOLESTEROL.

THE SEARCH FOR A LOW-FAT VINAIGRETTE

Vinaigrette is one of the cornerstones of French cuisine, but it's also been adopted with gusto by a new generation of chefs on both sides of the Atlantic as a way to provide flavor without the artery-clogging richness of such classics as hollandaise sauce and mayonnaise. Light, fresh, and quick to prepare, vinaigrette does indeed seem like a panacea, but the traditional recipe (and most modern variations) still contains a great deal of oil. In trying to come up with a low-fat vinaigrette, I took a cue from the great French chef Joel Robuchon, who sometimes enriches his vinaigrettes with a spoonful of juices from a roast. I went one step further, replacing a substantial part of the oil with chicken stock. I've given a sliding scale for oil measurements in the following recipes; you know what your health requirements dictate.

LOW-FAT VINAIGRETTE

Use this recipe on salads, grilled fish or meat, steamed vegetables, or any dish that needs a quick, flavorful sauce. For an especially rich version, use Brown Bone Stock (page 238).

1 or 2 shallots, minced
1 small clove garlic, minced (½ teaspoon)
2 teaspoons Dijon-style mustard
salt and freshly ground black pepper

1 tablespoon red wine vinegar
1 tablespoon fresh lemon juice
2–6 tablespoons olive oil
2–6 tablespoons chicken stock

Combine the shallots, garlic, mustard, salt, and pepper in a large bowl. Add the vinegar and lemon juice in a thin stream, whisking until all the salt is dissolved. Gradually whisk in the oil and stock in a thin stream. (Or the ingredients can be combined and shaken in a jar with a tight-fitting lid.) There should be ½ cup liquid in all. Correct the seasoning, adding salt and lemon juice to taste.

Makes ¾ cup.

24 CALORIES PER TABLESPOON: 0 G PROTEIN, 2 G FAT, 1 G CARBOHYDRATE; 20 MG SODIUM; 0 MG CHOLESTEROL.

TOMATO VINAIGRETTE

*In this recipe, puréed tomato takes the place of much of the oil in traditional
vinaigrette. It complements poached fish, grilled fowl, and a wide
range of vegetables, including my Eggplant Cake (page 15).*

3 or 4 very ripe tomatoes (about 2 pounds),
  or 1 28-ounce can plum tomatoes
1½ tablespoons olive oil
salt and freshly ground black pepper
2 tablespoons balsamic vinegar

1 teaspoon cornstarch
1 tablespoon water
3 tablespoons chopped fresh dill
1 tablespoon minced fresh chives

Peel and seed the tomatoes (see Cook's Notes). Place the tomatoes in a blender or food processor with the oil, salt, and pepper. Purée until smooth.

In a small saucepan, combine the vinegar and ½ cup of the puréed tomato, and bring to a boil. Dissolve the cornstarch in the water and whisk it into the vinegar mixture. Bring to a boil and remove the pan from the heat. Add this mixture back to the puréed tomatoes and blend again.

Transfer the vinaigrette to a bowl and whisk in the herbs. Correct the seasoning, adding salt, pepper, and vinegar to taste.

Makes 2 cups.

12 CALORIES PER TABLESPOON: 0 G PROTEIN, .7 G FAT, 2 G CARBOHYDRATE; 3 MG SODIUM; 0 MG CHOLESTEROL.

ASIAN VINAIGRETTE

*Ginger, garlic, and scallions give this vinaigrette an Asian accent.
Serve it with salmon, tofu, or cucumber salads.*

2 cloves garlic, minced (2 teaspoons)
1 tablespoon minced fresh ginger
2 scallions, minced
¼ cup chicken stock

2 tablespoons rice wine vinegar
1 tablespoon soy sauce
1 tablespoon sesame oil (optional)

Combine all the ingredients in a jar with a tight-fitting lid. Shake until well blended.

Correct the seasoning, adding soy sauce to taste.

Makes ½ cup.

4 CALORIES PER TABLESPOON: 0 G PROTEIN, 0 G FAT, 1 G CARBOHYDRATE; 131 MG SODIUM; 0 MG CHOLESTEROL.

VIETNAMESE DIPPING SAUCE

Nuoc cham is a sweet-sour-salty dipping sauce made with fish sauce (see Cook's Notes), lime juice, and sugar. It's as indispensable on the Vietnamese table as ketchup and mustard are on our own.

1 carrot
2 cloves garlic, minced (2 teaspoons)
1 shallot, minced
1 fresh hot chili, minced
2 tablespoons sugar

¼ cup fish sauce
¼ cup fresh lime juice
¼ cup water
3 tablespoons rice wine vinegar

Cut the carrot into the thinnest imaginable shreds. (I mean really thin. The easiest way for a Westerner to do this is to shave the carrot into thin strips with a vegetable peeler. Stack the strips up 3 or 4 high and cut lengthwise into hair-thin slivers.)

Combine the garlic, shallot, chili, and sugar in a mortar and pestle, and pound to a smooth paste. Work in the fish sauce, lime juice, water, and vinegar. (Or the ingredients can be combined and shaken in a jar with a tight-fitting lid.) Transfer the sauce to a pretty bowl (or several bowls) and stir in the carrot.

Makes 1 cup.

17 CALORIES PER TABLESPOON: 1 G PROTEIN, 0 G FAT, 4 G CARBOHYDRATE; 52 MG SODIUM; 1 MG CHOLESTEROL.

SPICY MIGNONETTE SAUCE

This piquant sauce takes its name from the French word for coarsely cracked peppercorns: mignonette. Spoon it over raw oysters and clams on the half shell, or serve as a dipping sauce for cooked seafood.

2 teaspoons black peppercorns
3 tablespoons minced shallots
1 or 2 pickled or fresh jalapeño chilies
(or to taste), minced

½ cup red wine vinegar
½ cup dry white wine
salt (optional)

Coarsely crush the peppercorns in a mortar and pestle or under a rolling pin or heavy pot. (The idea here is to obtain large pieces of pepper.) Combine the cracked pepper in a bowl with the remaining ingredients. Correct the seasoning, adding salt to taste, if desired.

Makes 1¼ cups.

6 CALORIES PER TABLESPOON: 0 G PROTEIN, 0 G FAT, 1 G CARBOHYDRATE; 7 MG SODIUM; 0 MG CHOLESTEROL.

HORSERADISH "CREAM"

Here's another low-fat remake of a high-calorie favorite. This attractive sauce makes a great accompaniment for smoked fish, boiled shrimp (or any sort of raw or cooked seafood), steaks, and roast beef.

2 cups nonfat yogurt
1 tablespoon white horseradish or finely
grated fresh root
1 clove garlic, minced (1 teaspoon)
1 shallot, minced

1 tablespoon minced fresh chives
1 teaspoon Dijon-style mustard
1 teaspoon fresh lemon juice
salt and freshly ground black pepper

Drain the yogurt in a yogurt funnel (see Mail-Order Sources) or a cheesecloth-lined colander for 2 hours. Gently stir the remaining ingredients into the yogurt. Correct the seasoning, adding salt and horseradish to taste. The sauce should be very spicy.

Makes 1¼ cups.

15 CALORIES PER TABLESPOON: 2 G PROTEIN, 0 G FAT, 2 G CARBOHYDRATE; 32 MG SODIUM; 0 MG CHOLESTEROL.

LEMON CHILI SAUCE

I first tasted this sauce at the Royal Orchid Sheraton Hotel in Bangkok. It was meant to be served with grilled seafood, but I soon found myself eating it straight with a spoon. For a truly authentic version, use cilantro root, which tastes like a cross between cilantro leaves and parsnips. (Asian and Hispanic markets often sell the whole plant.) Cilantro leaves produce a tasty sauce, too.

1 head fresh garlic, minced (¼ cup)
4 or 5 fresh hot red chilies, minced (¼ cup)
3 tablespoons minced cilantro root or leaves

½ cup fresh lemon juice
½ cup fish sauce
2 tablespoons sugar (or to taste)

Combine all the ingredients in a glass bowl and stir until the sugar is completely dissolved. Add more sugar as necessary. The sauce should be tart, salty, and sweet.

Makes 1¼ cups.

17 CALORIES PER TABLESPOON: 1 G PROTEIN, 0 G FAT, 2 G CARBOHYDRATE; 147 MG SODIUM; 3 MG CHOLESTEROL.

MOLASSES BARBECUE SAUCE

Molasses is hardly what one would call a fashionable ingredient these days, but unlike the sugar, fructose, and dextrose used in most commercial barbecue sauces, it has flavor behind its sweetness. This sauce goes particularly well with pork and duck.

1 tablespoon olive oil
1 small onion, minced (½ cup)
1 clove garlic, minced (1 teaspoon)
1 jalapeño chili, seeded and minced

⅔ cup molasses
⅔ cup distilled white vinegar
⅓ cup Dijon-style mustard
1 tablespoon soy sauce

Heat the oil in a large saucepan over medium heat. Add the onion, garlic, and chili, and cook, stirring well, for 2 to 3 minutes, or until soft but not brown.

Stir in the remaining ingredients and simmer for 5 minutes. Let the sauce cool before serving.

Makes 2 cups.

25 CALORIES PER TABLESPOON: 0 G PROTEIN, .5 G FAT, 5 G CARBOHYDRATE; 73 MG SODIUM; 0 MG CHOLESTEROL.

ROMESCO SAUCE

A specialty of Tarragona, Spain, romesco is a reddish sauce made of chilies, nuts, and tomatoes. I've reduced the amount of fat by cutting back on the nuts, substituting chicken stock for part of the oil, and toasting rather than frying the bread. Romesco isn't a pretty sauce (it's brown), but it has a wonderful flavor. Serve it with grilled chicken, baked fish, pork or veal, or even on pasta. I like to eat it straight with a spoon!

2 dried red chilies (preferably anchos
  or pasillas)
1 fresh jalapeño chili, seeded
4 ripe tomatoes, halved and seeded
4 cloves garlic, peeled
2 tablespoons slivered or chopped almonds
2 tablespoons chopped hazelnuts
1 slice country-style white bread (about
  ¼ cup crumbled)

1 tablespoon olive oil
¼ cup chopped flat-leaf parsley
2 tablespoons red wine vinegar (or to taste)
½ teaspoon sugar
¼ cup chicken stock (approximately)
salt and freshly ground black pepper

Soak the dried chilies in warm water for 1 hour.

Preheat the oven to 350 degrees F. Place the jalapeño, tomatoes, and garlic on a piece of lightly oiled foil in a roasting pan. Roast for 30 minutes, or until the garlic is soft. Toast the nuts on a baking sheet in the oven for 6 to 8 minutes, or until lightly browned. Toast the bread to a dark golden brown in a toaster and crumble it into small pieces.

Drain and chop the soaked dried chilies. (If a milder sauce is desired, remove the seeds.) Sauté the chilies in the oil in a small frying pan for 1 to 2 minutes, or until crisp and fragrant. Let cool.

Grind the nuts and toast to a fine powder in a food processor. Add the fried chilies, jalapeño, tomatoes, garlic, and parsley, and purée to a thick paste. Add the vinegar, sugar, and enough stock to obtain a pourable sauce. Correct the seasoning, adding salt, pepper, and vinegar to taste.

Makes 2 cups.

16 CALORIES PER TABLESPOON: 0 G PROTEIN, 1 G FAT, 2 G CARBOHYDRATE; 32 MG SODIUM; 0 MG CHOLESTEROL.

LEMON MUSTARD

This recipe calls for two optional ingredients: brown mustard seeds and green peppercorns. The former are smaller and hotter than yellow mustard seeds. Look for them at Indian markets. Green peppercorns are the fruit of the pepper tree. (When allowed to ripen and dry, they become black pepper.) Green peppercorns are available freeze-dried and pickled at gourmet shops.

4–5 lemons (¾ cup juice)
½ cup yellow mustard seeds
2 tablespoons brown mustard seeds
    (optional)
½ cup dry white wine

¼ cup dry mustard
2 tablespoons green peppercorns (optional)
1 teaspoon salt (or to taste)
2 teaspoons honey (or to taste)

Grate the zest of 1 lemon. Juice all the lemons. Combine ½ cup lemon juice with the mustard seeds, wine, and zest in a bowl. Let stand for 2 hours. In another bowl, stir the dry mustard into the remaining ¼ cup lemon juice to make a smooth paste.

Coarsely purée the mustard seed mixture in a blender or spice mill. (Don't worry if a few seeds remain.) Return it to the bowl with the pepper-corns, salt, and honey. Set the bowl in a pan of simmering water and cook for 6 to 8 minutes.

Remove the bowl from the heat and stir in the dry mustard paste. Correct the seasoning, adding salt and honey to taste. The mustard can be served right away, but the flavor will improve if you allow it to ripen in a jar for a few days. Store it in the refrigerator.

Makes 1½ cups.

10 CALORIES PER TEASPOON: 0 G PROTEIN, .5 G FAT, 1 G CARBOHYDRATE; 59 MG SODIUM; 0 MG CHOLESTEROL.

Banana Raita

Raita is a cooling condiment made from yogurt, mint, and cucumber. Patrons of Indian restaurants will be familiar with its ability to soothe a palate inflamed by chili hellfire. The twist in this recipe is the addition of a sweet touch: banana. Serve in a bowl with your favorite curry.

2 cups nonfat yogurt
¼ teaspoon ground cardamom (optional)
1 small cucumber, peeled, seeded, and
   grated or coarsely chopped

1 ripe banana, peeled and coarsely chopped
salt and freshly ground black pepper
¼ cup chopped fresh mint leaves
2 teaspoons sugar (or to taste)

Drain the yogurt in a yogurt funnel (see Mail-Order Sources) or a cheesecloth-lined colander for 2 hours.

Fold the remaining ingredients into the drained yogurt. Correct the seasoning, adding more salt to taste.

Makes 2 cups.

12 CALORIES PER SERVING: 1 G PROTEIN, 0 G FAT, 2 G CARBOHYDRATE; 11 MG SODIUM; 0 MG CHOLESTEROL.

Yemenite Hot Sauce

Zehug is a hot sauce from Yemen, served much the way bottled salsa is in North America. You can use almost any hot chili to make this sauce, including jalapeños, serranos, and Thai peppers. To make a red sauce, use red chilies; to make a green one, use green.

6 fresh red or green chilies, seeded
6 cloves garlic, peeled
2 tablespoons fresh lemon juice
   (approximately)

½ cup finely chopped cilantro or flat-leaf
   parsley
1 teaspoon ground cumin
salt and freshly ground black pepper

Purée the chilies and garlic in a spice mill or blender, adding enough lemon juice to obtain a smooth paste. (The ingredients can also be pounded to a smooth paste in a mortar and pestle.)

Transfer the chili paste to a bowl and stir in the cilantro, cumin, salt, and pepper.

Makes 1½ cups.

Note: This is a hot one. Use it sparingly and wear gloves when handling the chilies.

4 CALORIES PER TABLESPOON: 0 G PROTEIN, 0 G FAT, 1 G CARBOHYDRATE; 1 MG SODIUM; 0 MG CHOLESTEROL.

PICKLED OKRA
....

Who says okra has to be soft and slimy? These pickles are crisper and crunchier than many cucumber pickles. This recipe is a great way to introduce people who don't think they like okra to this pretty, finger-shaped vegetable. For the best results, choose small, firm, unblemished okra.

1 pound small okra
2 dried red chilies
2 cups white vinegar
1 cup water
1 tablespoon salt

2 teaspoons sugar
2 bay leaves
1 teaspoon each black peppercorns, coriander seeds, and dill seeds
½ teaspoon celery seeds

Wash the okra and trim off the ends of the stems. Place in a large, clean jar with the chilies. Combine the remaining ingredients in a nonreactive saucepan and bring to a boil. Let this mixture cool slightly, then pour it over the okra. Place a small dish or sealed, water-filled plastic bag on top to keep the okra submerged.

Let the okra stand at room temperature for 2 to 7 days. The pickles are ready to eat after 2 days, but the flavor will improve with age. (I've never been able to wait more than a week to see whether they continue to improve!)

Makes 1 pint.

Note: Nutritional values for pickled foods are imprecise and, therefore, no analysis is given.

PICKLED LEMONS
....

Salt-cured lemons are a popular flavoring in Morocco, where they are added to everything from salads to stews. Their explosive flavor is great for enlivening seafood, pasta, and grain dishes, or even for nibbling straight. Pickled lemons will keep almost indefinitely, and a little goes a long way. A tiny spoonful of the juice makes a wonderful addition to salad dressing.

3 whole lemons
½ cup kosher salt

½–1 cup fresh lemon juice
extra-virgin olive oil (optional)

Scrub the lemons and dry well. Cut each lemon into 8 wedges and each wedge in half. Remove any seeds. Place the lemons in a bowl with the salt and mix well. Transfer the lemon mixture to a clean glass jar with a glass or plastic-coated lid. Add lemon juice to cover.

Seal the jar and let the lemons pickle at room temperature for at least 5 days, shaking the jar from time to time to mix the juices. For extra flavor, stir in a tablespoon or two of olive oil. Store the pickled lemons in the refrigerator.

Makes 1 pint.

Note: Nutritional values for pickled foods are imprecise and, therefore, no analysis is given.

....
Pickled Okra, Pickled Lemons, Pickled Onions (page 190)

PICKLED ONIONS

Homemade pickles are a great way to spice up normally bland low-fat foods such as chicken breasts and fish fillets. I like to use cipollinas—small, flat Italian onions— for pickling, but pearl onions and small silverskins work well, too.

2 cups distilled white vinegar
⅔ cup water
2 teaspoons salt
1 tablespoon sugar

1½ pounds cipollinas or other small onions, peeled
1 or 2 fresh jalapeño chilies, thinly sliced

Combine the vinegar, water, salt, and sugar in a large bowl and whisk until smooth. Place the onions and chilies in a large, clean jar. Add enough of the vinegar mixture to cover the onions completely. If necessary, place a small dish or sealed, water-filled plastic bag on top to keep the onions completely submerged. Let the onions pickle at room temperature for 2 to 3 days.

Makes 1 pint.

Note: Nutritional values for pickled foods are imprecise and, therefore, no analysis is given.

BRAZILIAN HOT SAUCE

This molho de companha *(country hot sauce) could be described as a mildly spicy relish. To be strictly authentic, you'll need an aromatic African chili called* pimenta malagueta, *whose fiery bite is inversely proportional to its tiny size. But the sauce is perfectly good made with readily available jalapeño or serrano chilies. Serve with grilled meat.*

1 large red onion, finely chopped
1 large ripe tomato, seeded and finely chopped
1 green bell pepper, cored, seeded, and finely chopped
2 cloves garlic, minced (2 teaspoons)
2 *malagueta* or other chilies, minced (or to taste)

¼ cup finely chopped flat-leaf parsley
1 tablespoon extra-virgin olive oil
3 tablespoons fresh lime juice (or to taste)
2 tablespoons wine vinegar
salt and freshly ground black pepper

Combine all the ingredients in a bowl and stir to mix. Correct the seasoning with lime juice and salt to taste. If the sauce seems too thick, stir in a few tablespoons ice water.

Makes 2 cups.

8 CALORIES PER TABLESPOON: 0 G PROTEIN, .5 G FAT, 1 G CARBOHYDRATE; 1 MG SODIUM; 0 MG CHOLESTEROL.

HOMEMADE KETCHUP

Modern ketchup derives from a Chinese pickled fish sauce called ket-tsiap. *British mariners acquired a taste for this sauce in Malaysia in the 18th century and brought samples back for their compatriots. English chefs tried to recreate* ket-tsiap *using local ingredients such as mushrooms and walnuts. It wasn't until the 19th century that tomatoes entered the picture and the ketchup we know and love was born. This homemade ketchup isn't hard to prepare, and it will make you want to throw stones at the commercial brands.*

1½ tablespoons extra-virgin olive oil
1 large onion, chopped (1 cup)
3 cloves garlic, minced (1 tablespoon)
2 stalks celery, finely chopped
1 red bell pepper, cored, seeded, and
  finely chopped
3 pounds fresh ripe tomatoes, peeled
  and seeded (5 cups), or 3 28-ounce cans
  imported peeled plum tomatoes (reserve
  liquid)
½ cup brown sugar (approximately)

½ cup cider vinegar (approximately)
2 tablespoons tomato paste
2 teaspoons Tabasco or other hot sauce
1 tablespoon Dijon-style mustard
1 bay leaf
1 teaspoon celery seeds
1 teaspoon ground coriander
½ teaspoon ground allspice
¼ teaspoon ground cloves
salt, freshly ground black pepper, and
  cayenne pepper

Heat the oil in a large saucepan. Cook the onion, garlic, celery, and pepper over medium heat for 3 to 4 minutes, or until soft but not brown. Add the remaining ingredients, plus 1 cup water or reserved tomato liquid, and bring to a boil. Reduce the heat and gently simmer for 1 hour, stirring from time to time, adding tomato liquid or water as necessary to keep the mixture moist. Correct the seasoning, adding brown sugar, vinegar, salt, and pepper to taste. The ketchup should be a little sweet, a little sour, and quite spicy.

Purée the ingredients in a blender, adding water or tomato liquid as needed to obtain a smooth, thick sauce. Put the ketchup in clean jars and store in the refrigerator.

Makes 5½ cups.

13 CALORIES PER TABLESPOON: 0 G PROTEIN, 0 G FAT, 3 G CARBOHYDRATE; 10 MG SODIUM; 0 MG CHOLESTEROL.

BANANA-TAMARIND CHUTNEY

Tamarind is a tall tropical tree with a large curved seedpod. The pod contains a sour pulp used in Indian, Asian, and Caribbean cooking. The pulp combines the tartness of lime juice with the sweetness of stewed prunes. To make tamarind water, combine 4 ounces pulp and 2 cups warm water in a blender. Blend for 1 minute and strain well. If you can't find tamarind, substitute balsamic vinegar.

4 ripe bananas
juice of 1 lime
¼ cup tamarind water or tamarind purée
 (or ¼ cup balsamic vinegar)
2 tablespoons minced fresh ginger
1 or 2 jalapeño chilies, seeded and minced
1 red bell pepper, cored, seeded, and cut
 into ½" dice
1 green bell pepper, cored, seeded, and cut
 into ½" dice

½ cup light brown sugar (or to taste)
¾ cup raisins or currants
2 tablespoons coarsely chopped pecans
1 teaspoon ground cumin
1 teaspoon ground coriander
salt, freshly ground black pepper, and
 cayenne pepper

Peel and dice 3 of the bananas and sprinkle with lime juice. Prepare the tamarind water.

Combine all the ingredients (except the 4th banana) in a heavy saucepan and gently simmer for 5 minutes. Correct the seasoning with sugar, lime juice, and cayenne to taste. The chutney should be a little sweet, a little sour, and a little spicy.

Let the chutney cool to room temperature. Peel and dice the 4th banana and stir it in. Refrigerate until ready to serve. This chutney tastes best the first week.

Makes 4 cups.

24 CALORIES PER TABLESPOON: 0 G PROTEIN, 0 G FAT, 6 G CARBOHYDRATE; 10 MG SODIUM; 0 MG CHOLESTEROL.

CORN CHUTNEY

To most people, chutney implies fruit, but fine chutneys are made from onions and other vegetables and herbs. Here's a corn chutney that goes especially well with seafood and roast pork. Dried cherries can be found at gourmet shops or purchased by mail (see Mail-Order Sources).

4 ears fresh corn (2 cups kernels)
3 shallots, minced
1 or 2 jalapeño chilies, seeded and finely
  chopped
1 tablespoon minced fresh ginger
1 small green bell pepper, cored, seeded,
  and chopped
2 stalks celery, finely chopped

¼ cup dried cherries or raisins
3 tablespoons honey (or to taste)
¼ cup cider vinegar
1–2 teaspoons hot sauce
salt and freshly ground black pepper
3 tablespoons chopped fresh chives or
  scallions

Cut the corn kernels off the cob with a sharp knife. (The easiest way to do this is to lay the ears on their side on a cutting board and make lengthwise cuts with a chef's knife.)

Combine the corn with the remaining ingredients (except the chives) in a saucepan and simmer for 8 to 10 minutes, or until the vegetables are tender. Correct the seasoning, adding salt, honey, vinegar, and hot sauce to taste. The chutney should be a little sweet, a little sour, and decidedly spicy. Remove the pan from the heat and stir in the chives. Transfer the chutney to a clean jar and store in the refrigerator.

Makes 3 cups.

15 CALORIES PER TABLESPOON: 0 G PROTEIN, 0 G FAT, 4 G CARBOHYDRATE; 3 MG SODIUM; 0 MG CHOLESTEROL.

GINGER PEACH CHUTNEY

Chutney (from the Hindu word chatni) is a fruit-, vegetable-, or herb-based condiment traditionally served with Indian food. North American chefs use it to spice up everything from roast chicken to baked ham to grilled fish. Try making this chutney with ripe summer peaches. It's good enough to eat plain with a spoon! (You can also make it with nectarines, pears, or other fruits.)

2 pounds ripe peaches (5 cups diced)
4 slices candied ginger, minced
1 cinnamon stick
4 allspice berries
4 whole cloves
10 black peppercorns
½ red onion, diced (½ cup)

½ red bell pepper, cored, seeded, and diced
½ green bell pepper, cored, seeded,
  and diced
½ cup raisins
¼ cup rice wine vinegar
3 tablespoons brown sugar (or to taste)

Plunge the peaches in a pot of boiling water for 20 seconds. Rinse under cold water and slip off the skins. Pit and cut into ½" dice. Tie the ginger, cinnamon stick, allspice, cloves, and peppercorns in a piece of cheesecloth.

Place the peaches, spice bundle, and remaining ingredients in a heavy saucepan. Simmer, stirring frequently, for 10 minutes, or until the peaches are soft. Correct the seasoning, adding vinegar and sugar to taste. The chutney should be a little sweet and a little sour.

Let the chutney cool to room temperature, then transfer it to a clean jar. Store in the refrigerator.

Makes 5 cups.

Note: The amount of sugar used depends on the sweetness of the peaches.

10 CALORIES PER TABLESPOON: 0 G PROTEIN, 0 G FAT, 3 G CARBOHYDRATE; 0 MG SODIUM; 0 MG CHOLESTEROL.

CRANBERRY CHUTNEY

Here's an Indian twist on a Thanksgiving favorite.
It's a great accompaniment to Smoked Holiday Turkey (page 138).

1 12-ounce bag cranberries
1 tablespoon olive oil
3 shallots, minced
1 tablespoon minced fresh ginger
1 or 2 jalapeño chilies, seeded and minced
1 green bell pepper, cored, seeded, and cut into ½" dice
1 yellow bell pepper, cored, seeded, and cut into ½" dice
½ cup cider vinegar
½ cup brown sugar (or to taste)
½ cup raisins
salt and freshly ground black pepper

Wash and pick through the cranberries, removing any stems. Heat the oil in a large saucepan. Cook the shallots and ginger over medium heat for 30 seconds, or until soft but not brown. Add the remaining ingredients and gently simmer for 5 minutes, or until the cranberries are just tender. (They shouldn't be too soft.) Correct the seasoning, adding sugar and vinegar to taste. The chutney should be a little sweet and a little sour.

Store the chutney in clean jars. Refrigerated, it will keep for several months.

Makes 3 cups.

21 CALORIES PER TABLESPOON: 0 G PROTEIN, .5 G FAT, 5 G CARBOHYDRATE; 1 MG SODIUM; 0 MG CHOLESTEROL.

DESSERTS

BANANA CREAM PIE

Like most traditional American desserts, banana cream pie is loaded with fat and calories. To reduce the fat in the crust, I use zwieback crumbs, oil, and cider. A teaspoon of gelatin allows for a substantial reduction of eggs in the filling, while banana liqueur provides the yellow color lost by reducing the egg yolks.

FOR THE CRUST
¾ cup zwieback crumbs (3 ounces cookies)
¾ cup graham cracker crumbs (6 whole crackers)
1 tablespoon brown sugar
½ teaspoon ground ginger
¼ teaspoon ground cinnamon
¼ teaspoon freshly grated nutmeg
1 tablespoon canola oil
1 tablespoon butter, softened
3 tablespoons apple cider or water

FOR THE FILLING
3 small ripe bananas
1 teaspoon fresh lime juice
1 teaspoon gelatin
2 tablespoons water
1 cup skim milk
3 tablespoons light brown sugar
2 tablespoons flour
2 eggs, separated, plus 1 egg white
1 tablespoon grated fresh ginger (or 1 table-spoon chopped candied ginger)
2 tablespoons banana liqueur
1 teaspoon vanilla extract
⅛ teaspoon cream of tartar
¼ cup granulated sugar

To make the crust, preheat the oven to 375 degrees F. Combine the zwieback and graham cracker crumbs, brown sugar, and spices in a food processor and process for 1 minute. Add the oil, butter, and cider, and process until the ingredients come together into a crumbly dough. Add a little more cider if necessary. Press the dough into the bottom and sides of a lightly oiled 9" pie pan or 10" tart pan with a removable bottom. Bake for 10 minutes, or until lightly browned. Remove the pan from the oven and let cool.

To make the filling, peel and thinly slice the bananas. Toss with lime juice to prevent discoloring. Arrange the bananas over the bottom of the

A NICE JEWISH COMPOTE

Every family has at least one great cook. Ours is my Aunt Anette. My favorite of her specialties is this dessert of startling simplicity. Fruit juice makes it sweet, cloves and cinnamon sticks make it fragrant, and sliced lemons lend just the right touch of acidity.

2 cups dry red wine
2–3 cups apple cider or apple juice
3 cinnamon sticks
5 whole cloves
5 allspice berries
2 lemons

½ pound dried apricots
½ pound dried figs
½ pound prunes
½ pound sultanas
¼ cup sugar (or to taste)

Combine the wine, cider, and spices in a large pot and bring to a boil. Meanwhile, remove the zest from the lemons with a vegetable peeler and add it to the wine mixture. Cut the white inner rind off the lemons and cut the flesh into ¼" slices.

Add the dried fruit and sugar to the wine mixture, cover the pan, and gently simmer for 15 minutes, adding cider or water as necessary to keep the fruit moist. Add the lemon slices and simmer, uncovered, for 10 minutes, or until the fruit is soft and the juices form a thick syrup. Add sugar to taste. Let the compote cool to room temperature before serving.

Serves 6 to 8.

Note: We Raichlens like our compotes rustic, with whole spices and strips of lemon zest. Fastidious cooks could tie these ingredients in cheesecloth for removal before serving.

412 CALORIES PER SERVING: 4 G PROTEIN, 1 G FAT, 98 G CARBOHYDRATE; 18 MG SODIUM; 0 MG CHOLESTEROL.

BAKED APPLES

Is there any dish more evocative of autumn than baked apples? Unfortunately, most recipes are loaded with butter. My low-fat version uses banana to provide some of the moistness traditionally supplied by the butter. The rose water lends a Near Eastern accent.

2 cups apple cider
4 dried apricots, finely chopped
3 tablespoons raisins
6 firm, tart apples (such as Granny Smiths)
¼ cup toasted bread crumbs, Grape-Nuts,
   or other crunchy cereal
3 tablespoons brown sugar (or to taste)

¼ teaspoon ground cinnamon
freshly grated nutmeg
1 banana
1 teaspoon rose water or vanilla extract
2 tablespoons maple syrup
1 teaspoon cornstarch
1 tablespoon rum

Warm the cider in a saucepan. Remove the pan from the heat and add the apricots and raisins. Let soften for 20 minutes.

Meanwhile, core the apples, using an apple corer or melon baller, but don't cut all the way through the bottom. The idea is to create a cavity for stuffing. Preheat the oven to 350 degrees F.

Drain the apricots and raisins, reserving the cider. Combine the apricots, raisins, bread crumbs, brown sugar, cinnamon, and nutmeg in a bowl and crumble with your fingers. Finely chop the banana. Stir the banana and rose water into the crumb mixture. Stuff the filling into the apples. Make a few small holes in each filling with a skewer and pour in the maple syrup.

Place the apples in a baking dish. Pour in enough drained cider to cover the bottom inch of the apples. Reserve any excess cider. Bake the apples for 1 hour, or until soft. If the filling starts to get too brown, cover the apples with a piece of foil.

Transfer the apples to shallow bowls. Strain the pan juices and reserved cider into a small saucepan and bring to a boil. Dissolve the cornstarch in the rum. Whisk this mixture into the pan juices and bring to a boil. Pour the sauce over the apples and serve at once.

Serves 6.

216 CALORIES PER SERVING: 1 G PROTEIN, .7 G FAT, 53 G CARBOHYDRATE; 49 MG SODIUM; 0 MG CHOLESTEROL.

MELON WITH CARDAMOM YOGURT SAUCE

The idea for this recipe came from the intriguing book The Brilliant Bean *by Sally and Martin Stone. The combination of yogurt, lime, and cardamom is one of those culinary synergisms in which the whole is greater than the sum of the parts.*

1 cup nonfat yogurt
¼ teaspoon ground cardamom
3 tablespoons brown sugar
2–3 tablespoons fresh lime juice

4–5 cups melon balls (cantaloupe, honeydew, and/or watermelon)
½ bunch lemon verbena or mint (about ⅓ cup leaves), cut into thin slivers, plus 4 sprigs for garnish

Combine the yogurt, cardamom, brown sugar, and lime juice in a large bowl and whisk to mix. Gently stir in the melon balls and slivered lemon verbena. Taste the dressing, adding cardamom and sugar to taste. Garnish the salad with lemon verbena sprigs and serve at once.

Serves 4.

130 CALORIES PER SERVING: 5 G PROTEIN, .6 G FAT, 29 G CARBOHYDRATE; 63 MG SODIUM; 1 MG CHOLESTEROL.

PEAR SAUCE

Fruit sauces are known as coulis *in French. They became fashionable during the reign of nouvelle cuisine and remain so to this day. I like to make this sauce with fresh pears, but in a pinch you can use canned.*

2 ripe pears
1 tablespoon fresh lemon juice
2 strips lemon zest
1 cup water

2–3 tablespoons sugar (or to taste)
1 teaspoon cornstarch
1 tablespoon pear brandy or water

Peel, core, and dice the pears. Toss them with lemon juice to prevent browning. Combine the pears, zest, water, and sugar in a heavy saucepan. Simmer for 3 to 4 minutes, or until the pears are very soft.

Dissolve the cornstarch in the brandy and whisk it into the pears. Bring the mixture to a boil and remove the pan from the heat. Remove the zest and purée the pear mixture in a blender. Let cool to room temperature, then refrigerate until cold.

Makes 1½ cups.

14 CALORIES PER TABLESPOON: 0 G PROTEIN, 0 G FAT, 3 G CARBOHYDRATE; 0 MG SODIUM; 0 MG CHOLESTEROL.

GINGER FLOATING ISLAND WITH SHOCKING RED RASPBERRY SAUCE

....

Here's a modern twist on classic French île flottante, "floating island." The island is made by baking meringue in a soufflé dish. To lighten the recipe, I've replaced the traditional custard sauce with a colorful raspberry coulis. (A cranberry coulis is nice when cranberries are in season in the fall.)

FOR THE MOLD
1–2 teaspoons butter, melted (or vegetable oil spray)
2 tablespoons sugar

FOR THE MERINGUE
4 extra-large egg whites, at room temperature
1 tablespoon minced candied ginger
1 teaspoon grated fresh ginger
1 teaspoon vanilla extract
½ teaspoon cream of tartar

1 cup sugar
1 teaspoon freshly grated lemon zest

FOR THE SAUCE
3 cups fresh raspberries (or 1 12-ounce package frozen)
3–4 tablespoons confectioners' sugar (or to taste)
2 tablespoons fresh lemon juice (or to taste)

FOR THE GARNISH
1 cup fresh raspberries, or 2 ounces toasted, slivered almonds

To prepare the mold, brush the bottom and sides of a 5-cup soufflé dish or charlotte mold with melted butter and freeze for 5 minutes. Brush again with melted butter. (This technique is called double buttering, and it helps keep the meringue from sticking.) Alternatively, thoroughly coat the inside of the mold with vegetable oil spray. Sprinkle the inside of the mold with the 2 tablespoons sugar. Preheat the oven to 350 degrees F. Bring 1 quart water to a boil.

To make the meringue, combine the egg whites, candied ginger, fresh ginger, vanilla, and cream of tartar in the bowl of a mixer. Beat to soft peaks, starting at low speed and increasing to medium. Increase the speed to high, add ¼ cup sugar in a thin stream, and continue beating until the whites are firm and glossy.

Fold in the remaining sugar and the zest, using a rubber spatula. Work as gently as possible so

as not to deflate the whites. Spoon the meringue mixture into the soufflé dish. Place the dish in a roasting pan with ½" boiling water. Bake for 25 minutes, or until puffed and firm but not brown.

To make the sauce, purée the raspberries in a food processor, running the machine as little as possible so as not to crush the seeds. (Crushing the seeds will make the purée bitter.) Strain the puréed raspberries into a bowl and whisk in the confectioners' sugar and lemon juice.

Remove the floating island from the oven and let cool for 10 minutes. Invert it onto a round platter or shallow bowl, and let cool to room temperature. Just before serving, spoon the raspberry sauce around the floating island and garnish the top with raspberries or toasted almonds. Cut into wedges for serving.

Serves 4 to 5.

313 CALORIES PER SERVING: 5 G PROTEIN, 2 G FAT, 74 G CARBOHYDRATE; 96 MG SODIUM; 3 MG CHOLESTEROL.

Strawberry Tart with Lemon Lavender Cream

In this remake of a cholesterol-laden French classic, I replace the traditional puff pastry crust with phyllo dough. I lighten the crust by cutting the butter with olive oil and sprinkle bread crumbs between the layers to give them lift without fat. Lemon-flavored yogurt cheese replaces the traditional pastry cream. The lavender is a whimsical touch.

FOR THE FILLING
16 ounces nonfat yogurt
3–4 tablespoons sugar
2½ teaspoons freshly grated lemon zest
2 teaspoons Grand Marnier or other orange liqueur
1 teaspoon dried lavender

FOR THE CRUST
5 sheets phyllo dough (about ¼ pound)
1 tablespoon butter, melted
2 tablespoons olive or canola oil

3 tablespoons toasted bread crumbs
2 tablespoons sugar
¼ teaspoon ground cinnamon

FOR THE TOPPING
3–4 pints fresh strawberries (30 gorgeous berries)
¼ cup red currant jelly
1 tablespoon Grand Marnier or water (if needed)
1 tablespoon chopped pistachio nuts

To make the filling, drain the yogurt in a yogurt funnel (see Mail-Order Sources) or a cheesecloth-lined colander for 2 hours. Place the drained yogurt in a mixing bowl and whisk in the sugar, zest, Grand Marnier, and lavender.

To make the crust, lay the phyllo dough on a work surface and cover with a slightly damp dish towel. Combine the melted butter and oil in a small saucepan. Mix the bread crumbs, sugar, and cinnamon in a small bowl. Lightly brush a 10" round tart pan with removable sides or a 14-by-3" rectangular pan with the butter mixture. Preheat the oven to 400 degrees F.

Lay a sheet of phyllo dough in the pan. Brush with a little butter mixture and sprinkle with a spoonful of crumb mixture. Place another sheet of phyllo on top, brush with butter, and sprinkle with crumbs. Continue in this fashion until all 5 sheets of dough are used. Fold any overhang back into the crust to obtain neat edges. Line the crust with foil and fill it with dried beans.

(This holds the crust in shape as it bakes.)

Bake the crust for 6 to 8 minutes, or until the edges are lightly browned. Remove the foil and beans, and continue baking for 3 to 4 minutes, or until the whole crust is nicely browned. Transfer the pan to a wire rack to cool.

To make the topping, wash and stem the strawberries and blot dry on paper towels. Melt the currant jelly in a small saucepan over medium heat, adding Grand Marnier if needed to obtain a pourable glaze.

Just before serving, assemble the tart. Spoon the yogurt mixture into the crust. Arrange the strawberries on top. Brush the tops of the strawberries with the red currant glaze and sprinkle with pistachio nuts. Remove the sides of the tart pan and place the tart on a doily-lined platter. Cut the tart into slices or wedges for serving. (It's best to assemble the tart at the last minute so the crust doesn't become soggy.)

Serves 6 to 8.

284 CALORIES PER SERVING: 7 G PROTEIN, 8 G FAT, 49 G CARBOHYDRATE; 156 MG SODIUM; 6 MG CHOLESTEROL.

Strawberry Tart with Lemon Lavender Cream

GASCON CRÈME CARAMELS

Here's a low-fat version of another classic French dessert. To replace the richness of the egg yolks, I've added prunes soaked in Armagnac. You can substitute cognac or any other grape brandy.

⅓ cup Armagnac
6 pitted prunes
1 cup plus 3 tablespoons sugar
3 cups skim milk
1 vanilla bean, split

1 cinnamon stick
3 strips lemon zest (removed with a vegetable peeler)
6 egg whites (or 2 whole eggs and 3 whites), lightly beaten

Warm the Armagnac in a small saucepan. (Do not boil.) Add the prunes, cover the pan, and let soak for 30 minutes.

To make the caramel, combine ⅔ cup sugar with 3 tablespoons water in a heavy saucepan. Cook the mixture, covered, over high heat for 2 minutes. Uncover the pan and continue cooking until the sugar caramelizes (turns a deep golden brown). Pour the caramel into 6 ½-cup ramekins (or an 8" cake pan) and tilt to coat the bottoms and sides. (You may wish to wear heavy gloves during this procedure; molten caramel gives a terrible burn.)

Combine the milk, vanilla bean, cinnamon stick, and zest in the top of a double boiler and cook over low heat for 15 minutes. In a heatproof bowl, whisk together the egg whites and the remaining sugar. Strain the hot milk into the egg mixture, little by little, whisking constantly.

Bring 1 quart water to a boil. Preheat the oven to 350 degrees F.

Drain the prunes. (Save the Armagnac for another purpose. You can add it to the Nice Jewish Compote on page 200, for example.) Place 1 prune in the center of each ramekin (or arrange the prunes evenly around the cake pan). Strain the custard mixture on top, filling each ramekin to within ¼" of the top. Set the ramekins in a roasting pan with ½" boiling water. This is called a water bath, and it helps the flan cook at a moist, even heat.

Bake for 30 to 40 minutes, or until just set. (A skewer inserted in the center should come out clean. The cake pan will take slightly longer.) Remove the ramekins from the roasting pan and let cool to room temperature. Refrigerate for at least 6 hours, preferably overnight. (The recipe can be prepared up to 2 days ahead to this stage.)

Just before serving, run the tip of a paring knife around the inside of each ramekin. Place a dessert plate over the ramekin, invert, and give the ramekin a firm shake. Lift the ramekin, and the flans will slide right out. If using a cake pan, unmold it onto a platter and cut into wedges for serving.

Serves 6.

236 CALORIES PER SERVING: 8 G PROTEIN, 0 G FAT, 48 G CARBOHYDRATE; 119 MG SODIUM; 2 MG CHOLESTEROL.

It Shouldn't Be Like Pulling Teeth.

When you're ready to buy or sell your special home, we can make it so much easier for you. One call and you'll have a team of highly experienced professionals who know condominiums, luxury highrises, cluster and townhomes. We'll give you a full market update on the best opportunities available. And we'll give you a free Competitive Market Analysis. So call The Condo Store today and let our experience give you a beautiful smile.

EQUAL HOUSING OPPORTUNITY

TWO CONVENIENT LOCATIONS

BUCKHEAD:
2140 Peachtree Road NW, Suite 360
(404) 26-CONDO (262-6636)

NORTH ATLANTA:
1010 Huntcliff, Suite 1275
(770) 55-CONDO (552-6636)

http://www.condostore.com

Please disregard if your home is currently listed with another broker.

ATLANTA'S REAL ESTATE EXPERTS IN CONDOMINIUMS, LUXURY HIGHRISES, CLUSTER AND TOWNHOMES.

Bulk Rate
U.S. Postage
PAID
Permit No. 3396
Atlanta, GA

You Wouldn't Buy Jewels From A Dentist Just Because He Knows About Crowns.

So why use a real estate generalist for your special home?

THE Condo STORE

PUMPKIN FLAN

Here's a low-fat alternative to Thanksgiving pumpkin pie. The purist may wish to make the purée from scratch. To do so, bake a halved, seeded pumpkin, cut side down, on a lightly oiled baking sheet in a moderate oven for 1 hour, or until soft. Peel off the skin and purée the flesh in a food processor.

⅔ cup granulated sugar
2 cups pumpkin purée
¼ cup brown sugar (or to taste)
¼ cup molasses
2 teaspoons vanilla extract
2 teaspoons grated fresh ginger
1 teaspoon ground cinnamon

¼ teaspoon freshly grated nutmeg
⅛ teaspoon ground allspice
⅛ teaspoon ground cloves
6 egg whites (or 3 whites and 2 whole eggs), lightly beaten
1 cup skim milk or evaporated skim milk
2 tablespoons dark rum

To make the caramel, combine the granulated sugar with 3 tablespoons water in a heavy saucepan. Cook the mixture, covered, over high heat for 2 minutes. Uncover the pan and continue cooking until the sugar caramelizes (turns a deep golden brown). Pour the caramel into a 9" cake pan, gently swirling the pan to coat the bottom and sides with caramel. Work quickly, or the caramel will harden. (Take care not to let the molten caramel touch your skin.)

To make the filling, place the pumpkin in a large bowl and beat in the brown sugar, molasses, vanilla, and spices. Whisk in the egg whites, little by little, followed by the milk and rum. Pour this mixture into the caramel-lined pan.

Bring 1 quart water to a boil. Preheat the oven to 350 degrees F.

Set the cake pan in a roasting pan with ½" boiling water. (This is called a water bath, and it helps the flan cook at a moist, even heat.) Place the roasting pan in the oven and bake for 1 hour, or until set. (A skewer inserted in the center should come out clean.) Remove the flan from the roasting pan and let cool to room temperature. Refrigerate for at least 6 hours, preferably overnight.

To unmold the flan, run the tip of a paring knife around the inside of the pan. Place a large round platter over the pan, invert, and give the pan a firm shake. The flan should slide right out. Spoon the caramel sauce around the flan and serve at once.

Serves 8 to 10.

170 CALORIES PER SERVING: 4 G PROTEIN, 0 G FAT, 37 G CARBOHYDRATE; 64 MG SODIUM; 1 MG CHOLESTEROL.

LOW-FAT CHOCOLATE FONDUE

I always serve chocolate fondue at my Cook and Ski cooking classes at the Snowvillage Inn in New Hampshire. Despite its decadent reputation, it's really just a fresh fruit salad whose parts are dipped in chocolate sauce. To make the low-fat version, I substitute low-fat vanilla yogurt for the traditional heavy cream. You'd never know the difference!

2 bananas
2 apples or ripe pears
2 kiwis
juice of ½ lemon
2 oranges or tangerines

½ pound seedless red grapes
1 pint strawberries
½ cup nonfat vanilla yogurt
6 ounces semisweet chocolate
2 tablespoons rum or cognac

Peel the bananas, apples, and kiwis, and cut into bite-sized pieces. Sprinkle the banana and apple pieces with lemon juice to keep them from browning. Peel the oranges, break into segments, and carefully remove the seeds. Stem the grapes and hull the strawberries. Attractively arrange the fruit on a platter.

Combine the yogurt and chocolate in the top of a double boiler. Cook over low heat, whisking, until the chocolate is melted and the mixture is hot. Stir in the rum. Keep the chocolate warm over the double boiler until serving.

Serve the fondue warm but not hot. (Do not place it directly over the flame.) Invite guests to dip the fruit in the chocolate.

Serves 4.

448 CALORIES PER SERVING: 6 G PROTEIN, 13 G FAT, 85 G CARBOHYDRATE; 23 MG SODIUM; 1 MG CHOLESTEROL.

LOW-FAT CHOCOLATE PUDDING

*This creamy pudding is actually part of the next recipe (Low-Fat Chocolate Soufflé), but it's
so tasty (not to mention easy to make) that I decided to run it as a recipe in its own right.
Mexicans use cinnamon and vanilla in their hot chocolate as a counterpoint to the flavor
of the cocoa. If you use a fresh vanilla bean, you can rinse it off and use it again.*

⅓ cup unsweetened cocoa
⅓ cup sugar
1 tablespoon cornstarch
½ teaspoon ground cinnamon

⅛ teaspoon ground cloves
1 cup skim milk
½ vanilla bean, split (or 1 teaspoon vanilla
extract)

Combine the cocoa, sugar, cornstarch, cinnamon, and cloves in a bowl and whisk until smooth. Scald the milk with the vanilla bean in the top of a double boiler.

Whisk the scalded milk into the cocoa mixture in a thin stream. Return this mixture to a heavy saucepan and boil for 1 minute, whisking constantly. (Continuous whisking is important, or the milk will scorch.) Remove the pan from the heat and remove the vanilla bean. (If you're not using a vanilla bean, whisk in the vanilla extract at this point.)

Transfer the pudding to a bowl and press a piece of plastic wrap on top to prevent a skin from forming. Let cool to room temperature, then chill. Spoon into bowls for serving. For a decorative touch, top each pudding with a spoonful of sweetened Yogurt Cheese (page 241).

Serves 2.

Note: If you wish to serve 4, simply double the ingredients.

214 CALORIES PER SERVING: 7 G PROTEIN, 2 G FAT, 51 G CARBOHYDRATE; 73 MG SODIUM; 2 MG CHOLESTEROL.

LOW-FAT CHOCOLATE SOUFFLÉ

In my house, Valentine's Day isn't complete without a chocolate soufflé. It wasn't hard to create a low-fat version by eliminating the egg yolks and replacing the chocolate with unsweetened cocoa. Serve with Pear Sauce (page 202) on the side.

½ tablespoon butter, melted (or vegetable oil spray)
¼ cup sugar
Low-Fat Chocolate Pudding (page 209)

5 egg whites
½ teaspoon cream of tartar
confectioners' sugar

Brush the inside of a 5-cup soufflé dish with the melted butter (or spray with vegetable oil), taking special care to brush the inside rim. Freeze the dish for 5 minutes and brush it again. (This is called double buttering and helps prevent the soufflé from sticking as it rises.) Sprinkle the inside of the mold with ½ tablespoon of the sugar. Preheat the oven to 400 degrees F.

Prepare the Low-Fat Chocolate Pudding and keep it hot. Beat the egg whites at low speed for 20 seconds. Add the cream of tartar and gradually increase the mixer speed to high. Beat the whites to stiff peaks, adding the remaining sugar as the whites stiffen.

Stir ¼ of the whites into the hot pudding mixture to lighten it. Fold the pudding mixture into the remaining whites as gently as possible. Spoon the soufflé mixture into the dish. Smooth the top with a wet spatula. Run the tip of a paring knife around the inside edge of the dish to keep the rising soufflé from sticking.

Bake for 15 minutes, or until puffed and cooked to taste. (I like my soufflés a little runny in the center.) Dust the top with confectioners' sugar and serve at once.

Serves 4.

186 CALORIES PER SERVING: 8 G PROTEIN, 2 G FAT, 38 G CARBOHYDRATE; 120 MG SODIUM; 5 MG CHOLESTEROL.

REDUCED-FAT CHOCOLATE MOUSSE

This chocolate mousse is as rich and creamy as any I've tasted, but it contains not one gram of cholesterol and a reduced amount of fat. The secret is using Italian meringue to thicken and bind the mousse. The meringue has another advantage. Being cooked, it eliminates the risk of salmonella.

6 ounces semisweet chocolate, coarsely chopped
2 ounces unsweetened chocolate, coarsely chopped

FOR THE MERINGUE
1 cup sugar
6 egg whites
½ teaspoon cream of tartar

Place the semisweet and unsweetened chocolate in a large bowl over a pan of hot water and stir until melted. Let cool slightly.

To make the meringue, combine ¾ cup of the sugar and 3 tablespoons water in a heavy saucepan. Cook over high heat, covered, for 2 minutes. Uncover and cook the sugar to the softball stage (239 degrees F on a candy thermometer).

Meanwhile, beat the egg whites at low speed for 1 minute. Add the cream of tartar and beat until the mixture is frothy. Increase the speed to high and beat the egg whites until they form soft peaks. Add the remaining sugar and beat for 30 seconds, or until the whites are firm and glossy.

Pour the hot sugar mixture into the whites in a thin stream and continue beating until almost cool. Gently fold the melted chocolate into the meringue and let cool. Using a piping bag with a large star tip, pipe the chocolate mousse into ramekins or wine glasses.

Serves 8.

Note: For a more fanciful presentation, transfer 4 to 6 tablespoons meringue to a second piping bag fitted with a large star tip before incorporating the chocolate. Pipe rosettes of meringue on top of each serving. It will look exactly like whipped cream.

239 CALORIES PER SERVING: 5 G PROTEIN, 10 G FAT, 39 G CARBOHYDRATE; 42 MG SODIUM; 0 MG CHOLESTEROL.

PECAN DACQUOISE WITH CHOCOLATE MOUSSE

A dacquoise is a cake made with nut-flavored meringues. This one features Reduced-Fat Chocolate Mousse in place of the traditional buttercream icing. The recipe may seem complicated, but actually it's a series of simple steps. The meringues can be made a day ahead and stored in an airtight cookie tin. Be sure they are completely cool before storing. The pecans raise the fat content but even the most conscientious fat watchers are entitled to an occasional splurge.

2 teaspoons butter, melted (or vegetable oil spray)
1 tablespoon flour
1 cup pecans or other nuts
1 cup sugar
2 tablespoons cornstarch
6 egg whites
¼ teaspoon cream of tartar
Reduced-Fat Chocolate Mousse (page 212)
½ cup unsweetened cocoa

Line 2 or 3 large baking sheets with parchment paper and brush them with the melted butter (or spray with vegetable oil). Sprinkle the paper with flour, shaking off any excess. Cut an 8" circle out of cardboad and cover it with foil. Using a pot lid, trace three 8" circles on the paper-lined baking sheets, leaving 3" between each. (The meringues will spread.) Preheat the oven to 300 degrees F.

Lightly brown the pecans on a baking sheet in the oven. (This will take 4 to 6 minutes.) Grind them with ¾ cup of the sugar to a fine powder in a food processor. (Run the machine in brief spurts. Don't overgrind, or the nuts will become oily.) Mix in the cornstarch.

Beat the egg whites at low speed for 20 seconds. Add the cream of tartar and gradually increase the mixer speed to high. Beat the whites to stiff peaks, adding the remaining ¼ cup sugar as the whites stiffen. Gently fold in the nut mixture. Using a piping bag with a ½" round tip, pipe the meringue in circles on the parchment.

Bake the meringues for 50 to 60 minutes, or until firm. Let cool 3 minutes. Using a long spatula, gently loosen the meringues from the parchment paper. Place a plate or pot lid on top of the meringues and trim the edges with a sharp knife to form perfect circles. Transfer to a wire rack to cool.

Prepare the Reduced-Fat Chocolate Mousse.

To assemble the dacquoise, affix one of the meringue rounds to the cardboard with a dab of chocolate mousse. Spread half the mousse on top. Place the second round on top and spread most of the remaining mousse on it. Place the third round, smooth side up, on top. Mask the sides of the dacquoise with the leftover mousse. Sift the cocoa in a thick layer on top.

Let the dacquoise stand for at least 30 minutes before serving to soften the meringue. Cut into wedges and serve with espresso or a tall glass of milk.

Serves 8 to 10.

454 CALORIES PER SERVING: 9 G PROTEIN, 21 G FAT, 69 G CARBOHYDRATE; 116 MG SODIUM; 3 MG CHOLESTEROL.

CINNAMON ROSE ANGEL FOOD CAKE

This ethereal, uniquely American cake isn't difficult to make, but there are a few tricks to keep in mind. First, let the egg whites warm to room temperature before beating. Second, beat the whites to soft peaks only. You will need a 9" tube pan with removable sides for this recipe. Make sure it is completely free of grease. If in doubt, rewash and dry it. Rose water is available at Indian and Middle Eastern grocery stores and at many pharmacies.

1 cup plus 2 tablespoons cake flour (approximately)
1½ cups sugar
1 teaspoon ground cinnamon
¼ teaspoon salt
12 egg whites (about 1½ cups)
1 teaspoon cream of tartar
2 teaspoons rose water

Preheat the oven to 350 degrees F. Sift the cake flour onto a sheet of wax or parchment paper. Measure out 1 level cup (without packing the cup). Sift the sugar the same way and measure out 1½ cups. Combine the flour with ½ cup sugar and the cinnamon and salt. Sift three times.

Beat the egg whites at low speed for 1 minute. Add the cream of tartar and rose water, and beat until the mixture is frothy. Increase the mixer speed to high and beat the egg whites to soft peaks, adding the remaining 1 cup sugar in a thin stream. Do not overbeat. Sift ¼ cup of the flour mixture into the whites and fold in as gently as possible. Continue sifting and folding in the flour mixture, ¼ cup at a time, until all is used up.

Pour the batter into an ungreased 9" tube pan. Bake for 45 minutes without opening the oven door. To check the cake for doneness, press the top with your finger. The top should feel firm to the touch and spring back when you lift your finger. If necessary, cook the cake for 5 to 10 minutes more.

Remove the cake from the oven, invert, and let cool. (Many tube pans have leglike supports on the top to allow the air to circulate underneath when the cake is inverted. If your pan doesn't, invert it onto an upright bottle, with the neck of the bottle in the tube.) Let cool completely.

Gently run a sharp knife around the inside of the pan and around the tube to loosen the cake. Turn the cake out onto a platter. (You may need to give it a gentle shake.) Slice for serving.

Serves 10.

169 CALORIES PER SERVING: 5 G PROTEIN, 0 G FAT, 38 G CARBOHYDRATE; 120 MG SODIUM; 0 MG CHOLESTEROL.

TOFU CHEESECAKE WITH STRAWBERRY SAUCE

*The tofu cheesecake served at the Five Seasons restaurant in Boston is simply the best
I have ever tasted. What makes it so good is the addition of tahini (sesame paste),
white miso (fermented soybean paste), and umeboshi (Japanese pickled) plum
paste, which give the tofu the mildly fermented flavor of real cream cheese.*

FOR THE CRUST
1½ cups zwieback crumbs (1 6-ounce box)
1½ cups graham cracker crumbs (11 whole
   crackers)
3 tablespoons maple syrup
2 tablespoons apple cider
1 tablespoon canola oil

FOR THE FILLING
3 pounds tofu (preferably soft or medium),
   drained
½ cup soy milk
1¼ cups maple syrup
3 tablespoons tahini
1½ teaspoons freshly grated lemon zest
1 tablespoon vanilla extract

1½ teaspoons almond extract
1 rounded tablespoon white miso
1 rounded tablespoon umeboshi plum paste
2 tablespoons arrowroot powder or
   cornstarch
1 tablespoon Grand Marnier or other
   orange liqueur

FOR THE SAUCE
1 quart fresh strawberries, washed, hulled,
   and thinly sliced
¼–½ cup sugar, maple sugar, or maple
   syrup
½ cup fresh orange juice or water
2 teaspoons cornstarch dissolved in 1
   tablespoon water

Preheat the oven to 350 degrees F.

To make the crust, place the zwieback and graham cracker crumbs in a food processor. Work in the maple syrup, cider, and oil. Press the crumb mixture into the bottom and partway up the sides of a lightly oiled 10" springform pan. Bake for 10 minutes.

To make the filling, purée all the ingredients to a smooth paste in a blender or food processor. (You'll need to work in several batches.) Pour the filling over the crust. Bake for 50 to 60 minutes, or until the filling rises slightly and the top is lightly browned.

To make the sauce, combine the strawberries with ¼ cup sugar and the orange juice. Gently simmer for 4 to 6 minutes, or until the strawberries are soft but not mushy. Add more sugar to taste. Stir the dissolved cornstarch into the sauce and bring it to a boil. Remove the pan from the heat and let the mixture cool.

Let the cheesecake cool to room temperature, then refrigerate. Cut into wedges and serve with sauce.

Serves 10 to 12.

430 CALORIES PER SERVING: 15 G PROTEIN, 13 G FAT, 67 G CARBOHYDRATE; 237 MG SODIUM; 4 MG CHOLESTEROL.

ALMOND BISCOTTI
....

These hard, dry Italian cookies have taken the country by storm. This recipe comes from a friend and fellow food writer, Lucy Cooper, who lives in Fort Lauderdale, Florida.

2½ cups flour
½ cup yellow cornmeal
1 cup sugar
2 teaspoons baking powder
¼ teaspoon salt
3 egg whites, lightly beaten

¼ cup canola oil
1 teaspoon almond extract
finely grated zest of 1 lemon
finely grated zest of 1 orange
¼–½ cup dry white wine

Preheat the oven to 350 degrees F. Combine the flour, cornmeal, sugar, baking powder, and salt in a large bowl and whisk to mix. In another large bowl, combine the egg whites, oil, almond extract, zests, and ¼ cup of the wine. Whisk to mix.

Gradually stir the flour mixture into the wine mixture, adding wine as necessary to obtain a soft, pliable dough. Divide the dough in two and roll each half between your hands into a 12" log. Place the logs on a baking sheet lined with parchment paper, leaving 5" between them. Gently flatten the logs with your fingertips to form a ½"-thick rectangle.

Bake for 35 to 40 minutes, or until the tops are firm to the touch. Remove from the oven and let cool for 3 minutes.

Using a serrated knife, cut each log on the diagonal into ½" slices. Place the slices, cut side down, on the baking sheet and bake for 10 to 15 minutes, or until golden brown. Turn the biscotti and bake for 10 to 15 minutes more.

Completely cool the biscotti on a wire rack and store in an airtight container. The traditional way to eat biscotti is to dip them in coffee or wine, but I like to munch them straight.

Makes 40 biscotti.

72 CALORIES PER BISCOTTI: 1 G PROTEIN, 1 G FAT, 13 G CARBOHYDRATE; 34 MG SODIUM; 0 MG CHOLESTEROL.

CHAMOMILE GRANITA

Granitas are the world's simplest frozen dessert, consisting of frozen flavored water or wine. The name comes from the Italian granita, meaning "small seed," a description of the tiny ice crystals that give this dessert its crunch. Cool, light, and refreshing, granitas are perfect for warm weather. This recipe is from my assistant Didi Emmons.

2¼ cups water
¼ cup loose chamomile tea (or 4 tea bags)

¼ cup fresh lemon juice (or to taste)
¼ cup honey (or to taste)

Bring the water to a boil and remove the pan from the heat. Add the tea and let steep for 5 minutes. Strain into a bowl and stir in the lemon juice and honey to taste.

Place the bowl in the freezer for 6 to 8 hours.

Scrape the mixture 2 or 3 times with a fork as it freezes. Just before serving, scrape the mixture again with a fork to obtain loose ice crystals. Serve in chilled wine glasses.

Serves 4 to 6.

86 CALORIES PER SERVING: 0 G PROTEIN, 0 G FAT, 23 G CARBOHYDRATE; 3 MG SODIUM; 0 MG CHOLESTEROL.

EARL GREY TEA SORBET

This unusual sorbet is a great summer refresher. I like to think of it as a really icy iced tea. Earl Grey owes its distinct fragrance to the oil of the bergamot flower.

4 tablespoons loose Earl Grey tea (or 4 tea bags)
1 quart boiling water

1 cup sugar
1 cup fresh lemon juice

Steep the tea in the boiling water for 10 minutes. Strain into a saucepan and add the sugar. Boil the mixture for 8 to 10 minutes, or until thick and syrupy. Let cool, then stir in the lemon juice.

Freeze the mixture in an ice cream machine, following the instructions for your particular machine. Serve the sorbet in chilled teacups or wine glasses.

Serves 6 to 8.

132 CALORIES PER SERVING: 0 G PROTEIN, 0 G FAT, 36 G CARBOHYDRATE; 5 MG SODIUM; 0 MG CHOLESTEROL.

BASIL SORBET

Try this offbeat sorbet when you're tired of raspberry or lemon. The recipe will also work with tarragon, mint, rosemary, or lemon verbena. The terms sorbet *and* sherbet *come from the Turkish word* sorpa, *"a refreshing drink."*

1 bunch basil
4–6 lemons

1½ cups sugar
3 cups water

Stem and wash the basil. Set aside 8 small sprigs for garnish. Lightly bruise the remaining leaves by pounding them with the back of a spoon. Remove the zest of 1 lemon with a vegetable peeler. Juice the lemons. (There should be about 1 cup juice.)

Combine the basil, zest, sugar, and water in a heavy saucepan and bring to a boil. Reduce the heat and simmer for 8 to 10 minutes, or until thick and syrupy. Strain the syrup into a bowl, pressing the leaves with the back of the spoon to extract the juices. Let cool to room temperature, then stir in the lemon juice.

Freeze the mixture in an ice cream machine, following the instructions for your particular machine. Serve in chilled martini glasses, garnishing each with a sprig of basil.

Serves 8.

99 CALORIES PER SERVING: 0 G PROTEIN, 0 G FAT, 27 G CARBOHYDRATE; 5 MG SODIUM; 0 MG CHOLESTEROL.

....

BEVERAGES

....

MEXICAN HOT CHOCOLATE
....

Mexicans flavor their hot chocolate with cinnamon, cloves, and vanilla, a practice already popular when Cortès visited the court of Montezuma in the 16th century. Thanks to these spices, you won't miss the richness of whole milk. For a prettier presentation, sprinkle cinnamon or grate a little chocolate on top.

4 cups skim or 1 percent milk
⅓ cup unsweetened cocoa
⅓ cup sugar (or to taste)
1 teaspoon ground cinnamon

⅛ teaspoon ground cloves
1 vanilla bean, split (or 2 teaspoons vanilla extract)

Combine all the ingredients (except the vanilla extract, if using) in a heavy saucepan. Slowly bring the mixture to a boil, whisking constantly. Remove the vanilla bean (you can rinse it off and reuse it) and pour the hot chocolate into mugs. (If using vanilla extract, add it to the hot chocolate after removing the pan from the heat.)

Serves 4.

188 CALORIES PER SERVING: 10 G PROTEIN, 4 G FAT, 28 G CARBOHYDRATE; 125 MG SODIUM; 10 MG CHOLESTEROL.

THAI FRUIT SHAKE

This refreshing drink can be found at street stalls and open-air markets throughout Southeast Asia. Because of the hot climate and general lack of refrigeration, sweetened condensed milk is the dairy product of choice. Similar shakes can be made with virtually any other fruit.

1 cup diced watermelon
1 ripe banana, peeled and diced
1 cup diced fresh pineapple
1 tablespoon fresh lime juice (or to taste)

2 tablespoons sugar (or to taste)
2 tablespoons sweetened condensed milk
2 cups crushed ice

Combine all the ingredients in a blender and blend until smooth. Correct the flavoring, adding lime juice and sugar to taste.

Serves 2.

225 CALORIES PER SERVING: 3 G PROTEIN, 3 G FAT, 52 G CARBOHYDRATE; 27 MG SODIUM; 7 MG CHOLESTEROL.

BANANA SMOOTHIE

Made with yogurt, this drink is both refreshing and nourishing. To tell when a banana is ripe, look for tiny brown spots, called sugar spots, on the peel. If you use a banana slice for garnish, sprinkle it with lime juice to prevent browning.

1 ripe banana
½ cup nonfat yogurt
1 tablespoon sugar (or to taste)
1 tablespoon banana liqueur (optional)

1 cup crushed ice
1 teaspoon fresh lime juice
lime wedge or banana slice, for garnish

Combine the first 6 ingredients in a blender and blend until smooth.
Pour the smoothie into a large glass and garnish with a lime wedge or banana slice.

Serves 1.

215 CALORIES PER SERVING: 8 G PROTEIN, 1 G FAT, 48 G CARBOHYDRATE; 88 MG SODIUM; 2 MG CHOLESTEROL.

Thai Fruit Shake, Banana Smoothie

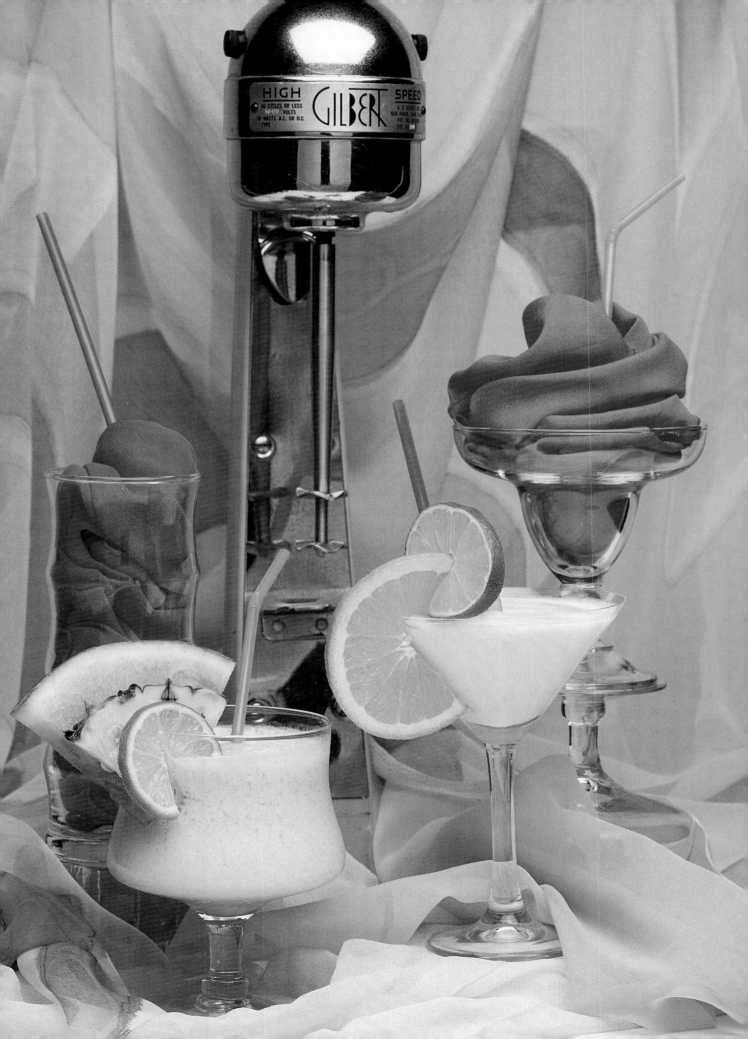

SOURPUSS LEMONADE

Nothing goes to waste in this lemonade, which uses both the sour juice and the fragrant zest of the lemon. When choosing lemons, avoid fruits with knobby ends (they tend to be dry) and those with a greenish tinge (they tend to be sour, even for lemons).

**4–6 lemons (1 cup juice), plus 1 lemon
for garnish**
⅓ cup sugar (or to taste)

4 cups water
ice

Wash the lemons and remove the zest of all but the lemon for garnish with a vegetable peeler. (Be sure to take only the yellow outer rind, not the bitter white pith beneath it.) Combine the zest, sugar, and 1 cup of the water in a saucepan. Simmer the mixture for 10 minutes. Strain it into a heat-proof pitcher and let cool.

Cut the zested lemons in half and extract the juice. Stir it and the remaining water into the lemon syrup. Correct the flavoring, adding sugar and lemon juice to taste.

Serve the lemonade in tall glasses with ice. Cut the remaining lemon into wedges or slices for garnish. For a fancier presentation, rub the rim of each glass with cut lemon and dip it in sugar.

Serves 4.

75 CALORIES PER SERVING: 0 G PROTEIN, 0 G FAT, 21 G CARBOHYDRATE; 8 MG SODIUM; 0 MG CHOLESTEROL.

CRANBERRY-PEACH PUNCH

This drink was invented by my friend Janet Meakin, a longtime resident of Norway. Instead of cranberry juice, she uses lingonberry juice, which can be found in health food stores and gourmet shops. (The lingonberry is a tiny European cousin of the cranberry.) For tea, I like to use Celestial Seasonings Country Peach Spice Tea.

2½ cups water
2 cinnamon sticks
2 bags peach-flavored tea

1 tablespoon fresh lime juice
1 tablespoon honey (or to taste)
2 cups cranberry or lingonberry juice

Bring the water to a boil in a large pan with the cinnamon sticks and tea bags. Remove the pan from the heat and let the tea steep for 10 minutes. Remove the tea bags and cinnamon sticks. Stir in the lime juice, honey, and cranberry juice. Transfer the mixture to a pitcher and chill.

Serves 4.

91 CALORIES PER SERVING: 0 G PROTEIN, 0 G FAT, 23 G CARBOHYDRATE; 7 MG SODIUM; 0 MG CHOLESTEROL.

MINT FIZZ

This drink is a booze-free twist on a classic cocktail made with gin. The mint and lemon flavors are so intense that you won't miss the alcohol.

3 or 4 lemons
¼ cup fresh mint leaves, plus 4 sprigs for garnish
⅓ cup sugar

1 egg white
3½ cups sparkling water
2 cups crushed ice

Juice the lemons. (There should be ¾ cup juice.) Wash and stem the mint leaves. Combine the lemon juice, mint leaves, sugar, and egg white in a blender. Blend at high speed for 1 minute.

Add the sparkling water and ice. Blend until the mixture is smooth. Pour into glasses and garnish with mint sprigs.

Serves 4.

76 CALORIES PER SERVING: 1 G PROTEIN, 0 G FAT, 20 G CARBOHYDRATE; 59 MG SODIUM; 0 MG CHOLESTEROL.

MINTED LIMEADE

This drink combines the cooling properties of fresh mint with the thirst-quenching tartness of lime. It's more refreshing than all the beer at Budweiser. Pounding the lime zest and mint with the sugar helps release the fragrant oils.

6–8 limes (1 cup juice)
15 fresh mint leaves, plus 4 sprigs for garnish
⅓–½ cup sugar (or to taste)

4 cups water
ice

Using a vegetable peeler, remove the zest from 3 of the limes. Cut all the limes in half and extract the juice. Combine the zest, mint leaves, and sugar in a mortar or sturdy bowl, and crush with a pestle or the end of a rolling pin to release the aromatic oils.

Place the sugar mixture in a pitcher and whisk in the lime juice and water. Whisk until all the sugar crystals are dissolved. Correct the flavoring, adding sugar to taste. The limeade can be served right away, but the flavor will improve if it stands for 15 minutes. To serve, strain the limeade into ice-filled glasses, garnishing each with mint sprigs.

Serves 4.

76 CALORIES PER SERVING: 0 G PROTEIN, 0 G FAT, 21 G CARBOHYDRATE; 8 MG SODIUM; 0 MG CHOLESTEROL.

COOK'S NOTES

A guide to foods, flavors, basic recipes, and techniques

ANISEED
A small brown seed with a sweet licorice flavor, aniseed is widely used in European cooking. It is available at Italian markets and in the spice section of most supermarkets.

ARUGULA
A member of the radish family, this peppery green can liven up an otherwise dull green salad. Once rare, it's now available at most supermarkets.

BALSAMIC VINEGAR
This is a sweet, intensely flavored vinegar from the province of Emilia-Romagna in north central Italy. Unlike most other vinegars, balsamic vinegar is made from must (fresh or partially fermented grape juice), not wine. This gives it a fruity sweetness beloved by chefs on both sides of the Atlantic. The best balsamic vinegar comes from the Reggio Emilia district, where it's aged in farmhouse attics for years (often decades) in a succession of fruit-wood casks. Only vinegars made this way and aged for at least 12 years are allowed to be called *tradizionale*. Expect to pay dearly for them—up to $20 an ounce! Vinegar makers in the city of Modena make a respectable commercial-grade balsamic vinegar aged for 3 years that's fine for everyday use.

BASMATI RICE
Grown in the foothills of the Himalayas, this slender grain has a distinctly aromatic nutty, milky flavor. The rice is aged in storage bins for several years to develop the flavor; this accounts for its high price. True basmati is recognizable by its slim, slightly curved grains, which taper to sharp points. It also has the unusual property of doubling in length, not width, when cooked. Several basmati-type rices are grown in North America, including Texamati from Texas.

BAY LEAF
Used to crown poets in ancient Greece, bay leaves are an essential flavoring in European, North American, and Indian cooking. Never crumble bay leaves into a dish; their sharp edges make them difficult to digest. Tie them up in cheesecloth along with other herbs, leave them whole to flavor soups and stews and remove just before serving, or use ground bay leaves.

For pictorial reference, see pages 242–245.

Basic Chicken Stock (page 237)

BEANS

Beans are good for you. (They're loaded with protein, vitamins, and minerals, and they've been shown to help reduce everything from cholesterol levels to the risk of cancer.) Dried beans cooked from scratch are better for you—and better tasting—than canned beans. Home-cooked beans have a firmer consistency and richer flavor. They're also lower in sodium, as most canned beans contain a staggering amount of salt.

• Beans should be soaked in water to cover for 4 to 6 hours prior to cooking. The soaking helps shorten the cooking time and eliminate some of the complex sugars (oligosaccharides) that cause flatulence. (Changing the soaking water a few times helps remedy the flatulence problem further.) Use 3 to 4 times as much water as beans.

Lentils and split peas don't need to be soaked before cooking.

• Salt should be added only when the beans are soft. Otherwise, it toughens the skins. Acidic ingredients such as vinegar and tomatoes have a similar effect. Add them only when the beans are soft.

• The cooking time for beans varies widely, from 30 minutes for lentils to 3 hours for fava beans. The time can be shortened dramatically in a pressure cooker. To test a bean for doneness, squeeze it between your thumb and forefinger. It should crush easily. One of my pet peeves as a restaurant critic is being served undercooked beans.

COOKED BEANS

*Here's my basic recipe for cooking beans. One cup dried beans
will cook up to about 2½ cups—enough to serve 4.*

1 cup dried beans
1 bay leaf
1 onion, quartered

1 whole clove
1 carrot, cut into 1" pieces
salt and freshly ground black pepper

Pick through the beans, removing any pebbles or debris. Rinse the beans thoroughly and place them in a large bowl with 4 cups cold water. Soak the beans for 4 to 6 hours, changing the water 2 or 3 times.

Pour off the soaking liquid and place the beans in cold water to cover by at least 3 inches. Pin

the bay leaf to one of the onion quarters with the clove. Add the onion quarters and carrot to the beans and gradually bring to a boil.

Cook the beans at a brisk simmer for ½ to 1 hour, or until soft, adding the salt and pepper during the last 5 minutes. Drain the beans and refresh under cold water. Discard the vegetables.

CARDAMOM

This greenish tan, coffee bean–sized pod has a perfumed scent and haunting flavor that endears it to cooks from India to the Middle East. (The latter use it to flavor Arabic coffee.) Cardamom is sold in 3 forms: whole pods, the hard black seeds found inside the pod, and powdered. Cardamom is available at most supermarkets but is quite expensive. For the best price, buy it in bulk from a Middle Eastern or Indian grocery store. At the latter, you'll also find black cardamom, which has a smoky flavor and comes in a black pod the size of a plum pit.

CHEESE

Because of its high saturated-fat content, I don't use much cheese in this book. The notable exception is the Italian grating cheese Parmigiano Reggiano, made from partially skimmed cow's milk. The lengthy aging process gives this cheese an intense flavor, so a little goes a long way.

This cheese has spawned numerous imitators. While there are some tasty Parmesan-style cheeses, none has the dictinction of the Italian original. For the best results, make every effort to use the real Parmigiano Reggiano. It comes from strictly delimited regions in Italy, where it is made following a time-honored tradition and submitted to rigorous quality control. To recognize the real McCoy, look for the words *Parmigiano Reggiano* stamped into the rind.

CHILI PASTE/SAUCE

The wide distribution of this condiment attests to its popularity. Every nation in Asia has one: Chinese hot bean paste, Thai chili paste, Indonesian sambal ulek, and Vietnamese hot sauce (chili garlic sauce). The basic ingredients are chili peppers, salt, and garlic. Chinese hot bean paste is made with fermented soybeans. Another Chinese condiment is chili purée with garlic. My favorite—Thai chili paste—often contains fresh basil. (The Thais also make a hot sauce called *sriracha*, which tastes like radioactive ketchup.) Indonesian sambal ulek is a fiery paste of chilies, garlic, and salt. Vietnamese hot sauce is a piquant mixture of bright red chilies and vinegar. The flavor of each is quite different, so try to use the one called for in a particular recipe. If you can't find the type you need, substitute one of the others rather than do entirely without.

CHILI PEPPERS

The last decade has witnessed the spontaneous combustion of North America. Chili peppers, once regarded with suspicion if not downright terror, have become mainstays of American cooking. As our palates have become emboldened, we have realized that there's more to chili peppers than hotness. Each pepper has a distinctive flavor, from the smoky sting of a chipotle to the bitter-chocolate flavor of an ancho chili.

The hottest part of any chili is the seeds. Since people have widely varying tolerances for chilies (I've been accused of having an asbestos tongue), I've tried to give a range of chilies called for in a particular recipe, and I suggest omitting the seeds. *If you like really spicy food, leave the seeds in and increase the number of chilies.*

Here's a guide to some of the more common chilies in today's culinary arsenal. Most of the fresh chilies mentioned below can be found in the produce section of major supermarkets.

- **Ancho:** A dried poblano chili 3 to 4" long, 2 to 3" wide, and dark red to almost black in color. It is sweet, a little bitter, and moderately hot. There's something about it that reminds me of unsweetened chocolate.

- **Chinese Dried:** Small dried red chili in the cayenne family. Sold at Asian markets, they're used extensively in Sichuan cooking.

(continued)

Chili Peppers *(continued)*

• **Chipotle:** Smoked jalapeño chilies, chipotles are often sold canned in a spicy sour orange sauce. You can also buy them dried. Look for chipotles at Mexican markets and gourmet shops.

• **Jalapeño:** This bullet-shaped pepper is our most readily available chili, sold at supermarkets as well as specialty shops. Despite its reputation, the jalapeño is relatively mild as chilies go. The heat of a chili is measured in units called Scovilles. Jalapeños ring in at about 5,000 Scovilles. Compare that to the 200,000 Scovilles of the scotch bonnet chili!

• **Pasilla:** Often confused with anchos, which have a similar flavor. Pasilla chilies make great chili powders and moles.

• **Poblano:** A large (4 to 6" long, 2 to 3" wide), dark green, tapered chili often used for stuffing. Similar in flavor to a green bell pepper, but hotter and more aromatic. If unavailable, you can use green bell peppers mixed with minced jalapeños.

• **Scotch Bonnet:** Red, orange, yellow, or green, the scotch bonnet is about an inch long and shaped vaguely like a Highlander's bonnet. There's nothing about its handsomely crinkled exterior to suggest its tongue-torturing heat. Scotch bonnets and their Mexican cousins, *habañeros*, are the world's hottest chilies—50 times hotter than jalapeños! The tiniest taste of a raw one is like biting a high-voltage cable. Widely used in the Caribbean, scotch bonnets can be found at West Indian markets and at an increasing number of supermarkets.

• **Serrano:** Literally, "mountain chili." A thin, tapered, bright green chili, smaller and slightly hotter than a jalapeño. I use the two interchangeably.

• **Thai:** There are two Thai peppers: the short (1" long), slender, bumpy *prik kee nu* (literally "mouse dropping") and the longer (2 to 3"), slightly milder, horn-shaped *prik chee far*. Both are members of the cayenne family and are exceedingly hot. The shorter Thai peppers are often called bird peppers. Look for them at Asian markets, or use jalapeños or serranos instead.

CILANTRO

This pungent, aromatic herb turns up in everything from Thai curries to Mexican salsas. Also known as Chinese parsley, cilantro is the leafy part of the coriander plant. The plant's roots are used in Southeast Asian cooking. The seeds (see description below) are an ingredient in corned beef and kosher-style pickles. Cilantro can be found at Asian, Indian, and Hispanic markets; specialty greengrocers; and an increasing number of supermarkets. There is no substitute for the fresh herb, and it doesn't dry particularly well. Nonetheless, fresh mint can be substituted in many recipes. Cilantro is one of those flavorings people either love or hate. If the herb tastes like soap to you, you may be mildy allergic to it.

CINNAMON STICK

Most spices are seedpods; cinnamon is the bark of a tropical tree. What often passes for cinnamon in this country is actually its close cousin, cassia. Whole cinnamon sticks have a more subtle and pleasing flavor than powdered cinnamon. To save money, buy them in bulk at Hispanic or Indian markets.

CORIANDER SEED

This small, round, ridged, highly aromatic seed is a primary ingredient in pickling spice. Coriander seeds are a mainstay in Indian cooking. The leaf of the plant, cilantro (see description above), is a delicacy in its own right. Look for coriander seeds in the supermarket spice rack.

CUMIN

A small, crescent-shaped seed with an earthy, musky flavor, cumin is widely used in Cuban, Mexican, Middle Eastern, and Indian cooking. It is generally sold ground at the supermarket. Buy it in bulk at Hispanic or Indian markets.

EGGS

Eggs are among the worst fat offenders. Fortunately, there are 2 sides to an egg: the yolk and the white. Yolks give custards their solid but soft consistency, but whites also have the ability to set custards and other creamy desserts—without the fat. (An egg white is almost pure protein.)

• Egg whites are drier than yolks, so you may wish to add 1 teaspoon or so of water or oil per white for extra moistness.

• When separating egg whites, do so 1 at a time, using 3 bowls. (The yolks go into 1 bowl, the whites in the other 2.) Check to make certain each white is yolk-free, then add it to the 3rd bowl. There's nothing worse than having 11 clean whites for an angel food cake, then ruining the whole batch with yolk from the 12th.

• To use up egg yolks, feed them to your dog or cat, add them to your favorite shampoo, or make tempera paint.

FENNEL SEED

Elongated, greenish tan seeds with a sweet, anise-like flavor, fennel seeds are the principal flavoring in Italian sweet sausage. (They are also a key ingredient in birdseed!)

FISH SAUCE

A salty, clear brown condiment made from pickled anchovies, fish sauce is used in Southeast Asia the way soy sauce is in China and Japan. Known as *nam pla* in Thai and *nuoc mam* in Vietnamese, it serves as both a cooking ingredient and a table sauce. The strong, cheesy aroma can be off-putting, but the flavor quickly becomes addictive. Fish sauce is available at Asian markets and in the Oriental food section in most supermarkets. The best grades are sold in glass bottles (avoid those in square plastic bottles); good brands include Flying Lion, Three Crabs, and Squid Brand.

GALANGAL

Used widely in Southeast Asian cooking, this looks like its cousin, ginger, but features zebralike markings on its skin. Galangal has the peppery hotness of ginger but not the sweetness. If you live in a city with a large Southeast Asian population, you may be able to find it fresh or frozen at a Thai or Vietnamese market. Dried galangal is available at Asian markets and many gourmet shops. Ginger makes an acceptable substitute.

GARLIC

The recipes in this book call for a LOT of fresh garlic. I prefer fresh, whole-clove garlic to the minced, oil-packed garlic sold at the supermarket for 2 reasons: it has a superior flavor, and it's free of preservatives and fat.

• To peel a clove of garlic, smash it lightly with the side of a chopping knife or cleaver. This loosens the skin so you can slip it off.

• To mince garlic, cut each clove widthwise into ¼" slices. Stand these slices upright and smash them with the side of a chopping knife or cleaver. (Be sure the knife handle extends over the edge of the cutting board.) The garlic will disintegrate into tiny pieces.

• One average-sized garlic clove makes about 1 teaspoon minced.

GINGER

Ginger is one of the cornerstones of Asian cooking. It's hard to think of a savory Chinese dish without it. You'll need a lot of fresh ginger for the recipes in this book. When buying ginger, choose hands (as whole gingers are called) that are firm, plump, and heavy. Avoid any that look shriveled, moldy, or dried up.

• Peel the ginger with a paring knife. (Some chefs omit this step, but I like my ginger peeled.) Using a sharp knife or cleaver, thinly slice the ginger across the grain. Pile the slices 3 or 4 high and cut them into thin slivers. Turn the knife 90 degrees and cut into a fine mince.

• A walnut-sized piece of fresh ginger makes about 2 tablespoons minced.

HERBS

Fresh herbs are a cornerstone of my high-flavor, low-fat cooking. The emphasis here is on fresh. If fresh tarragon is unavailable, I'm more likely to substitute fresh basil or flat-leaf parsley than to use dried tarragon. Fresh herbs aren't inexpensive, but when stored properly, they'll keep for a week to 10 days.

Wrap the herbs in a paper towel and moisten with cold water. Place them in an unsealed plastic bag (the unsealed bag lets the herbs breathe), and store the bag in the refrigerator.

Fresh herbs may not be available at certain times of the year in some parts of the country. Dried oregano, basil, summer savory, rosemary, and mint have almost as much flavor as fresh (albeit a different flavor). Generally, substitute 1 to 2 teaspoons dried herbs for 1 tablespoon fresh.

If you don't have fresh or dried mint, open a mint tea bag.

Cilantro, chervil, and tarragon lose their flavor when dried. Use fresh mint or even flat-leaf parsley instead. A great way to pep up any dried herb is to chop it with a little fresh parsley or scallion.

HOT BEAN PASTE

This spicy condiment is made with chilies, soybeans, and spices. Look for it in Chinese markets and gourmet shops. There are several possible substitutes: Chinese chili garlic sauce (which contains vinegar); Thai chili paste (which contains basil and garlic); Vietnamese hot sauce (a loose red purée of chilies, garlic, and salt); and Indonesian sambal ulek.

JERUSALEM ARTICHOKE

Also known as sunchokes, these small, lumpy tubers are members of the sunflower family. The name "Jerusalem" is a corruption of the Italian word for sunflower—*girasol*. Their white flesh is deliciously crisp, with an earthy flavor that hints at artichoke. When buying them, choose the largest tubers with the fewest possible knobby protuberances, since these will be the easiest to peel.

LEMONGRASS

Another Southeast Asian gift to contemporary American cooking, lemongrass has a haunting aroma and delicate citrus flavor that have endeared it to Eastern and Western chefs alike. At first glance, lemongrass looks like a large, dry scallion with a bulbous base tapering to sharply pointed leaves. The top ⅔ of the fibrous stalks are generally discarded, as are the outside leaves covering the base and the root. The remaining core has a mild lemon flavor that goes well with seafood, chicken, and beef. Fresh lemongrass can be found at Asian markets and an increasing number of upscale supermarkets. Dried lemongrass can be found at most natural food stores. There's no equal substitute, but fresh lemon zest makes an acceptable stand-in.

MACE

The lacy membrane surrounding a nutmeg, mace is sold powdered and in blades (twisted orange-tan chips). It's a little sweeter than nutmeg, but the two are interchangeable.

MILK

Skim milk works in virtually any recipe calling for whole milk, provided you bolster the flavor in some way (using herbs, condiments, or puréed vegetables). Skim milk burns easily when cooked. When possible, heat it in a double boiler. If you cook it over direct heat, whisk constantly to prevent it from scorching.

MUSTARD SEED

These tiny round seeds are ground or crushed to make mustard. There are 3 types: white, brown, and black, listed in ascending order of hotness. White and brown mustard seeds are used to make mustard (the condiment); black mustard seeds are a common ingredient in Indian cooking.

NUTMEG

An aromatic, brown, finely veined nut the shape and size of your thumbprint, nutmeg is prized for its unique flavor and fragrant, musky aroma that hints at cinnamon and vanilla. Freshly grated nutmeg has a much more intense flavor than the ground spice.

OLIVE OIL

Medieval alchemists hunted in vain for the elixer of life, but modern cooks have no farther to go than their local supermarket or gourmet shop. Olive oil is my preferred fat for cooking because, in addition to its nutritional value and broad culinary applications, it has a wonderful taste.

There are 3 grades of olive oil: extra-virgin, virgin, and olive oil. The first is the best. Technically speaking, extra-virgin olive oil has an acidity (oleic-free fatty acid content) of 1 percent or less. Practically speaking, this means it's made with the choicest olives, which are pressed in a machine designed to minimize heat (which denatures the flavor of the oil). In the past 10 years, extra-virgin olive oil has inspired the sort of connoisseurship once reserved for wine. Italy, France, Spain, and California all make wonderful oils—some of them even dated with the vintage, like wine. Each oil has its own character, so I hesitate to recommend a single brand. Half the fun is discovering your own favorite.

Virgin olive oil, which is seldom seen in North America, contains 1 to 3 percent acidity and is less expensive than extra-virgin. I prefer to spend a few dollars more for the extra-virgin olive oil.

Olive oil, sometimes called pure olive oil, is a highly refined oil that, for reasons of excess acidity or a poor flavor, can't be sold in its natural state. After refining, the oil has less than 1.5 percent acidity. Often the manufacturers add virgin oil to bolster the flavor. Compared to extra-virgin, regular olive oil seems bland—even tasteless—but it's considerably less expensive, and it does have the health benefits of all monounsaturated oils. I strongly recommend that you use extra-virgin olive oil in salads and dishes where taste is important; use regular olive oil for cooking.

OYSTER SAUCE

This is a salty brown sauce flavored with oysters and used extensively in Cantonese cooking. Look for it at Asian markets and in the exotic food section of most supermarkets.

RICE STICKS

These translucent white noodles are made from rice flour and water. Some are as slender as vermicelli, others as wide as pappardelle. Once available only in Asian markets, rice sticks can be found today in gourmet shops and most large supermarkets. Soak the rice sticks in cold water to cover for 30 minutes, or until they are pliable. Drain and cook in boiling water for 20 seconds, or until tender. Asians like to eat these noodles long, enjoying each bite with a slurping sound. North American cooks may choose to cut the cooked noodles with scissors before serving.

ROSE WATER

A perfumed extract of rose petals, rose water is used in many Middle Eastern and Indian desserts. Look for it at Middle Eastern, Indian, and Armenian grocery stores, as well as at some pharmacies and cosmetic stores.

SAFFRON

Botanically speaking, saffron is the fragrant, rust-colored stigma of a crocus grown in southern Spain. Nicknamed "the herb of the sun," it's an essential ingredient in sunbelt cuisines from the Mediterranean to India. Seventy thousand flowers are needed to make a single pound of saffron (each must be processed by hand), which accounts for its high price. Always buy saffron threads, not powder (the latter is easier to adulterate), preferably in small quantities in tiny glass tubes. Tightly sealed and stored away from bright light, saffron will keep for several months. If it lacks an intense aroma when you open the bottle, it's past its prime. To activate saffron, soak the threads you'll need for a recipe in 1 tablespoon of hot water.

SALTED BLACK BEANS

Salted and fermented black soybeans are used by the Chinese as a flavoring for steamed dishes and stir-fries. The aging process gives them a tangy, salty, almost cheesy flavor. They keep almost indefinitely, and a little goes a long way. Contrary to the advice of many cookbooks, I don't rinse black beans before using. (Why dilute the flavor?) Salted black beans are generally sold in plastic bags at Asian markets.

SESAME OIL

This dark and very flavorful oil is extracted from roasted sesame seeds and used extensively in Japanese, Chinese, and Korean cooking. One good brand is Kadoya from Japan. Look for it at Asian markets and natural food stores. Steer clear of domestic sesame oils, most of which lack the intense flavor of the Asian brands.

SICHUAN PEPPERCORNS

Native to China, Sichuan peppercorns are rust-colored with hair-thin stems and open ends. They're not in the pepper family, however, and they aren't particularly hot. Endowed with a clean, woodsy flavor, Sichuan peppercorns go especially well with poultry. Look for them at Asian markets and gourmet shops.

SOUR ORANGES

If you live in a city with a large Hispanic population, you may be able to find sour oranges (naranjas agrias), also known as Seville oranges. They can be smooth-skinned or bumpy, orange or green, but all have a sharp citrus flavor similar to lime juice. Fresh lime juice is a suitable substitute.

STAR ANISE

This dried, star-shaped fruit comes from a small evergreen tree that grows in southwest China and Vietnam. Its smoky, licorice flavor is as distinctive as the 8 points on its pod. A member of the magnolia family, star anise is one of the spices in Chinese five-spice powder. Look for it at Asian and Hispanic markets and gourmet shops.

STOCK

Stock is the cornerstone of all the world's great cuisines. It's particularly valuable in low-fat cooking because it can be used as a substitute for oil, butter, or cream. Many people are intimidated by the idea of making stock, but nothing could be easier. All you do is simmer a meat of some sort with spices and aromatic vegetables. I think of stock as the ultimate recycler. I save chicken necks and backs, turkey carcasses, meat trimmings, tomato peels, vegetable scraps, and the like in a plastic bag in the freezer. Whenever I have enough, I put on a pot of stock. The preliminary boiling and rinsing helps remove impurities and fat.

There are two important watch points. First, after the initial boiling, never let the stock boil. (If you do, the fat will homogenize, and the stock will become cloudy.) Second, skim the stock often with a shallow ladle (not a slotted spoon). This removes more fat and impurities, and it keeps the stock clean. Store-bought stock is loaded with sodium, and it can't touch the flavor of homemade. Add making stock from scratch to your culinary repertoire. I promise you'll be glad you did.

BASIC CHICKEN STOCK

4-5 pounds chicken parts (scraps, backs, or wings)
1 leek
1 onion
1 parsnip
2 carrots
2 stalks celery

1 tomato (optional)
4 cloves garlic
4 large sprigs parsley (or parsley stems)
4 sprigs fresh thyme (or 2 teaspoons dried)
2 bay leaves
10 peppercorns
2 whole cloves

Place the chicken parts in a stockpot with cold water to cover. Bring to a boil and cook for 1 minute. Drain the chicken in a colander and rinse well. Wash out the pot.

Remove one dark outside leaf from the leek and wash well. Trim the top (the dark green leaves) off the leek and discard. Thoroughly wash the bottom. Cut the leek, onion (with skin intact), parsnip, carrots, celery, and tomato (if using) into 1" pieces. Cut the garlic cloves in half. Gather the parsley, thyme, bay leaves, peppercorns, and cloves into a bunch and wrap them in the leek leaf. Tie into a neat bundle with string. (Alternatively, the herbs and spices can be tied in cheesecloth.)

Place all the ingredients for the stock in the stockpot with cold water to cover. Bring to a boil and skim off any foam that rises to the surface.

Lower the heat and simmer gently, skimming often, for 2 to 3 hours, or until well flavored. (You'll need to skim more frequently at the beginning, less at the end.) Add cold water as needed to keep the ingredients covered. (Skim the stock right after adding water. The cold water helps bring impurities to the surface.)

Strain the stock into a large bowl, let cool to room temperature, and refrigerate until cold. Scrape off any fat that congeals on the surface. I like to transfer the stock to 1- and 2-cup containers for freezing so I always have premeasured amounts on hand. Stock will keep for several months in the freezer, although if you use it as much as I do, you'll need to make a fresh batch every week.

Makes 2 quarts.

• **Chicken Broth:** Chicken broth is the richer brother of stock. Make it as described above, using a whole chicken instead of bones and parts. Cook the chicken for 1 hour, transfer to a platter, and let cool. Pull the meat off the bones (save it for salads or sandwiches). Return the bones to the pot and simmer another 1 to 2 hours.

• **Veal Stock:** Make as described for Basic Chicken Stock, using veal bones instead of chicken. Try to choose bones with some meat on them, such as neck or shin bones.

• **Brown Bone Stock:** This is my favorite stock because roasting gives the meat extra flavor. There's another advantage: roasting the meat on a rack melts the fat away. Prepare Basic Chicken Stock, but instead of boiling the bones, place them on a wire rack in a large roasting pan. Roast in a 400 degree F oven for 1 to 1½ hours, or until dark golden brown. Add the vegetables the last 30 minutes so that they roast, too.

Transfer the bones and vegetables to the stockpot. Pour the fat out of the roasting pan and discard. (If necessary, scrape out any leftover fat with a rubber spatula.) Deglaze the roasting pan with 1 cup dry white wine (i.e., place the pan over high heat and add the wine; bring the wine to a boil, scraping with a whisk to dissolve any congealed meat juices). Add this liquid to the stock. Also add 2 tablespoons tomato paste for color. Add the herb bundle and cold water to cover, and simmer the stock for 2 to 3 hours, skimming often.

FISH STOCK

As much as I'm a purist about chicken stock, I almost never make fish stock. The reason is simple: bottled clam broth (sometimes called clam juice) usually tastes better. It's easy to use, relatively inexpensive (particularly if you can buy it by the quart at a discount food market), and has a briny, shellfish flavor that's more interesting than that of fish stock. The only drawback is that it's quite salty, so cut back on the salt in the recipe. Once in a while, for old times' sake (after all, I did go to cooking school in Paris), I make a traditional fish stock. For the best results, I use the frames (skeletons) or trimmings of delicate white fish, such as halibut, snapper, or haddock. (Sometimes fish stores sell cheap, cubed white fish fillets under the name "chowder fish." This works great.) Salmon stock works for salmon dishes, but it's too strong for most dishes. Do not make stock from dark, oily fish such as mackerel or bluefish.

2 pounds chowder fish, fish frames, or fish heads
1 onion
2 stalks celery
2 cloves garlic
3 large sprigs parsley (or parsley stems)

2 sprigs fresh thyme (or 1 teaspoon dried)
1 bay leaf
10 peppercorns
2 whole cloves
1 tablespoon olive oil
1 cup white wine

Cut the chowder fish into 1" pieces. If using fish frames, cut into 2" pieces. If using fish heads, have your fishmonger cut them in half and discard the gills. Rinse the fish in cold water until all traces of blood are gone. Finely chop the onion, celery, and garlic. Tie the herbs and spices in a piece of cheesecloth. (Or wrap them in a square of foil and perforate the foil with a fork.)

Heat the oil in a large saucepan. Add the onion, celery, and garlic, and cook over medium heat for 2 to 3 minutes, or until soft but not brown. Increase the heat to high and add the fish. Cook, stirring well, for 1 to 2 minutes to sear the fish.

Add the wine and boil for 1 minute. Add the spice bundle and water to cover. Bring the stock to a boil and skim off any foam that rises to the surface. Lower the heat and gently simmer the stock, skimming often, for about 30 minutes. (You don't need to cook fish stock as long as chicken stock.)

Strain the stock into a large bowl and let cool to room temperature. Refrigerate until cold. Skim off any fat that congeals on the surface. I like to transfer the stock to 1-cup containers for freezing so I always have the right amount on hand.

Makes 1 quart.

LOBSTER STOCK

Lobster bodies make a wonderful stock for fish stews. If you live in New England (or anywhere that sells cooked lobsters), you may be able to buy them. (I used to get them for a quarter apiece in Boston.) Whenever I cook lobster at home, I save the heads in the freezer. You'll need 8 lobster bodies to make 1½ to 2 quarts stock.

Prepare lobster stock as you would Basic Chicken Stock. Finely chop the vegetables. Lightly brown them in 1 tablespoon olive oil. Add 1 cup wine and ¼ cup cognac, and bring to a boil. Add the herb bundle, 2 tablespoons of tomato paste, and 2 coarsely chopped tomatoes.

Cut the lobster bodies in half. (If you're in a hurry, leave them whole.) Add them to the wine mixture with water to cover. Bring to a boil, reduce the heat, and simmer for 30 minutes, skimming often. Strain the stock into a large bowl, let cool to room temperature, and refrigerate. (Crab stock is made the same way.)

INSTANT STOCK

Although there's no substitute for a lengthily simmered, conscientiously skimmed stock made of meat and vegetables, the following mixture will work in a pinch— especially in soups, stews, and other dishes that contain lots of ingredients.

4 cups warm water
2 tablespoons fish sauce

1 teaspoon soy sauce

Combine all the ingredients in a large pan or bowl, and whisk to mix.

Makes 1 quart.

Note: To make an instant vegetarian stock, replace the fish sauce with miso (Japanese fermented soybean paste).

SUMAC

A purplish berry with a tart, lemony flavor, sumac is usually sold ground. Look for it in Middle Eastern and Armenian markets.

TAHINI

Popular in the Middle East, this chalky paste is made of sesame seeds. Tahini thinned with water and lemon juice is the traditional sauce for falafel. It can be found at Middle Eastern markets, at natural food stores, and in the ethnic food section of most supermarkets. You can store tahini at room temperature, but when it sits for any length of time, the oil tends to separate. Before using, stir it with a fork until smooth. Tahini is relatively high in fat, but thanks to its intense flavor, a little goes a long way.

TAMARIND

The pulp of a large tropical seedpod, tamarind tastes like puréed prunes mixed with lime juice. Most North Americans ignore its very existence (although it's an ingredient in Worcestershire sauce), but its sweet-sour flavor is highly prized in the Caribbean, Middle East, India, and Southeast Asia. If you live in a city with a large Hispanic or Asian population, you may be able to find fresh pods. (Peel them with a paring knife.) Asian and Indian markets sell sticky balls of peeled tamarind paste. For instructions on using tamarind, see page 193.

TOMATILLO

A tomatillo is a small, green tomatolike fruit recognizable by its papery husk. There's nothing quite like its tart, perky flavor. A mainstay of Mexican cooking, tomatillos are widely available at produce shops and most supermarkets.

TOMATO

In the best of all possible worlds, we would have year-round access to fresh, vine-ripened tomatoes. Unfortunately, we don't. Sometimes good canned tomatoes have more flavor than the anemic hothouse variety. There's a trick for boosting the flavor of a marginally fresh tomato: add a teaspoon of tomato paste.

• To peel a fresh tomato, cut out the stem end and cut a small **x** in the rounded end. Plunge the tomato in a pot of rapidly boiling water for 20 to 60 seconds (depending on the ripeness of the tomato), or until the skin feels loose. Rinse the tomato under cold running water and pull the skin off with your fingers.

• To seed a tomato, cut it in half widthwise. Squeeze each half in the palm of your hand, cut side down, to wring out the liquid and seeds. (These can be added to stock.) The tomato is ready for chopping or dicing.

• Two pounds fresh tomatoes (4 or 5 tomatoes) make about 2 cups peeled, seeded, and chopped.

TURMERIC

This fragrant, orange-fleshed rhizome (underground stem) is closely related to ginger. Sometimes you can find it fresh at Southeast Asian markets. Dried and powdered, it's available in any supermarket spice rack. Turmeric is an important ingredient in curry powder. It's also the coloring agent that turns ballpark mustard bright yellow. The most economical way to buy it is in bulk at an Indian market.

UMEBOSHI PLUM PASTE

Umeboshi are Japanese pickled plums flavored with a tangy herb called *shiso*. Their distinctive tart flavor lends vibrancy to salad dressings and sauces. The paste is also great for basting grilled meats. Umeboshi paste is available at Japanese markets and natural food stores.

VANILLA BEAN

Vanilla comes from an orchid native to Central America. The part of the plant we use is the long, slender seedpod, which is filled with innumerable dustlike black seeds. Whole vanilla beans provide a subtler but richer flavor than the extract. Cut the bean in half lengthwise and infuse it in warm milk or sugar syrup. Another great way to use vanilla is to bury a split bean in a canister of granulated or confectioners' sugar for a few days to make vanilla sugar. The bean can then be rinsed off, dried, wrapped in plastic, and reused.

WASABI

If you've ever eaten sushi, you've tasted wasabi. It's the excruciatingly hot stuff that looks like a blob of green toothpaste. Often described as Japanese horseradish, wasabi is a light green, parsnip-shaped root known as mountain hollyhock. Outside Japan, it's most readily available in powdered form, sold in tiny cans. To reconstitute dried wasabi, blend ½ teaspoon warm water with 1 heaping teaspoon powder. Let the paste stand for 5 to 10 minutes to allow the flavor to develop. Occasionally, you can find premixed wasabi paste in toothpastelike tubes. Wasabi is available at Japanese markets, natural food stores, and gourmet shops.

YOGURT

One of the biggest challenges facing the low-fat cook is finding acceptable dairy products. In writing this book, I tried to eliminate butter, cream, sour cream, and cream cheese. Nonfat yogurt has become one of the cornerstones of my new style of cooking. Its sharp flavor recalls the tartness of crème fraîche and sour cream. Custardlike in its natural state, it takes on the consistency of heavy cream when whisked. Best of all, you can turn it into a sort of cream cheese.

YOGURT CHEESE

Use as a base for dips, sauces, and even creamy desserts. To make it, drain the yogurt in a yogurt funnel (see Mail-Order Sources) or a cheesecloth-lined colander. Both low-fat and nonfat yogurt can be turned into cheese. Whichever you use, be sure it contains no gelatin. The longer you drain it, the firmer the cheese will be.

Line a colander with several layers of cheesecloth. Drain 1 quart (2 pounds) yogurt for at least 2 hours (as long as overnight). I don't bother to refrigerate the yogurt for shorter periods, but I do when draining it overnight.

Two hours of draining will produce a soft, creamy cheese. Twelve hours will produce a firmer, drier curd.

Makes 2 cups.

YOGURT CREAM CHEESE SPREAD

Here's a low-fat accompaniment to Wok Smoked Salmon (page 115).

1 cup Yogurt Cheese (the drier the better)
3 tablespoons chopped fresh chives or
　scallions

3 tablespoons chopped pimiento (optional)
1 teaspoon lemon juice
salt and freshly ground white pepper

Place the yogurt cheese in a bowl and fold in the remaining ingredients. Correct the season-ing, adding salt and pepper to taste.

Makes 1 cup.

HIGH-FLAVOR INGREDIENTS

1. vanilla bean
2. turmeric
3. galangal (dried)
4. sumac
5. cilantro
6. star anise
7. aniseed
8. wasabi
9. saffron
10. nutmeg
11. Sichuan peppercorns
12. cardamom pods
13. coriander seed
14. cumin seed
15. cinnamon sticks
16. lemongrass (fresh)

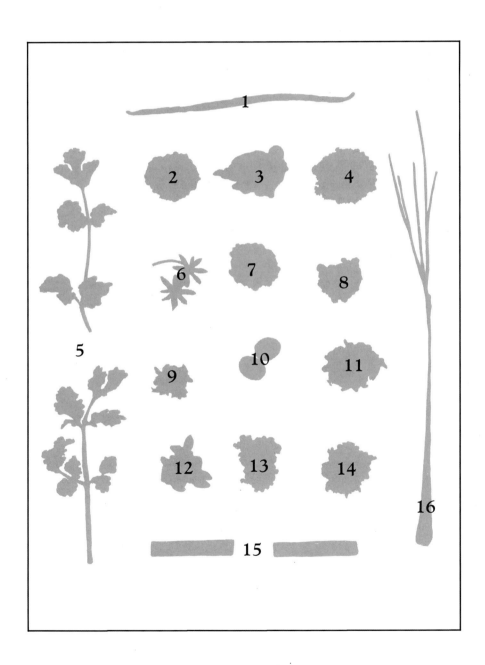

HIGH-FLAVOR INGREDIENTS

(continued)

1. sesame oil
2. extra-virgin olive oil
3. fish sauce
4. rose water
5. balsamic vinegar
6. chili paste
7. salted black beans
8. umeboshi plum paste
9. chipotle chilies
10. ginger (fresh)
11. ancho chili
12. Chinese dried red chilies
13. jalapeño chilies
14. scotch bonnet chili
15. Thai chilies

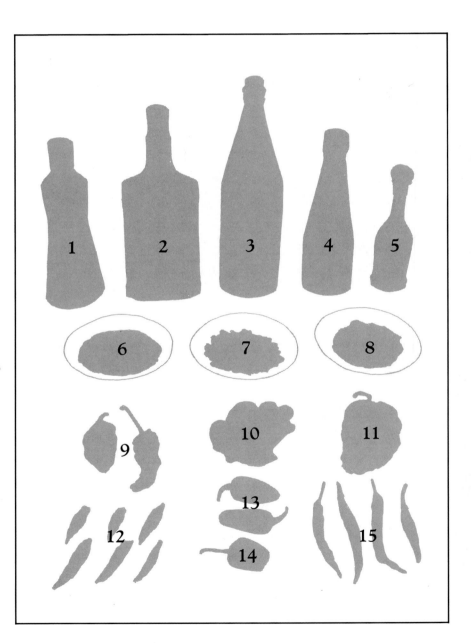

Mail-Order Sources

Contact the following companies for catalogs
and price lists for specialty foods and equipment.

Adobe Milling Company
P.O. Box 596
Dove Creek, CO 81324
(800) 54-ADOBE
*Anasazi and other dried beans;
blue cornmeal; popcorn; spices;
Beano, an enzyme that helps reduce
flatulence in beans.*

American Spoon Foods
P.O. Box 566
Petoskey, MI 49770
(800) 222-5886
*Dried cherries, blueberries, and
cranberries; sugarless preserves;
fat-free salad dressings; barbecue
sauces.*

Aux Délices des Bois
4 Leonard Street
New York, NY 10013
(212) 334-1230
*Exotic mushrooms: truffles; morels;
shiitakes; oyster and portabello
mushrooms; black trumpets; hen-
of-the-woods; others.*

Bland Farms
P.O. Box 506
Glennville, GA 30427
(800) VIDALIA
*Vidalia onions; onion products;
Georgia peaches; peach products.*

Joyce Chen Unlimited
423 Great Road
Acton, MA 01720
(508) 263-6922
*A wide range of Oriental ingredi-
ents and cookware.*

C.M. International
P.O. Box 60220
Colorado Springs, CO 80960
(719) 390-0505
*Manufacturer of the Camaroons
Stovetop Smoker Cooker, an in-
genious device that enables you to
smoke fish, turkey, and countless
other foods indoors on top of your
stove.*

Coyote Café General Store
132 West Water Street
Santa Fe, NM 87501
(505) 982-2454
*A wide range of Southwestern in-
gredients: dried chilies (anchos,
chipotles, etc.); chili powders;
spices; salsas; condiments; cookbooks.*

Dean & DeLuca, Inc.
560 Broadway
New York, NY 10012
(800) 221-7714
A large selection of international ingredients for Italian, Mexican, Oriental, and Indian cooking; cocoas; mustards; herbs and spices; oils and vinegars; pastas, rices, and other grains; flours; cookware.

De Wildt Imports, Inc.
RD 3, Fox Gap Road
Bangor, PA 18013
(800) 338-3433
Indonesian, Thai, Vietnamese, Indian, and Oriental foods and equipment: rice paper; Oriental noodles; mirin; chili paste; tamarind concentrate; Oriental cookware.

G.B. Ratto International
    Grocers
821 Washington Street
Oakland, CA 94607
(800) 325-3483
A wide variety of ethnic foods: mustards; spices; tamarind concentrate; dried chilies; pastas; vinegars; arborio and basmati rice; flours.

Gray's Grist Mill
P.O. Box 422
Adamsville, RI 02801
(508) 636-6075
Organic stone-ground flours and meals, including johnnycake meal.

Maine Seaweed Company
P.O. Box 57
Steuben, ME 04680
(207) 546-2875
Kelp and other dried seaweed.

Millhopper Marketing
1110 N.W. 8th Avenue
Gainesville, FL 32601
(904) 373-5800
Yogurt cheese funnels and yogurt-making supplies.

Old Southwest Trading Co.
P.O. Box 7545
Albuquerque, NM 87194
(800) 748-2861
A wide range of Southwestern ingredients: dried chilies (anchos, chipotles, etc.); chili powders; spices; salsas; condiments; cookbooks.

Williams-Sonoma
100 North Point Street
San Francisco, CA 94133
(415) 421-4242
A large selection of cookware; oils; vinegars; other gourmet products.

METRIC GUIDELINES

These guidelines were developed to simplify the conversion from Imperial measures to metric. The numbers have been rounded for convenience. When cooking from a recipe, work in the same system throughout the recipe; do not use a combination of the two.*

Metric Symbols

Celsius: C
liter: L
milliliter: mL
kilogram: kg
gram: g
centimeter: cm
millimeter: mm

Oven Temperature Conversions

IMPERIAL	METRIC
250 degrees F	120 degrees C
275 degrees F	140 degrees C
300 degrees F	150 degrees C
325 degrees F	160 degrees C
350 degrees F	180 degrees C
375 degrees F	190 degrees C
400 degrees F	200 degrees C
425 degrees F	220 degrees C
450 degrees F	230 degrees C
475 degrees F	240 degrees C
500 degrees F	260 degrees C

Length

IMPERIAL	METRIC
¼ inch	5 mm
⅓ inch	8 mm
½ inch	1 cm
¾ inch	2 cm
1 inch	2.5 cm
2 inches	5 cm
4 inches	10 cm

Volume

IMPERIAL	METRIC
¼ teaspoon	1 mL
½ teaspoon	2 mL
¾ teaspoon	4 mL
1 teaspoon	5 mL
2 teaspoons	10 mL
1 tablespoon	15 mL
2 tablespoons	25 mL
¼ cup	50 mL
⅓ cup	75 mL
½ cup	125 mL
⅔ cup	150 mL
¾ cup	175 mL
1 cup	250 mL
4 cups	1 L
5 cups	1.25 L

Mass (Weight)

IMPERIAL	METRIC
1 ounce	25 g
2 ounces	50 g
¼ pound	125 g
½ pound (8 ounces)	250 g
1 pound	500 g
2 pounds	1 kg
3 pounds	1.5 kg
5 pounds	2.2 kg
8 pounds	3.5 kg
10 pounds	4.5 kg
11 pounds	5 kg

Some Common Can/ Package Sizes

VOLUME

4 ounces	114 mL
10 ounces	284 mL
14 ounces	398 mL
19 ounces	540 mL
28 ounces	796 mL

MASS

4 ounces	113 g
5 ounces	142 g
6 ounces	170 g
7 ounces	220 g
15 ounces	425 g

*Developed by the Canadian Home Economics Association and the American Home Economics Committee.

INDEX

(Page numbers in boldface indicate color photographs.)

ABOUT THE AUTHOR

Ramona Martineau

STEVEN RAICHLEN IS A FOOD writer, cooking teacher, and syndicated columnist. His "New Foods" column, syndicated by the *Los Angeles Times* to 95 newspapers, won the Newspaper Food Editors and Writers Award for best food column in 1991. Raichlen writes regularly for *Bon Appetit, Food Arts, Eating Well,* and *Washingtonian* magazines, as well as *The Boston Globe* and *The Washington Post.*

In addition to his magazine and newspaper work, Raichlen has written six books on cooking and restaurants, including A CELEBRATION OF THE SEASONS: A COOK'S ALMANAC, BOSTON'S BEST RESTAURANTS, and A TASTE OF THE MOUNTAINS COOKING SCHOOL COOKBOOK.

He is director of "Cooking in Paradise," a unique cooking school in St. Barthelemy, specializing in healthful Caribbean cookery, and also gives classes at the Snowvillage Inn in New Hampshire.

Trained at the Cordon Bleu and La Varenne cooking schools in Paris, Steven Raichlen currently lives in Coconut Grove, Florida.